PEACE PILOT

Praise for
Peace Pilot

As someone who's risked his own neck in pursuit of high adventure, I can tell you that Robert DeLaurentis has the true grit. In "Peace Pilot," his gripping account of a polar circumnavigation flight to help save the planet, Rob encounters one dangerous obstacle after another—burst fuel tanks, navigation loss, brutal temperatures—deftly pushing through, and ultimately triumphing. This cat has more than 9 lives.

—**Jim Clash**, Forbes adventure writer

…Started reading your book—after the first few pages I'm captured and want to know more and read on—the mark of a good book!

—**Air Chief Marshal Sir Stephen Hillier**, Former Chief of the Air Staff, Royal Air Force

"Peace Pilot" is a thrilling and inspiring book that takes readers on an unforgettable journey. Through Robert's adventures in the Citizen of the World, this fast-paced read reveals how achieving the impossible is possible through global cooperation. It demonstrates that with faith, determination, and a belief in humanity, we can overcome any obstacle.

From facing mythical creatures to embarking on a vision quest, "Peace Pilot" keeps readers engaged from start to finish. Robert's encounters with dragons and the enchanting Sirens transform him into the embodiment of a Peace Pilot, offering valuable lessons on personal growth and becoming exemplary figures for our world.

For fans of true-life adventure stories, "Peace Pilot" exceeds expectations. It showcases how real adventurers lead the way even in the face of extreme danger, defying insurmountable odds with unwavering faith. Robert and his Angels fearlessly take on the world, highlighting the importance of a mission that sur-

passes individual ambitions. The magical plane, the Citizen of the World, *serves as a powerful symbol of unity and collaboration.*

Prepare for an exhilarating journey as you accompany Robert on his globe-spanning adventure, from Pole to Pole. "Peace Pilot" is an E-ticket ride that will leave you inspired and ready to embrace the spirit of Oneness and cooperation.

—**Prof. Brian Keating**, UC San Diego,
Author of Losing the Nobel Prize

At first you might think that the story of a flight from the South Pole to the North Pole would be a classic adventure tale, in the tradition of Homer's Odyssey in which the hero overcomes all manner of colossal challenges on a perilous journey toward a goal. Well it is that, and a whole lot more.

Initially it delves into the preparation of an aircraft for the long and brutal journey, and the many upgrades to navigation and fuel systems. Then there are the challenges of getting local government approval for the route, which could cancel the entire plan. We begin to learn that this is not just the story of one individual as we see the importance of gathering support from friends, and also from strangers along the way.

As the journey evolves we begin to understand the wisdom of the choice of the title for the book, "Peace Pilot," as the overcoming of the obstacles leads to an inner peace for the author. On the route back from the South Pole, across many environments and cultures, we also understand why the aircraft was named "Citizen of the World." To help address a growing problem in our era, an innovative data capture system was installed to measure the global distribution of airborne microplastics. Stops along the route provided many opportunities to engage the broader public on a host of critical issues for the planet.

—**Stephen Miller**, Scripps Institution of Oceanography,
now retired after 30 expeditions exploring the deep
sea, including Alvin submersible dives down 2800 m

"Peace Pilot" is an adventurous journey that takes the reader on a quest with Robert and the Citizen of the World through the gravity of external and internal challenges. With humility, and faith in humanity, Robert shows how the vision, determination and spirit of explorers continue to show us a way forward in spite of the obstacles.

—**Erik Lindbergh**, Chairman, The Lindbergh Foundation and co-founder, VerdeGo Aero

PEACE
PILOT

Robert DeLaurentis

To the Ends of the Earth and Beyond

Polar Circumnavigation

This book is dedicated to the brave people who have dreamed of and acted to make the world a better place. It is for those who have overcome obstacles, ignored those who said it could not be done, and discovered their path forward in life. These dreamers found their supporters, persisted, doubted themselves and everything they believed in along the way, but emerged on the other side fuller and more complete human beings with greater knowledge, more confidence, and a wider perspective on the world.

These are the Citizens of the World.

This book was written for pilots and non-pilots knowing that some aviation terms that are common for pilots are not for everyone. We have attempted to make it an enjoyable read for all. The Appendices at the end of the book provide details about my flight and plane which will interest pilots in particular.

Contents

Appendices

Foreword
By Susan Gilbert

British novelist and Nobel Peace Prize recipient Doris Lessing said, "Whatever you want to do, do it now. The conditions are always impossible." Her statement resonates with me and mirrors the story you are about to read.

I've known Robert DeLaurentis for more than thirty years, going back to when he was in the Navy but had not yet shipped out for the Gulf War. We met at Bodyworks, a gym in San Diego, California, where we both worked out regularly, and he began to frequent my café, Lil' Miss Muffins, which was around the corner from the gym. When he returned from the Gulf after completing his commitment to the Navy, he went to work for one of the "big six" accounting firms. This was the career path that had been set for him by his father and by his undergraduate degree in accounting from the University of Southern California.

But the corporate world was not for Robert. He envied my entrepreneurship, the fact that I was my own boss, and what he longed to do was get out from behind his desk and invest in houses he would renovate and then rent. By then we'd become friends, and we spent a lot of time talking about what he could do to make his dream come true. It wasn't an easy decision, and he encountered considerable pushback from his family. But the choice he made set the stage for the rest of his life.

He quit his job, and from then on he'd come into the café covered in rehab dust and flakes of paint after spending the day tearing out cabinets and repainting the interior of his newly-acquired homes. Following a formula he'd developed, the number of single-family homes increased. Then he added duplexes, then four-plexes, then apartment buildings. That's how he built his business—one step at a time. Although I didn't know it then, Robert turned out to be the first person I coached to reach for his dreams. He had outgrown who he was, what he was doing and why. He wanted to do something that had more impact and gave him more joy, but he was stuck. He credits me as a pivotal mentor who helped him take the leap.

Shortly after Robert began recreating himself, I set out on a life-changing path of my own. I was attending the Unity Church, and from time-to-time Robert would come with me even though he was not yet fully engaged in his own spiritual growth. In 2001

I published a gift book called *The Land of I Can*, which was very successful, and I created a book-marketing website that was ahead of its time. As a result, I was sought out by the publisher of the Idiot's Guides to co-author *Starting and Running a Coffee Bar*. Based on what I had learned while writing those two books, I found that I was in a position to help other entrepreneurs write and publish their books, build their platforms, and achieve their heart's calling.

During that time, I was also taking another leap—learning to fly an airplane. When I got my pilot's license, Robert was one of the few people who trusted me enough, a new and low-time pilot, to be a passenger on jaunts to Palm Springs or Big Bear.

I had visited Seattle in 1990 to attend a meeting at Starbucks' headquarters to assess the possibility of using the kiosks they had developed as prototypes for expanding my own cafe business, and I fell in love with the Pacific Northwest. I could see myself living there, but at the time I was still entrenched in running my café business in San Diego. By 2005, however, my publishing business had become my core focus. I sold my cafés and moved to Seattle, but Robert and I stayed in touch. He began taking flying lessons and was soon far more qualified than I—moving up in ratings and aircraft. At the same time, his business had become so successful that he was able to step back from the day-to-day operation of the company. With all that newfound time on his hands, his father told him to join a country club and learn to play golf. But that was not in the cards for Robert.

It was also about this time he began working toward an advanced graduate degree in Spiritual Psychology with an emphasis in Consciousness, Health and Healing at the University of Santa Monica. Robert was growing, expanding his horizons and looking for his next great adventure.

He'd been flying to the Caribbean and many other places far away from San Diego, which, as a pilot myself, I know that very few of us ever do. Because this was so unusual, FBOs (Fixed Base Operators, who handle private aviation aircraft services) were asking him to speak to their pilots and pass along tips and inspiration from his flying adventures.

One weekend, he rented a plane and flew up to Seattle to brainstorm what he should do next. I knew he wanted to combine his love of business with helping others, and that whatever he did, he would do it in a big way. I told him that all speakers (which he was already becoming) should be authors and suggested that we build a brand around books, speaking, and other aviation opportunities. The brand I created for him was **Flying Thru Life | Achieving Altitude in Your Business and Life**. We developed a website to support his new venture and began posting to his blog and social media to build his influence as a thought leader in the aviation industry and someone who was committed to giving back to others.

When Robert completed his first circumnavigation in 2015, we released his book *Flying Thru Life* to an eager audience of folks who had been following his quest. The following year, we published his second book, *Zen Pilot*, an adventure story that describes both the outer and inner experience of that journey, what he had learned and how he had grown along the way.

Robert DeLaurentis is one of my "Messengers on a Mission," someone who has heard a Calling, heeded the Call, and supports that Calling by taking it out into the world to others with whom it will resonate. He and his fellow messengers have a core message to share and are on a mission to reach people in a big way.

Have you ever noticed that when you commit to something, magic unfolds? While the vision Robert and I had was incredibly big right from the beginning, it continued to expand with each committed step along the way. Our initial impossibly big dream—the mission—was for Robert to circumnavigate the globe flying solo in his single-engine Malibu Mirage, *The Spirit of San Diego*. An inordinate amount of preparation is required to undertake such a journey, but how do you prepare for an engine outage over the Strait of Malacca? Robert averted that disaster by flying without an engine (dead sticking in aeronautic jargon) back to Kuala Lumpur International Airport 2 twenty minutes after takeoff and lived to tell the story.

When he returned from that circumnavigation and published his books, Robert's speaking engagements grew from local FBO gatherings to large organized fly-ins like Sun 'n Fun, Oshkosh, and Aircraft Owners and Pilots Association (AOPA) regional gatherings. He became one of AOPA's Thought/Opinion blog writers, and his social media platforms continued to grow.

It was time for us to use that visibility to plan a new worldwide trip. This time it would be in a heavily refurbished twin-engine Turbo Commander 900 that would become a global billboard for peace, a cause that the world needs now more than ever. The new mission became One Planet, One People, One Plane, connecting the only two places where there has never been a war—the North and South poles. Robert named this plane, *Citizen of the World*.

If we thought preparing for his 2015 circumnavigation was challenging, what Robert accomplished over the next two years required Commitment with a Capital C and neon flashing lights.

You'll read the details of that preparation in this book, along with the story of the journey itself. I don't want to say too much here, but what I can tell you is: along with telling the story of his adventures, Robert offers "Peace Moments," pearls of wisdom he earned in unexpected ways.

Modern-day thought leaders like Robert have incredible courage. Courage to tell their story. Courage to say something that not only sounds good but also makes an impact in the world.

Your brand is your story—and Robert's life personifies his brand, **Flying Thru Life**.

The Big Go No-Go Decision

Courage is being scared to death ... and saddling up anyway.

—John Wayne

I had come to the longest, hardest and most challenging part of my trip to circumnavigate the poles. I was on a mission of peace, but I was feeling anything but peaceful. After taking off from San Diego, doing test flights in the Mojave, then down into Central and South America, I landed in Ushuaia, Argentina. After losing sleep and worrying about my chances for survival for almost 18 months, I was walking the last 100 feet to my plane to take off for the South Pole, and I was literally at the point where I could no longer silence the voices in my head screaming at me "Don't do this! This is crazy. You are going to get yourself killed!" I was terrified. What had I gotten myself into? But I had accepted more than half a million dollars in

Robert in his neoprene survival suit, terrified and standing next to the Citizen of the World, *fully loaded with fuel, a few minutes before departure for the South Pole*

sponsorship and had literally promised the world to 95 sponsors, so there was no way I could back out now.

Flying to the South Pole was by far the riskiest and most costly venture I had ever attempted. Financially this trip was breaking my back, just as the fuel load in the *Citizen of the World's* ten fuel tanks was threatening to break her dual wing spars. To cover the tremendous cash shortfall, I had instructed the people managing my business to "bleed it dry" in support of my global peace effort. I had put everything at risk: my livelihood, my life, my plane, my pilot's license, and my reputation were on the line. There was no going back.

My legs trembled as I walked awkwardly to the plane.

I had never before planned anything so carefully or in such detail—to the point where I kept finding new risks that had to be mitigated. The problem was that some risks cannot be mitigated when you are stretching your plane beyond its material limits. How do you make a plane designed to fly for 6 hours go 18+ safely? This was insanity and I knew it.

My nightmares leading up to this point had been absolutely brutal and graphic, predicting in detail over and over how I would die. The plane breaking apart on takeoff was the vision. I had only flown her at 70 percent fuel load and then projected her range and performance. I was told she could handle it, but what if the 89-year-old wing designer who did the feasibility study was wrong? All people make mistakes. I would crash and burn on the runway, hit the mountains that surrounded the airport, or get swallowed up by the chilly waters of the Beagle Channel.

I thought about how my entire life had been leading up to this moment: the previous circumnavigation, my time in the Navy during the Persian Gulf War, becoming a pilot, building a business, and eventually developing the skills I needed to win the support and confidence of so many sponsors. And, of course, the spiritual work I had done to put my own issues aside, find my peace in the world, and make a difference when others could or would not.

But, at this point, my personal peace seemed tantalizingly illusive, and the voices in my head that I had worked hard to silence were fighting to take control. No matter how carefully I had planned, it was as if the Universe had decided to stack the deck against me, tossing me a series of "impossible" challenges, warning me in every way possible that I should not go. The voices' message was clear: if you go, you will not survive.

About 50 feet from the plane, while I was still within Wi-Fi range of the flight plan office, I heard my phone chirp one last time. It was a text message, and I couldn't resist seeing what it said. This could be my last communication with the world before I set off for the South Pole. It was Super Fred Sorenson, the ferry pilot genius who had designed, built, and installed my ferry tanks, informing me that the FAA was concerned about my flight because of the recent crash of a Chilean Lockheed Martin C-130 Hercules that had gone down in the Drake Passage, a body of water located between South America's Cape Horn and Antarctica. It took four days to find the wreckage even with dozens of planes from several countries doing the searching. The C-130 was carrying its maximum payload of 42,000 pounds, and authorities speculated that perhaps it had suffered a structural failure of the wing. The FAA didn't want to have to deal with one of their planes having that same issue on the far side of the world, and Fred made it 100 percent clear that if I continued, I could lose both my pilot's license and the airworthiness certificate for the plane.

The Universe seemed to be doubling down on me at the precise moment when I was about to risk it all, issuing one final warning: "Just step across this line with your big brass balls and see what happens. I have given you every possible warning, and you are just going to get yourself killed." I was risking it all for my mission of peace and oneness. *Why does this need to be so damn hard?* I thought.

I realized I was mentally and physically already exhausted and I had not even started the trip. I had intended to leave at 9:00 am, but had been delayed by last minute unexpected issues with my flight plan, permit, and fueling, and it was now 2:30 pm.

It was one of those days when you look at your watch and think, how much longer before I can go home? Being so late in the day, it was a terrible time to start a brutally challenging eighteen-hour-plus flight to the most remote and dangerous part of the planet. The words of Super Fred rang in my head: "A ferry flight doesn't start until you are exhausted and the brass in your balls is equal to that in your ferry tanks." Why did Fred always have to be right?

I honestly didn't know if I would return. I held my odds of being alive in the next 36 hours at about 50/50. The night before, I had stacked my belongings in the hotel room with my family's address on top, in case the hotel manager needed to pack everything up and send it to them. I also showered and carefully groomed myself. I had flashbacks to the movie *Gladiator*, when the slaves prepared to enter the arena to fight the seasoned veterans. They knew they would die, and each one handled it differently, some trembling, others wetting themselves, and still others standing in shock, not knowing what to do next. All were terrified. I knew that feeling.

To add insult to injury, I noticed the wind had changed directions and was blowing at 15 to 20 knots in the opposite direction from what I had planned. That meant I had to change runways. Not only was the new runway uphill, requiring more power to build up speed and lift off, but it also pointed directly at the mountains. Turning a plane reduces the lift, and doing that when the plane is beyond its maximum gross weight is not only extremely dangerous but also violates all principles of flight.

However, what scared me the most at that moment was the crash of the Chilean Air Force C-130 on December 9th. Today is December 17th.

The aircraft that went down was the newest version of the C-130. I was flying a 1983 model 900 version of the Turbo Commander with a documented damage history. On the day of my departure, my aircraft was thirty-six years old. In addition:

- The Chilean aircraft had two experienced pilots. I was flying solo with no experience over Antarctica.
- The Chilean aircraft was on a 2-hour flight. I had an 18+ hour flight ahead of me.
- The Chilean aircraft was flying at its maximum gross weight. I was flying *over* mine.
- The C-130 had four engines. I had two.
- The C-130 was flying in relatively clear weather. I would be flying under instrument flight conditions and able to see the earth for only a portion of the flight. The weather at the pole was expected to be zero visibility.
- And worst of all, no bodies had ever been found following the C-130 crash.

All I could think was, *what were my chances?*

With my head spinning, I eventually got to the *Citizen of the World*. She was lower to the ground than she had ever been. She was loaded up like a pack mule whose owner had no idea how much she could actually carry. The *Citizen* only had only about 1 inch of travel remaining on the landing gear struts to absorb the bumps as I rolled down the runway. The struts function like shock absorbers and would normally have 6 to 8 inches of travel—a clear indication of how overloaded she was. If I hit any bumps, I would be slamming metal on metal, which could lead to a landing-gear failure.

"Super" Fred had suggested I fuel the day of departure, but based on the difficulty of getting the fuel truck to the plane, and the complexity of moving fuel using battery-powered pumps among the 10 tanks and 20 valves, I knew that would be impossible.

Jeremy La Zelle, the cinematographer who was filming our documentary of the Polar Circumnavigation, was standing next to the plane hoping to catch some last images of me before takeoff. I can only imagine what he saw on my face and heard in the tone of my voice. Jeremy had told me during the earlier test flights that I was as calm as some of the astronauts he had filmed, but I had him fooled. I was anything but calm inside. I explained the text I had received from Super Fred and I asked him what he thought I should do.

"I can't make that decision for you," he said. There was a long pause as I considered all the possible outcomes. Then I answered the way a child does when you ask a ridiculous question like, "Don't you think it would be fun to be shot out of a cannon?" and the child says in a loud and enthusiastic voice, "Sure!" As if I had not the slightest concern for my own safety or the consequences of my actions, I said, "Fuck it, I'm going."

I got into the plane in my bright red immersion suit, moving like one of the "penguinos" I had seen days before, and closed the hatch behind me. With shaking hands, I belted myself in for the 18-hour flight, said "God help me." and began the long series of engine start-up items on the checklist. With more than fifty modifications, of which every major component had failed in the past year and a half, I was attempting solo flight over the most remote part of the planet.

This was all too much to comprehend, easily the most stressful moment of my life. I was unsure if I would be alive in the next five minutes. The voices in my head kept saying *if you quit now at least you will be alive!*

I was not, however, going to walk away after two years of preparations, promises to sponsors and supporters, and so much money spent. This mission of peace was bigger than me, bigger than my license, and bigger even than the *Citizen of the World*.

I had no control over what the future held for me.

The words of a friend kept ringing in my ears: "Robert, you can't do a circumnavigation without breaking rules."

I just didn't know I would need to break them all.

Peace Moment

The Universe only gives us what we can handle no matter how difficult or impossible it may seem in the moment. Even at times when we feel we will be crushed by the enormity of the task at hand, we have the tools we need to find our way on our journey of learning at this earth school.

PART ONE

Preparing for Flight

Chapter 1

The Call to Adventure

Too often we race around in the physical world as if we're going to find somewhere outside of us these deep points of meaning and purpose that will really make our lives worthwhile and give it that satisfaction that we're craving, but all these things actually lie within us.

—Kathy Sullivan, Astronaut

"What's next?"

My restless soul had been asking me that from the minute I completed my equatorial circumnavigation in 2015. It seemed I had an inexhaustible desire for adrenaline, perspiration, and flying in the face of extreme danger.

As I was pondering all this, and wondering what God had been preparing me for, I had a chilling realization. I was standing in front of a statue I had bought fifteen years ago, before obtaining my pilot's license. It was a figure of Icarus made of spoons

Statue of Icarus about to take flight

mounted on a black marble base. According to the famous ancient Greek myth, Icarus's father had warned him not to fly too close to the sun, because if he did, his wax wings would melt and he would fall to earth. Icarus's father got that right, and, apparently, so had my father.

During my equatorial circumnavigation in a Piper Malibu Mirage named the *Spirit of San Diego*, I had suffered an engine failure. With oil spraying on the 1,500-degree exhaust, I was flying dead-stick (without power) for 19.6 nautical miles over the Strait of Malacca and the jungles of Malaysia with an over-speeding prop, trailing smoke. And I was doing it in a single-engine plane overloaded with 600 extra pounds of high-octane aviation fuel in the cabin. You can read the whole story in my book *Zen Pilot, Flight of Passion and the Journey Within.*

After that emergency, I was through with the risks of flying single-engine piston planes, but I wasn't ready to follow my dad's advice to join a country club and take up golf. I'd survived in 2015, so why should I stop now? I knew from my spiritual studies that the Universe keeps on sending you lessons until you've learned them. Had I learned my lesson, or was I still the rebellious youth doing things just because somebody told him not to?

I was walking in Balboa Park, San Diego one day when I decided to open myself up to what the Universe had in store for me instead of trying to figure things out intellectually—which often didn't work out anyway. I thought my first trip had perhaps been a warm-up for something much more epic, something that could change the world. Flying over the poles would be a continuation of our mission to dream impossibly big, which I'd written about in *Flying Thru Life.* It would also be a sensible next step after the equatorial circumnavigation.

My curiosity and passion to explore nudged me along, and I started researching the poles. I became more and more intrigued with what I might see, experience, and learn about myself in the most remote parts of the planet while pushing myself beyond my absolute limits. I had no idea how truly dangerous, challenging, or complicated such an endeavor would be or the amount of time and resources it would take to pull off such a venture.

There were many reasons to take on this level of risk.

1. I had become restless and needed another challenge. Once again, it was time to stretch my physical, emotional, and spiritual limits to grow and evolve.

2. This next trip would take a bold step beyond general aviation, and my new plane would become the vehicle for my message of oneness for the planet: "One planet. One people. One plane. Oneness for humanity."

3. My mission would further science by carrying experiments for NASA and the Scripps Institution of Oceanography

4. As before, we would promote the latest in aviation safety and technology—ceramic coating, propellers, turboprop engines, night vision, ADS-B (Automatic Dependent Surveillance Broadcast) In and Out, LED lighting, more efficient heating and cooling technology, and biofuels.

I told my dad about my intentions, and, despite his reservations, he sent me an article about the Antarctic Treaty and the poles from which I learned that the poles were the only two places on the planet where peace had always existed. How appropriate then to connect them on this mission of peace.

As the world was becoming more polarized by religion, politics, finances, and racial issues, my mission seemed to make more and more sense. A pole-to-pole circumnavigation had the potential to be the thread that joins all humanity together instead of breaking us apart. Our perceived separation from each other, ourselves, and our Creator drives us apart and away from love, compassion, and kindness for others. One of the core beliefs of the DeLaurentis Foundation is that humans are already united in many ways, something we often forget in the course of our busy and fragmented lives. Our commitment is to be a living example of all those connections and explore new ways to expand and deepen those relationships.

I felt I was being nudged to complete this part of my life's journey, and I decided to use all the resources at my disposal to improve my chances of surviving the flight. That included consulting two psychics. While I didn't intend to base my decisions on what they told me, I thought the readings could draw my attention to something I had missed or perhaps confirm that I had made the correct decision. Surprisingly, the psychic I had consulted before my first trip now told me I was searching the world for a mate, that I would meet this person during the first part of the trip, and that I would be raising hell at the time. My potential mate would see my lack of patience with what was happening as sensible. We would meet in a place I had not planned to visit but would out of necessity. When we first met, we would both be surprised, and she would say something like, "Where did you come from? Did you fall out of the sky?" And I would respond, "Actually, I did!"

On the recommendation of my mentor, Susan Gilbert, I spoke with that psychic again on the phone before starting the trip. She said that my future mate would moderate my intensity much the way Susan had since the first day I met her, and that I would know this person at first sight. Fast forward: while I met wonderful women on the trip, I never met the person who fit this description. That was the only thing the psychic told me that did not come true.

In retrospect, I realized that I had never married because I would never have made this trip and taken these risks if I had a family. It all made sense. I was hopeful that perhaps I would be free to find my special person after the trip. Certainly, by that time I would have scoured the earth, looked everywhere, and known there was not something more out there I had missed.

For now, however, I felt the call to adventure, to achieve an impossibly big dream. Could I complete a polar circumnavigation on a mission of peace? Would I be successful and inspire others or, like Icarus, would my wings melt and cause me to fall from the heavens?*

Peace Moment

It was clear to me that my curriculum on the planet had been laid out long before I lived it. The Universe was orchestrating something much bigger than I was aware of for my highest and best good as well as that of the planet. Perhaps this was an opportunity to confront the fear I had experienced years before undertaking a second flight—like doubling down on life, but with the added intention of helping the world focus on peace.

---

* To see an image of the entire trip as it unfolded, reference Appendix 2.

Chapter 2

Picking My Plane

"Your only job on the Polar Circumnavigation is to stay alive."

—Erik Lindberg

Private and commercial pilots fly over the North Pole every day. I had been within about 1,000 nautical miles while crossing the southern edge of the Polar Ice Cap in 2015. It felt readily attainable.

The South Pole, on the other hand, terrified me. Tackling it involved issues I hadn't encountered during my earlier circumnavigation: extreme cold (–67° C, ie –88° F), which could turn my fuel to gel and starve both engines, vast distances without a place to land, loss of GPS navigation at the poles, the worst weather in the world, snow blindness, and pilot fatigue on an 18-hour flight.

What type of aircraft could even make such a trip?

Years before, when I lectured at Scaled Composites, the premier experimental aircraft design and building company, I talked with the senior engineer, Robert Morgan. We were standing in front of an Adam Aircraft CarbonAero twin-engine inline plane, and he explained that the project had been handed off to junior engineers because Burt Rutan, the famous aircraft designer, wasn't interested, and that, by the time the Federal Aviation Administration (FAA) had finished making design demands, the plane was just too heavy, and it became a failed project.

Next, I asked him, "How much would Scaled Composites charge me to build a plane capable of flying over the Poles?"

His answer came so fast I thought he had to be joking. "One billion dollars."

I smiled at the absurdity, but he was serious. It was a bit of a buzzkill moment, but he's made it clear that my only option would be finding a general aviation aircraft capable of massive modification.

I decided to talk to Fred Sorenson of Flight Contract Services in Las Vegas, who had more than forty-six years of experience ferrying hundreds of planes vast distances across the globe. Fred is tall, with light skin and gray hair. He exudes quiet confidence, seems to know and be liked by everyone in the business, and operates with a sense of style—along with a dry sense of humor punctuated by pauses at the exact right time. Fred needed few words to make his points.

If you read *Zen Pilot*, you may recall that Fred is the highest-time ferry pilot in the world, with more than 575 Pacific crossings. He comes from a family of ferry pilots. It's in his blood. And, based on his extraordinary experience, he has the ability to move from one type of plane to another and somehow remember

"Super Fred" Sorenson and Robert DeLaurentis standing next to the Citizen of the World *after discussing the size and placement of ferry tanks*

how to fly each one. That is a skill that few pilots possess.

A ferry pilot normally delivers airplanes specially modified with extra fuel tanks, long range radios, and, for oceanic trips, equipped with rafts and survival equipment. Many ferry pilots get in a prepared airplane and fly it to its next destination. Fred goes above and beyond by actually doing the modifications to the planes he is going to fly.

Ferry pilots are a unique breed who repeatedly perform one the riskiest jobs in aviation. Many times, they are not flying a brand-new airplane, fresh from the factory, to be delivered to a foreign destination. Rather, they may be tasked with a recovery ferry flight, moving an aircraft that has been neglected, ignored, or poorly maintained, sometimes over vast distances.

In my opinion, it takes at least a year of flying a plane for it to reveal all its flaws and for you to know it completely. Fred felt that you never know an airplane completely, but you must always listen to it.

Ferry pilots like Super Fred (which is what I call him), who are also mechanics, assess the aircraft and make the repairs necessary to make the aircraft "safe" to fly to its destination. Then they may set out over oceans, mountains, and deserts, normally alone, to deliver it.

The pay isn't much compared to the risks they take on, but they are additionally compensated with the enjoyment of fear, adrenaline, and solitude. Their relationship with death can only be defined as respect but not fear.

My circumnavigations have included a handful of risky flights, while, as I've said, Super Fred has been ferrying planes for almost fifty years. He was a tremendous source of information, a sponsor, a mentor, and a friend I admire perhaps more than anyone in aviation. I once asked him, "How is it possible that you are still alive?" In a nonchalant voice, Fred responded, "I learned early to know when to go and when to turn around."

Robert DeLaurentis with "Super" Fred Sorenson pointing to the Flight Contract Services sponsorship logo on the Citizen of the World

I remember a story he told me about losing an engine on a twin-engine Cessna over the Pacific Ocean. With the remaining engine at full power and overheating under the load, he flew it fifty feet above the water for more than 300 miles. At fifty feet above the water you are subject to bird strikes, because they can only fly up into your props to get out of harm's way. Three hundred miles over water at fifty feet is terrifying, but Fred was neither reckless nor fearless, and he made it home.

When Fred speaks, I listen. So I asked him what plane I should use for a polar circumnavigation. He suggested a Fairchild Metroliner, which was used by many airlines. Its Garret gear-driven engines assured fantastic range. Doing my research, I learned that, since buying out Garret, Honeywell had improved these already-remarkably-efficient engines by putting the equivalent of a one-speed transmission between the engine and propeller, increasing their efficiency by 50 percent. Unfortunately, the plane didn't fly much higher than 25,000 feet, and few places that could service or repair it. The thought of flying an antique aircraft pole to pole didn't sit well with me.

Next, I looked at the Mitsubishi MU2, which used Honeywell engines as well. Unfortunately, it flew less efficiently at lower altitudes and lacked a fuselage large enough to carry extra fuel for long-range flights.

A Fairchild Swearingen Metroliner, which was considered for the Polar Circumnavigation

A Mitsubishi MU-2, considered for the Polar Circumnavigation

A Beechcraft King Air 100, another aircraft considered for the Polar Circumnavigation

Next was the King Air B100, which was older. It had a small fuselage, so it couldn't carry much extra fuel, and short wings that resulted in less efficient high-altitude cruise.

I hit pay dirt when I came across the Gulfstream Turbo Commander 900. It had efficient engines, a large fuselage for extra fuel, and long wings for efficient high-altitude cruising.

The Twin Commander line had evolved over the many years it was in production. Each successive

The Turbo Commander's 52-foot wing with winglets, MT Scimitar 5-bladed nickel-tipped composite propellers, and two Honeywell geared drive TPE331-10t engines—also found on Predator B drones—give the Citizen of the World *tremendous global efficiency and range.*

owner had infused it with their technology, making it better in performance and reliability. Rockwell, the maker of the B-2 bomber for the military, was one of those owners, so the plane was built stoutly, as if Rockwell had intentions of selling it to the military.

When Gulfstream bought the rights to build the Turbo Commander, the plane went through a remarkable transformation.

The first thing Gulfstream did was to put one of their wings on the plane. It was ten feet longer than the existing wing, with dual spars and almost laminar flow. This extension brought the wing to 52 feet

The Citizen's signature baby blue "smile" painted to match the DeLaurentis Foundation logo colors

¼ inch in length and allowed the plane to fly higher, more efficiently, and faster. It was one of the early planes with winglets that remain common today, some forty years later.

Gulfstream also upgraded the engines to the Honeywell TPE331-10t, which produced more horsepower at maximum altitude. The Citizen's Honeywell TPE 33-10t's (Formerly Garrett) had 4,900 hours on them, just 500 hours from their 5,400-hour TBO (time between overhaul). They still produced good horsepower, but a refurbishment would increase their power in the flight levels, giving more range and fuel efficiency. Honeywell had also made improvements to the engines, so it made sense to upgrade and get the best power possible out of them. TAE in Scottsdale did the refurbishment. They replaced several major components, including the second-stage impeller and wheels, combustion cases, combustion liners, and crossover ducts. The TPE engines' time between overhauls was 4,200 hours, which was much longer than the nearest competitor. These magical turboprop engines can be found on the Predator B drones. On the test stand, mine produced 1,147 horsepower and 1,150 horsepower.

I wanted to take the plane higher than it normally flew, where it could fly faster using less fuel. So I went to AeroMech Incorporated, an FAA ODA (Organi-

Bob Hoover's North American Shrike Commander, the smaller, older, piston version of what would become the Gulfstream Turbo Commander 900

A Predator B Drone engine from the Citizen of the World with a MT nickel-tipped composite scimitar propeller

zation Designation Authorization) company, which provided me with an STC (Supplementary Type Certificate) for RVSM (reduced vertical separation minima). The STC, along with a backup altimeter and other components, would allow the *Citizen of the World* to fly at up to 35,000 feet, 7,000 feet higher than it was originally designed to achieve. At this altitude over the South and North poles, the *Citizen* would burn only a fraction of the Jet A fuel required by the much thirstier Pratt and Whitney PT6 engines.

Mechanics Steve Rodriguez (left) and the late Morris Kernick (right) from Commander Services working hard on the Honeywell TPE 331-10T engines to get the Citizen of the World *ready for her Polar Circumnavigation.*

Flying at this higher RVSM altitude offers pilots many advantages, including more efficient fuel burn, generally better weather, obstacle clearance, sometimes a less crowded airspace, and more solitude. However, flying at these altitudes requires expensive equipment, which requires calibration, approval from the FAA, and is more likely to break due to the complexity.

Gulfstream also lowered the floorboard inside the plane by four inches, making the space roomier and increasing the cabin pressure so that you felt like you were at 10,000 feet while the plane was actually flying at 35,000 feet.

From the time it was built, the Twin Commander had tremendous ramp presence. People would see one and never forget it. As the Commander line evolved, it became bigger, faster, more powerful, higher flying, and able to carry huge payloads.

I once stood beside another pilot and commented on the great ramp presence of the plane. He corrected me by saying, "It's not great, it's badass." The plane's engineer, Ted Smith, had designed the A-20 Havoc bomber used in World War II and took the best from that 1945 warbird to create a civilian plane with far more performance than one would ever need.

The landing gear, which could handle the stress on dirt runways, was stout and taken from a larger plane.

The fuselage was low slung and like a long square tube. The Commander had been used by the Panamanian and Colombian militaries for counter-drug ops during which they carry up to eleven troops with gear. The 1,150-hp turboprop engines hung under the muscular wings and were distinguished by huge, five-

Susan Gilbert standing under the enormous tail of the Citizen of the World

bladed nickel-tipped composite Scimitar propellers. The plane also had a huge tail to counteract asymmetrical thrust if you lost an engine, and it flew quite nicely on one engine with only a trim adjustment.

While the *Spirit of San Diego*, from my equatorial circumnavigation in 2015 was like an elegant ballerina, the *Citizen of the World* was a toned Olympic sprinter with muscles bulging and veins popping out at the starting line ready to explode. If that weren't enough, she also had an infrared night vision sensor on her nose to help with scary night landings. The sensor looked like an extra eye that you would find on an attack helicopter. She was built for anything the South or North Poles could throw our way—or at least I hoped she was.

Truthfully, I was never completely comfortable flying the *Citizen of the World* either before or after the trip. She was a handful, and I was always a little bit afraid of her. The *Spirit of San Diego* had a single 350-hp piston engine, and the *Citizen* had two 1,150-hp turboprop engines—and more than 6 ½ times as much power. She was bigger and more intimidating. Each propeller was almost as tall as I am. She wasn't a casual flier.

As a complicated high-performance aircraft, the *Citizen* was also more likely to fail. With more than 8,800 hours of flight time, she wasn't a young lady either, and now I was going to push her way beyond what she was designed to do. She was considered "historic" by California tax laws, so it was like pumping Grandma full of steroids and telling her she was going to run three ultra-marathons in a row during the winter with no one around in case she needed help. At times, the route would be unmarked, the weather would be terrible, and she would carry more weight than she ever had before.

What this meant was that the aircraft was being called on to perform the impossible.

How much can you possibly ask of an aircraft before you've gone too far? How long can you keep making performance modifications until it becomes dangerous? At some point you need to say that's too much. The risk can become too great and it won't work. Find another way. Spend the 65 million and buy the Gulfstream G650ER.

Chapter 3

Aligning with Allies

"I'm sending angels."

God

When I realized I couldn't do it alone, I searched for renowned experts in various fields related to my journey. One of the many blessings of preparing for the polar circumnavigation was my aviation support team, who made my flying safer and more enjoyable. But building the team wasn't easy. It involved many moments of frustration and soul-searching that left me scratching my head, and course-correcting more often than I care to remember. In the end, however, with persistence and a relentless focus on the mission: "One planet, One people, One plane, Oneness for humanity" I found my perfect team. These people taught me many things, made me stronger, clearer, and I hope a little more "Zen" in the process. Knowing you have a reliable, caring foundation of earth angels allows you to be your absolute best both in the air and on the ground.

First and foremost, I found people who shared my passion 100 percent. In a time when we can have 5,000 Facebook "friends", I'm here to tell you just the opposite of what you might expect: To do the impossible, you only need a handful of dedicated, trusted supporters to get you started. Imagine a small circle of people with their arms outstretched, hands on your shoulders, championing you and your ideas without exception. The energy of that circle creates an upward spiral that at times, cheesy as it may sound, becomes the wind beneath your wings.

The day of departure from San Diego. Friends and supporters from all over the United States gather to offer a blessing for the challenging weeks and months ahead

Meet my Team of Angels

Susan Gilbert, Ground Control, Strategic Coach, and Book/New Media Guru

I have described Susan as a friend across the ages. She has directed me at key moments in my life, and stood by me through the best and worst that life could throw my way. I believe Susan is one of my an-gels who was put on this planet to help me get past my fears and challenges and to have an impact on the planet.

Professor Brian Keating, Science Advisor

I was introduced to Brian at a party years ago because we were flying similar aircraft. We joke that this was the point where our eyes met and our "bromance" officially began. Brian was nominated for the Nobel Prize in physics and had been to the South Pole, where his BICEP (Background Imaging of Cosmic Extragalactic Polarization) telescope is located. He was instrumental in helping to plan the best time to fly the mission over each pole as well as introducing me to many people, including NASA funded scientists. I consider Brian one of my closest friends and biggest supporters.

Eddie Gould, Global Flight Logistics, G.A.S.E. General Aviation Support Egypt

Eddie is the brains behind routing, flight plans, permits, overflight requests, fueling and acquiring parts anywhere in the world. He is the guy who stays up all night watching you on satellite-tracking to make sure you made it to your destination safely. Each country has different rules, tolerance for small aircraft, restrictions, and political climate. Eddie helped me navigate twenty-two countries on this trip and twenty-three on the previous equatorial circumnavigation. He always got me home safely. A pilot could not have a better friend and supporter than Eddie. He taught me what true generosity means.

Ahmed Hassan, Operations Manager, G.A.S.E. General Aviation Support Egypt

Ahmed was our flight logistics expert. He had the most technical expertise. When Eddie and I hit a wall and our flight plans were rejected, Ahmed could always give us a workable solution. In one case, transiting through political hot spots in the Middle East, his plan required more than twenty route changes, but of course, it worked perfectly.

Mary Marcdante, Community Outreach, Strategy, and Public Relations

Along with Susan and me, Mary was a critical part of our original team of three. She was my first editor and always made what I wrote even better. Mary has a fantastic spiritual intuition and was instrumental in helping to make the really hard decisions. I can remember her telling me many times when I was totally overwhelmed, "Robert, just breathe."

Dr. H. Ron Hulnick, Global Peace Advisor

Ron is a pilot, and one of the two Spiritual Psychology instructors who changed the way I see the world and my role in it. He was the first to suggest a global peace mission back in 2013, and he reminded me that the Universe doesn't distinguish between big and small goals, so, when you go for it, why not go for it all. Ron taught me that the best way to inspire is by being a living example.

Captain Mike Jesch, Commercial Airline Advisor

I met Mike through aviation friends and quickly realized that he was the smartest and most technically knowledgeable pilot I knew. Mike has been an airline pilot for over 37 years and has more than 25,000 flying hours. He helped me identify the risks I needed to mitigate, make the go-no-go weather decision for the South Pole leg, and was always available to answer equipment and fuel gelling questions.

Tim Kneeland, Global Survival Advisor

Tim was teaching a survival class at Corporate Air Parts when I first met him. He has been doing survival training since Vietnam, and is the type of guy who keeps you bent over laughing all the way through his training. I liked to call him the Bionic Instructor because he was "Faster, funnier, and more educational" than any other man alive. Tim designed my survival pack, introduced me to new survival sponsors, and trained me to survive in the most challenging climates on the planet.

Jeremy Là Zelle, Cinematographer

I met Jeremy and our other cinematographer, Kristin, at the Explorers Club—an organization that has been supporting scientific expeditions of all disciplines and uniting members worldwide in the bonds of fellowship for over a century. The club was showing short film segments from past expeditions, and one was clearly head and shoulders above the rest. I felt like I was having a Nat Geo moment, and it took my breath away. It turns out that Jeremy and Kristin had been the cinematographers for that segment. Jeremy also had experience working with National Geographic, Discovery, the History Channel, Bravo, and Animal Planet.

Dimitri D. Deheyn, Ph.D. Marine Biology Research Division Scripps Institution of Oceanography

Dimitri was the lead scientist for the expedition and played a major role on the board of Walter Munk's Foundation for the Oceans, leading international research projects in this era. I met him at the celebration of life for Walter Munk, perhaps the most famous ocean scientist ever. Dimitri was making a tribute and said that he considered himself a "Citizen of the World," which was the name of my plane. This was surely no coincidence. Dimitri loved our project and designed the plastic particle experiment we would use to test the atmosphere for microfibers all the way around the planet and over the poles.

Kristin Gates, Cinematographer

Kristin was part of our film crew and with us every step of the way. An adventurer herself, she had hiked the Brooks Range in Alaska solo. She was tireless, fearless, and the second camera on all scenes. Kristin also helped with the long hours of preparing equipment, organizing film, and coordinating interviews.

For detailed bios of individual team members, go to https://flyingthrulife.com/pole-to-pole/the-team/

More Angels Met Along the Way

Garrick Louie, San Francisco

It was about the time I was struggling the hardest that a new angel emerged. I'd taken out a second mortgage and realized our mission could only continue if we received ongoing financial support that I heard from Garrick Louie.

Garrick is an instrument pilot, business owner, philanthropist, and adventurous soul. He offered airline tickets to get me around the U.S. for plane modifications and speaking engagements. Those tickets allowed our team to allocate more of our valuable funds to important plane upgrades and took us many steps closer to realizing our goal.

I relied on Garrick for his sage advice, technical expertise, and for encouraging me to make aviation and the world stronger and safer.

Michel Gordillo, Campo Real, Spain

I have been humbled by the generosity and wisdom of this man whom I never met in person until I reached Spain. I consider Michel one of my aviation mentors. He was involved in many aspects of the planning and execution of the Polar Circumnavigation—everything from helping with polar permits, weather analysis, technical advice on airplane modifications, route planning, and providing encouragement when I felt defeated.

Robert DeLaurentis, Claes and Inger Martinsson-Bunge

By the time I took off from the Bunge Aviation Museum on the island of Gotland, Sweden, I felt like I was leaving my family. Claes and his mother Inger, the owners of the museum, took me in and showed me kindness and support I had never before known from people I had just met. Besides cooking for me and providing shelter, they also tended to the little things. Inger noticed I had used a piece of duct tape to do a field repair on my jacket, so she took the jacket and used her sewing machine to fix it properly. She also gave me an early edition of one of Charles Lindbergh's books to read and a tour of the historic control tower that had been used to control the movement of planes in and out of the airfield in the early days. Aviation inspiration was plentiful in their home and I'm deeply thankful to have met them.

Aviation Museum and Airport, Gotland, Sweden

Johan Wiklud (left) and Axel Leonhardt, Malmo, Sweden

Johan and Axel are definitely my Viking brothers. I will be forever thankful for the help they provided getting me into Sweden during the pandemic, fixing my ferry tanks, showing me around town, locating biofuel, and giving me the extra support I needed just before crossing over the North Pole.

Robert (wearing ball cap) with Mead Treadwell, and Ron Sheardown (next to floatplane) with Robert, Alaska

Mead and Ron made countless introductions during my time in Alaska and made sure my stay was enjoyable. They gave the *Citizen* a spot in the Alaska Aviation Museum for a time, which helped attract publicity. Both Ron and Meade shared their considerable wisdom related to aviation and, most importantly, life. I respect and admire these guys more than my words can express for what they are doing in the world, for peace, and for their support of aviation. They are great men and examples for all of us.

For more information on these angels see: https://www.flyingthrulife.com/pole-to-pole/calling-on-our-angels/

Peace Moment

You and your team must be strong enough to change and evolve with the times. This means letting go of who and what doesn't work to make room for new people and new experiences. Not everyone is intended to be with us forever. People come into your life for a season, a reason, or a lifetime.

Chapter 4

Preparing the Pilot

You start to understand that by accepting the unknown, the doubts and question marks become extremely powerful stimulations for creativity and performance.
—Bertrand Piccard, Pilot of the Solar Impulse

While speaking to the Santa Barbara pilot group Serious about Aviation, I asked, "What is the most likely part of the plane to fail during a polar circumnavigation?"

A retired 747 female pilot blurted out with all the confidence in the world, "The pilot."

The answer caught me off guard. The silence in the room was a reality check. We all knew her response was correct the instant she said it.

After that, I focused on reducing the risk of pilot failure to an acceptable level that would allow me to sleep at night. My goal was to get myself into the best condition, mentally and physically, that I could.

I started the process by attending an underwater egress course offered by Survival Systems. The training included getting tossed into the chilly waters of the Atlantic in a bright red neoprene survival suit also affectionately called a Gumby suit because you looked like the cartoon figure when wearing it. With the suit on you had to learn how to:

1. Operate various types of survival gear
2. Get into a life raft that was bobbing around while you were wearing the survival suit. This was not easy as it sounds, because the waves were high and you could only grip with your thumbs because your four fingers were joined together.
3. Survive the most terrifying simulator ever devised. A huge pool inside a warehouse, it was in reality part simulator and part torture chamber. The participants were strapped into various cockpits with a five-point harness, the hatch was closed, and the pitch dark cabin was filled with water in the midst of rain, thunder and gale force winds. Once the cabin filled with water and completely submerged, it flipped upside down in the dark, and you were instructed to hold your breath as you went under. To get out, you had to undo your

harness and, amidst the chaos and panic, follow a route you had memorized. About a third of the class failed and had to be rescued by divers when they didn't come up in the allotted time.

My first two egresses went smoothly, but on the third simulation my harness jammed and I ended up taking water in through my mouth and nose in the pitch black while inverted. and strapped in. I made it out and barely passed the test.

During the simulation we didn't have the Gumby suit on because the buoyancy would have stuck us to the floor of the inverted cockpit and we would never have been able to get out. Without the suit on you had about a minute to get out of the freezing water before you died from hypothermia. It was clear to me that I would be many times safer keeping the plane in the air and dealing with whatever challenges I had in flight than I would be if I had to deal with the icy water in the pitch dark.

Other things I did to prepare myself for the flight included surgically improving my eyesight.

Spotting an airport or hazards even a few seconds sooner can save you. Vision was a major focus of my preflight effort. I didn't want to depend on glasses or contact lenses that could fall off or out during a critical phase of the flight. I would be flying blind if that happened. To avoid that possibility, I had corrective surgery to replace the lenses in my eyes, as they do with cataract surgery. The new lenses are clearer, and one is set for distance, the other for close vision, so I can see the panel with one eye and out to infinity with the other.

A sponsor provided the latest noise cancelling headsets. The amount of time wasted in a cockpit saying "Say again all after" or worse yet, misunderstanding a critical communication, can be costlier than any amount of money spent on a noise-canceling headset. Today's technology is absolutely amazing. My Lightspeed Zulu "Zen" headset calculated the mathematical equation needed to cancel out noise based on the environment in which I was flying and the shape of my ear. Not only did this keep the cockpit "Zen," but it made the flying experience much more enjoyable.

I improved my physical conditioning. Pilots are rarely thought of as athletes. In my mind, however, pilots are athletes who play the game of life and death and can't afford to lose even once! Leading up to the flight, I spent 60 to 90 minutes a day walking, running, or riding my bike in San Diego's Balboa Park, and then hit the weights.

I took care of all medical issues so that I was as healthy as I could be. It's important to know what, if any, parts of your body could create a physical distraction in the cockpit. If you don't know, start with any pain you have. I had developed ingrown toenails from my days in the military and decided I was tired of dealing with the pain and having them cut out every month or two, which could be an issue on my polar expedition. After three procedures I was able to focus on my flying.

I improved my eating habits. While preparing for my flight, I changed my diet. After doing a few three-day fasts, and eliminating meat from two of my three daily meals, I dropped my weight by eight pounds. I also noticed that gluten made my stomach bloat and meals eaten late in the day caused me to sleep hot for half the night. Processed foods tasted great but made me tired. When I ate steamed veggies or drank a fruit shake, I performed better and felt that I was doing something good for myself.

My wardrobe needed to support my flying environment both in the plane and in many climates. For the flight, I focused on safety and comfort. I wore compression socks to prevent blood clots, a survival suit on ocean legs that was as hip as a survival suit can be, and custom sunglasses designed by Scheyden specifically for pilots to handle two different light conditions—one below the clouds and one above—with a simple flip of the frame.

I surrounded myself with supportive people. This one can be tricky, but is critical to your well-being, relationships, and productivity. I came to realize that some people in my life were not supporting my effort, and the clock was ticking down to take-off. To keep my plans on track, I needed to stay focused on my mission and myself. I let people know upfront that I would make time for them if they were emotionally supportive of my trip, but if not, they would have to wait until I returned.

I needed to face the things that concerned me. If you asked me what part of the 26,000 nautical mile, 22-country, 6-continent polar circumnavigation scared me the most, I wouldn't have to think about it very long. Antarctica! Per Wikipedia, the Earth's southernmost continent is 5.4 million square miles of extremes: the coldest and driest continent, the highest average elevation at 7,545 feet above sea level and 9,300 feet at the South Pole.

There were five things about flying to Antarctica that kept me up at night:

Weather

The Antarctic is known to have some of the worst weather in the world. Winds and temps are intense, and it is not uncommon to sit at Punta Arenas, Chile, for a week or two waiting for tolerable weather conditions. On an 18.1-hour leg, there would be multiple fronts to cross before I could make it safely home. On the positive side, Punta Arenas had a good weather reporting station, which allowed my team to monitor the weather a year in advance for temperatures, fronts, pressures, and winds.

Distances

The distance from Punta Arenas, at the southern tip of Chile, to the South Pole and back is 4,457 nautical miles (nm). My Gulfstream Turbo Commander 900 was originally designed to fly 2,000 nm. With the addition of six fuel tanks, 5-bladed MT nickel-tipped composite Scimitar props, RVSM (Reduced Vertical Separation Minima which allows planes to fly closer together in flight), and two zero-time refurbished Honeywell TPE 331-10T engines, we estimated a 5,000 nautical mile range, the equivalent of flying from San Diego to Hawaii and back nonstop. Sponsors and followers often asked where I could land if I had an issue on my longest leg to the South Pole.

The joke was always that a plane can land anywhere once. It's just taking off again that poses a challenge.

Navigation

A magnetic compass does not work at the magnetic North and South poles, and GPS does not work where the meridians meet at the true poles. I was told by a pilot with experience flying in Antarctica that an old-fashioned directional gyro with a metal ball spinning at 15,000 rpm was the solution. One expert told me, "Just fly the heading you are on for about 50 nm, and then everything will be fine." Engineers at the Avidyne Corporation, whose state-of-the-art system I had added to my equipment, told me that when they simulated the Poles, their GPS units did fine. Possible solution: use a GPS waypoint before the pole, and one after it, and the unit won't get confused.

Fatigue

How does one stay up for more than eighteen hours in an extremely cramped, stressful space loaded with six extra tanks of Jet A-1 (available outside the US) fuel expanding and contracting in the cabin near a high frequency (HF) radio and power supply? When I asked the pilot who had set a world record for flying for more than twenty hours, how he stayed awake, he answered, "Honestly, I was afraid the entire time."

The pilots of Solar Impulse, the first to fly around the world in a solar-powered plane, stayed up longer. But they were also flying at slower speeds and in friendlier conditions than the *Citizen of the World*. They took micro naps and were monitored by their team in different parts of the world. I was advised to bring a timer, set the STEC 2100 digital autopilot, and sleep in 30-minute intervals. But even the best autopilots can be persnickety at times.

Extreme Cold

With outside air temps as low as −67 °C at 35,000 feet, we were concerned that below freezing temps could impact my ability to function in the cockpit for up to 20 hours. The plane's 35-year-old environmental system was unreliable, inefficient, and incapable of handling extreme heat or cold, which presented a great opportunity to update. The new environmental system we installed worked when we needed it but failed both before and after the trip. It was a constant source of stress.

It was important to prepare for worst case scenarios.

The last pilot to make a similar trip didn't take any survival gear. He figured that the extra fuel was worth more than the weight of any survival gear. He thought that staying alive in the bitter cold would only prolong his misery. Even the great Super Fred Sorenson had a similar belief. I was and am more optimistic. I took three survival courses from Tim Kneeland, one of the foremost survival experts on the planet, who also prepared my custom survival kit. Thanks to the modern satellite technology installed in the *Citizen of the World*, my potential rescuers would know my location within twenty feet every three minutes if the plane went down, and my survival suit and gear would give me extra time to stay alive while they got to me.

I decided to address the biggest challenge first.
To help improve my chances for a successful trip, I would fly the longest and hardest leg over Antarctica at the front end of the trip. This would ensure that the *Citizen* was working the best she could rather than allowing her to degrade over five months and then attempting the hardest leg at the end. I learned this valuable lesson during my equatorial circumnavigation in 2015. *By the end of the trip, the plane had developed major mechanical issues and limped home on the longest hardest leg over the Pacific Ocean.*

My team and I continued to do everything humanly possible to plan every detail and mitigate the risks. I've learned that at some point you must either accept the risks you can't control or simply walk away. I chose to accept the risks and keep flying. The opportunity to expand the boundaries of general aviation, inspire present and future generations to live their impossibly big dreams, and to fly in the name of world peace made all the risks worthwhile.

I thought about what Bertrand Piccard had said about flying solo in the *Solar Impulse*:

In the middle of the Pacific or the Atlantic, alone in the cockpit of the Solar Impulse, I wondered why I felt so much more comfortable than any other moment of my life? I came to this conclusion, when you are in the routine, when you are in your habits, you are not obliged to attain performance. You just do business as usual. At that moment you are obliged to be performant because you lose all the habits and the routine, then you don't need just to be courageous when you fight against your fear, you go to a level that is much more important. You go to the level of being confident because connecting to yourself makes you find the solutions to succeed, sometimes even survive. What do you discover inside of yourself? You discover all the skills, all the potential, all the qualities that you need to be concentrated, to be in performance, to do exactly the right thing at the right moment.

I visualized what it would be like to crash in a frozen wasteland. I would keep the gear up so the fuselage could slide on the snow and ice, crack the hatch open so it wouldn't jam shut, keep my thumbs off the yoke (so they wouldn't break on impact), shut the fuel and power off, and fly through the crash. I knew any landing would be violent, and that I would likely be injured and knocked out for a time. My plan was to use the fuselage for shelter and pray that I could somehow move enough to reach my survival gear, which was just inches away.

The Spirit of San Diego crashed at the hands of the second owner after me, and he broke his back while landing at slow speeds in tame visual flight conditions. I would be traveling at much faster speeds with six fuel tanks loaded with enough fuel to drown—or burn me alive—strapped in behind me. I didn't want to dwell on that outcome and risk manifesting it. However, I knew I wasn't much of the rugged outdoorsy type, and it would be really ugly out in the cold.

Peace Moment

Once we get to the point where we have done everything humanly possible to reach a goal, what remains
is a test of our faith and our purpose, and most importantly, our faith in ourselves and a higher power.

Chapter 5

Preparing the Aircraft

It's a machine. It reacts. It breathes. It lives and evolves. Changes. Interacts with you and, if you listen, even speaks to you. And if you treat it like the living thing it is, it will love you back.
—Jiri Marousek, Vice President of Marketing for the Aircraft Owners and Pilots Association

I made a late decision to install an Avidyne flight management panel, because I was going for the safety margin. If the system could improve my chances of survival, bring it on. I had a fully functional Garmin avionics panel with a GTN 750/650 touchscreen combo, transponder, and communications that worked quite well, and I was familiar with it from my trip in 2015. Avidyne's new IFD 550/440 flight management system was a touchscreen. It was intuitive and light years ahead of Garmin, but required some training to use.

The Citizen of the World

The panel of the Citizen of the World *outfitted for the polar flight*

The most mission-critical feature was the coordinate system, which was able to calculate the exact geographical position of the North and South poles, where all the meridians met. Some pilots had cheated their navigation systems by putting a waypoint before the pole and eliminating the poles. Some relied on a directional gyro and "dead reckoning" as the ancient mariners did for about 50 miles until their GPS units reinitialized. The system also offered backup knobs in addition to touch screen controls, in case the cabin got too cold for the touchscreen to work. This backup feature gave me added comfort that I would be able to enter inputs at critical moments.

To help with the learning curve, I used Gary "GPS" Reeves's instructional DVDs and attended one of his wonderful classes. Avidyne also had a great iPad-based simulator, and I tried to do as much buttonology (The art of pushing buttons on avionics in a plane) work as possible. I certainly lacked the confidence I had with the Garmin, but I enjoyed the Avidyne system, which flew instrument approaches coupled to the STEC 2100 digital autopilot with remarkable precision.

To install the additional tanks I would need for the mission, I called upon Fred Sorenson. When I got the *Citizen* to Las Vegas for the ferry system install, Fred seemed to have a constant stream of people stopping in to visit and others there to help. They were mostly experienced pilots, machinists, or young pilots he was mentoring. Fred was not the introvert you would expect of a person who spent long hours flying planes from point A to point B all over the planet. When one of Fred's protégés asked me what my chances were of making my pole-to-pole journey, I told him I had no idea it could be done until Fred decided to take on the project. I knew he wouldn't take on something he thought was not possible. But I still wasn't 100 percent sure. Would the plane even leave the ground loaded with that much fuel? It just didn't seem that the laws of physics could support it.

I considered Fred an aviation mentor and one of the few people on the planet who could stop me in my tracks with comments that chilled me to the bone. One such comment came during the ferry tank design phase, when Fred told me I was crazier than him. I thought about that for weeks; we all knew nobody was crazier than Fred. Anybody trying to take that title from him would need a special contract with the Universe to stay on this planet, because the odds were seriously stacked against them.

At one point, Fred told me outright that he didn't think I should make the trip. When I asked him why he was helping me if my trip was too dangerous, he told me, "I knew you would do it anyway, and I'm just trying to keep you alive."

Fred also told me that people close to him had advised him not to install supplemental fuel tanks in my plane, and he was losing sleep trying to figure out how to make this mission work. With forty-two years of experience ferrying and tanking planes, and stories of harrowing experiences in the cockpit that would make your jaw drop, Fred did not scare easily. But I was still certain he would not assist me if he thought it was truly impossible. While comforting, I too was losing sleep right along with Fred.

While designing the ferry fuel system which allowed a plane to fly much further than originally intended, I located the original designer of the wing of the Gulfstream Turbo Commander 900. He did a feasibility study and told us the plane was structurally capable of carrying a total of 1,404 gallons of fuel rather than the original 454, but I would be carrying much less than the maximum because of FAA restrictions. Luckily, this model had an enormously large fuselage and would allow us to add five extra fuel tanks inside the cabin as well as one in the luggage compartment. Four were custom-made aluminum tanks, and the remaining two were rubber bladders. The aluminum tanks did not originally fit through the hatch, which was just the first of a series of problems we had with them. The second problem was that they didn't slide all the way down tightly between the heat-

Interior ferry tank #2 of 6 showing the tight fit inside the cabin

ing channels on either side of the cabin floor, so they required plywood supports. However, the plywood lifted the tanks a bit and made it impossible to fill all but the first one because of minimal clearance above.

When Fred and I had our first discussion about the clearance on the tank, I suggested that maybe I could slide in on top and fuel each one. Fred bet me $100 that I couldn't fit in there. I took the bet. A few minutes later I was stuck with half of my torso jammed between the tank and the fuselage. When I extracted myself a few minutes later, laughing out loud, Fred said dryly, "Told ya," and walked away with a smile on his face.

Filling the tanks was a delicate operation that took place inside the plane. Any misstep would result in fuel being spilled. For that reason, I would always do it myself. I would start by filling tank #1 and use either or both of two electric pumps to transfer the fuel to the tanks farther aft in the cabin and the one in the luggage compartment. The five tanks in the cabin could push fuel into the inboard wing tanks by using cabin pressurization as well. In the event that didn't work, I could use one or two electric pumps. This gave us three options for uploading fuel into the wings.

Further, to make the system work, there was a fuel manifold with twenty valves, each of which needed to be properly aligned to move the fuel to the proper location. Basically, two valves fed the inboard tanks on each side of the plane from the six extra fuel tanks. Depending on the alignment of the valves, I could move fuel into either the right- or left-side tank from any of the six ferry tanks. Ferry tanks are additional fuel tanks added to a plane to increase the range when moving the plane great distances.

Fred didn't want me to share pictures of the components of the ferry system. But what a thing of beauty! I had never seen so many fuel valves, fittings, and clear and black hoses organized in such an elegant and practical way. Several times I had to stop people from taking a picture of the valve set-up. It was proprietary, art with both form and function, meant to take me to the ends of the earth and back.

To call the ferry tank system "complex" was an understatement, given its twenty valves and what seemed like miles of hoses. The problem was that this system of valves and tanks could not dump fuel in the event of an emergency landing. To do so would require putting a hole in the pressurized skin of the plane. It would take hours to dump that amount of fuel anyway. The only solution would be landing heavy and potentially breaking the two wing spars (which are the central structures on the wings,

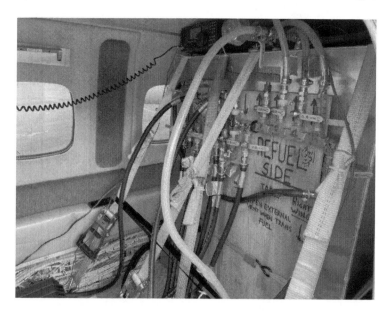

Fuel manifold for the ferry system designed by
Super Fred Sorenson

much like the keel of a ship), or flying around for up to 20 hours to burn off the fuel.

As we got closer to departure, I realized Fred and I had a major misunderstanding. After he installed the six extra fuel tanks and it was time to submit the paperwork to the FAA, he said, "Do you have the approval for the over gross weight for the tanks?" There was a long pause as I stared at Fred in total disbelief. He thought the engineer who did the feasibility study was getting permission from the FAA for the overweight permit. I thought Fred was doing it.

So I asked him what he thought our chances were of getting approval from the FAA at that point.

True to form, Fred thought for a second and then said, "Mmm 50/50." At which point he walked away. This of course sent me into a panic. I had spent two years of my life preparing myself and the aircraft, courting sponsors and accepting their money, losing sleep only to realize I had a 50/50 chance of getting approval. The only 50/50 issue I wanted to worry about was my chance of survival, which I already knew.

First Major Fuel Leak

To complicate matters even further, we suffered a major setback during the installation of the plumbing for the ferry tanks. One of the lines going to the inboard tank created a siphon effect from the higher wing tank into the cabin, and, on a flight from Las Vegas to Utah to visit a friend, fuel started leaking from two fittings with different thread patterns. By the next morning, 75 gallons of Jet A fuel had been dumped into the cabin, and I got a call from the FBO (Fixed base operator) that the plane was hemorrhaging fuel on their ramp. Two local mechanics and I spent two days with fuel containment barriers and kitty litter all over the ground as we removed the floorboards and used a child's Super Soaker to pump out the fuel by hand. Several times, we thought we had the issue resolved, only to find that the draining had temporarily stopped because dirt had clogged the drain holes.

The reality of having Jet A fuel sloshing around in the floorboards with a hot power supply just inches above it certainly shook me up. Knowing that the fumes could ignite kept me up at night and created more stress. The fumes in the cabin persisted despite the mechanic's efforts to evaporate the fuel by spraying rubbing alcohol on the exposed panels and using baby powder to absorb the smell. It was heartbreaking to think I'd be smelling Jet A for the entire trip and dealing with side effects like burning eyes and sinuses, nausea, headaches, and dizziness, not to mention the taste of fuel in my throat when I swallowed. This was a foreshadowing of things to come.

The process of tanking the plane was supposed to take five days, but I knew that Fred was being too optimistic. It ended up taking almost three weeks and multiple trips to Las Vegas to keep the project moving along. At first, I saw little progress and thought I was getting blown off. However, Fred was working overtime trying to figure out how he could get enough fuel into the plane to make the South Pole leg.

At one point, I expected him to explode under the pressure. As the chief pilot of a local charter company with ten corporate jets, he was getting pulled in many different directions. The company had just lost two pilots, and Fred was being asked to fill in while also trying to fulfill his commitment to me.

One night, as we were positioning the *Citizen* on the ramp after a long, hot day of work, Fred turned to it and, like a father talking to his child, put his hand on the nose and said, "It's okay, I know you are scared," he said. Truth is, I was just as scared as the plane.

What a touching moment. At that point, Fred became the "Plane Whisperer" to me.

In all, with the help of our sponsors we modified and upgraded the *Citizen of the World* in over fifty ways. At the completion of the trip, assuming it was successful, the DeLaurentis Foundation would have a battle-tested aircraft with all new systems that was capable of traveling to seven continents. Looking forward, we would have a mobile STEM platform to carry out global missions for the next twenty years.

That said, I was still dealing with natural human emotions. Despite the many high-tech and old-school modifications to the *Citizen of the World* that would improve my odds of survival, nothing could make the journey safe.

Peace Moment

Being Zen doesn't mean being cautious in challenging times. It means reaching within yourself when others are afraid and doing what is right and must be done for a higher cause. Having faith in your mission and in yourself is part of being "Zen" and leads to peace.

Chapter 6

Trial and Error

If you can dream it, you can do it and the only
way to fail is if you quit. Never give up.
　　　—Dick Rutan, Pilot of Voyager, Mojave
　　　　　　　　　　Desert, United States

I was quickly learning that I could seek out and work with the most qualified people on the planet who had the most experience and the best equipment, but they were still human and would occasionally make mistakes. To ensure my safety, I would have to learn about the systems we'd installed, what the mechanics had done, test the equipment, and be ready in case it failed. In truth, the plane had become so complex that it now carried a high probability of failure.

Charles Lindbergh had flown across the Atlantic in a fabric-covered plane with one radial engine, a magnetic compass, and two sandwiches. I was flying a plane with multiple turboprop engines, a panel full of high-tech avionics, pressurization, a heating and cooling system so complex that it took a Ph.D. to operate, and ten fuel tanks with twenty valves along with fuel pumps in pressurized and unpressurized areas. Instead of sandwiches, I typically took along some protein bars, bananas, a couple of cans of corn, some yogurt, lunchmeat, and almonds.

I chose the Mojave Air and Space Port also known as Rutan Field to conduct my test flights to measure the long-distance efficiency of the plane at 70 percent of fuel capacity. The aerospace company Scaled Composites had been using the facility for years to test their creations, including the *Voyager*, designed by Burt Rutan, that was flown nonstop around the world by Dick Rutan and Jeana Yeager in 1986. Mojave Airport had a 12,503-foot runway (international airport runways are typically between 9,000 and 13,000 feet), and was remote enough that nobody would bother me while I was filling the ferry tanks. During these flights, I maintained low fuel in the wings to keep the weight on the wing spars as light as possible. Only later did I learn that this was terrible for the wing and created additional stress on the dual wing spars.

Before the test flights, I was nervous. *Terrified* would be more accurate. I did not sleep well the night before, and while pre-flighting the plane, I got distracted and hit the front of my head on the sharp trailing edge of the aileron, which tilts the plane side to side in flight. I put my hand on my head; I was bleeding. I slapped on my black Lightspeed baseball cap to cover the cut and slow the bleeding before the film crew arrived. I wiped my bloody hand on my dark blue flight suit so nobody would see. I would have to deal with the cut later.

By the time the cinematographers were filming, I had my best poker face on and was connecting the ferry tank lines to the two inboard fuel tanks. My hands were shaking which made connecting the fuels lines difficult and caused fuel to start spraying all over the cabin—and me. I managed to kink the second line, which stopped the fuel from pouring out beneath the floorboards but the plane stank, and the fuel spill threw me off balance.

Cleaning it up would have required the floorboards and elaborate ferry system to be removed. That wasn't happening, so I would have to live with the smell and the fumes for what would be the next 8 months and 23 days. All we could find online was that prolonged exposure to jet fuel caused cancer, which meant prolonged over many years and not the 120 hours the trip was expected to take.

During a break, I made an excuse to go into the restroom to regain my composure, wash some fuel off, do calculations, and calm down. My hands were still shaking so hard that I dropped my iPad mini and cracked the screen. For an instant, I thought the many naysayers might be right. I shouldn't be flying with oily Jet A fuel on my flight suit. I was in heavy self-judgment at that moment, questioning myself, wondering *What are you doing? You are insane and this death wish of yours is about to manifest.*

The next day, Jeremy told me he'd been shocked at how calm I was. He compared me to an astronaut he had filmed. In reality, I was anything but calm. The voices in my head were screaming, "Don't do it! You are going to get yourself killed just like your father said!" But I had Jeremy fooled, and for that matter most others.

As luck would have it, I had met Scaled Composites' senior research and development engineer, Robert Morgan, years before at Burning Man, and annual event focused on community, art, self-expression, and self-reliance that draws tens of thousands of Burners to build Black Rock City, a participative temporary metropolis in the Nevada desert. Robert Morgan is a brilliant engineer and passionate about aviation. After the test flights, we talked over Thai food in Mojave, and he asked about the climb performance of the plane before and after each flight. I handed him a messy sheet with handwritten columns of numbers—my test data. Some information was missing, numbers were crossed out, and my writing looked like the work of a third grader. The data recorded varied from 15-minute to 45-minute intervals.

When Robert first saw it, he must have thought I was a Neanderthal, but he took it home and did calculations and projected the performance of the plane at the maximum fuel I was hoping to carry. He said that, based on a slower climb rate and less efficient cruise when heavy with fuel, I would have a 27 percent fuel reserve when at the maximum allowed amount of ferry fuel. I also did various calculations myself, and every way I looked at it, things looked good. I could see that I would have between 19 and 20 hours of range over 5,000 nm even with high winds. But Robert Morgan's conclusions mattered more. This brilliant engineer with experience had blessed my belief that the *Citizen* could fly to the South Pole. Knowing that Robert was an incredibly gifted aviation engineer and that he had taken a hard look at my performance data helped reduce my pre-departure stress and fear of running out of fuel on the way back from the South Pole.

I had noticed that the headwind at Mojave favored a departure to the north on runway 30. The problem was a mountain with windmills was in that direction, so I decided to do a wrong-way departure. This meant taking off with the wind at my tail as opposed to my nose. Whatever my rotation speed, I needed to overcome that 3-knot tailwind before the *Citizen* could start generating lift.

I had watched a video of the *Voyager* taking off in 1986 using all of the 15,024 feet of runway at Edwards Air Force Base just a few miles away. Another polar circumnavigator I knew had used 10,000 of the 12,000 available feet and barely lifted off in his Lancair experimental homebuilt plane. As I sat there looking out over 12,503 feet of runway at Mojave Air & Space Port/Rutan Field, smelling to high hell of Jet A, bleeding and shaking, in a plane with full tanks of fuel, I was ignoring my intuition and every sign the Universe was sending my way. I put the throttles to full and slowly started to move. I didn't know if the tires or the dual wing spar would hold. The plane seemed sluggish at first, but then continued to accelerate. I alternated between watching the airspeed indicator climb and keeping an eye on the end of the runway. I thought, *this could be where it ends… and it will all be on film. A privileged white guy with an overly ambitious and unrealistic goal gets stopped in his tracks. He ignored every warning sign the Universe sent his way and flew nonetheless.*

The engines emitted their characteristic thunderous roar, and, to my surprise, I lifted off about one-fourth to one-third of the way down the runway and climbed at 2,000 feet per minute, taking it easy on the plane. She definitely had more if I wanted it. I made a turn to the right, and the plane felt pretty good, even though the elevation was 2,801 feet above the ideal sea level altitude for takeoff. The *Citizen* was flying like it was no big deal. I was so happy. All the naysayers were wrong. My engines, which were also used on military Predator B Drones, delivered a ton of reliable fuel-efficient power, and the *Citizen's* Gulfstream wing was producing great lift.

I felt energized and proud—the exact feeling I would need to pull off a trip of this magnitude. The fatigue I had felt for eighteen months was, as one friend said, "Spirit using you in a different way."

This complex trip was dependent on me operating all the systems competently. A few people who had seen the tanks suggested I have a fuel engineer join me, but I wasn't willing to take on the extra weight. I also wanted to experience flying the South Pole solo. I had worked so hard, put in so much time and so many resources, that I felt I could be selfish and experience all the Universe had for me at the most remote part of the planet.

The risk of fuel gelling

The possibility of fuel gelling remained an issue. My team anticipated that at the South Pole the temperature could be as low as –67 °C, which was 17 degrees below the gelling point of my fuel and could potentially shut down both engines in flight. Larger commercial planes didn't have to deal with that issue very often, because their higher speeds created friction, heating the wings as air crossed over their surface and warming the fuel significantly. I was so concerned that the plane was equipped with three temperature gauges to help me keep myself out of the freezing air that could take me down. The problem was that the three gauges never agreed. Two were digital and one was analog. Which one should I believe? To make matters worse, the differences among the three gauges varied at different altitudes, so it was impossible to make sense of the readings. In the end, I worked with the average reading among the three.

We considered a fuel additive to keep the fuel from gelling but decided against it because it was highly toxic and would only stop water in the fuel from freezing, not the fuel itself. The advantage of having tanks in the cabin was that the fuel in them remained warmer and would not turn to gel. Thankfully, we were able to find a direct route from the interior fuel tanks to the engines that prevented any exposure to the outside freezing air. The heat from air friction, engine oil, and a pump also kept the fuel from gelling.

Test-Flight Problem

About thirty days before our scheduled departure, the *Citizen of the World* started throwing major fits. She was sending me a clear message that she was not ready—not even close. A lot of technology and new equipment, including the engines, airbags, props, avionics panel, and the environmental system, which handled heating the fuel, cooling, pressurization, and emergency pressurization, had come together in a short time, and I had not allowed enough time for debugging.

On Friday, December 21, 2018, we hit the wall hard north of Scottsdale, where I had flown to work with Rob Louviax, the senior mechanic and shop manager at Gemini Air Group. We were climbing through 33,500 feet to test a change in the fuel controller setting in order to get more horsepower at altitude.

I was flying the plane, watching for traffic, talking on the radios, and adjusting the engine rpm and torque settings while Rob made minor adjustments to the engine settings. At 34,000 feet, he said the fuel controllers had frozen and the engines were beginning to overheat due to an incorrect ratio of air to fuel. I looked over at him and saw that he was moving the throttles without getting any response. He pulled the throttles back. No response. He reached up to the right and left inlet heat and turned them on.

Again, no response on the engine temperature gauges. By this time, the temperature had topped the critical orange indicator range. I suggested shutting the hotter right engine down to save it from overheating and being damaged.

Based on the fact that the engines had only 160 of 4,200 hours on them, and considering the immense cost of replacing a turboprop engine, shutting down the hotter engine right seemed like a no-brainer. All I had to do was reach over and grab the propeller condition lever that controlled the rpm, pull it back to the stop, lift it over a gate and then another inch or two down. Alternatively, I could have reached up to the right and rotated the fuel hydraulic cutoff to shut off the fuel flow to the engine, which would have cooled it instantly with the huge amount of ram air flowing into it at close to 250 mph.

Rob, however, said he could get the temperature down. I watched him pull back the right propeller rpm condition lever. The temperature on the right engine was now well above the orange at 675 °C, some 155 degrees over the maximum temp. It stayed there for what was probably just over a minute but seemed like an eternity.

Eventually, the engine temperatures dropped. The right engine had overheated for about three minutes. I knew I was in trouble if the *Citizen's* fuel controllers stopped working at −30 °C, because in Antarctica, the temperatures would likely get as low as −67 °C. Rob said I just needed to turn on the right and left air inlet heaters at 0 °C to avoid that happening in the future. I said that in all the time I'd flown at 35,000 feet, the fuel controllers had never frozen up, and I had flown more than 60 hours on the newly refurbished engines. A friend later told me that he flew his engines at −60 °C and had never needed to turn on the air inlet heat. I felt we should send in the fuel controllers to be examined. I suggested that maybe we should return the engines to their previous settings, but Rob said they were not receiving enough fuel when the controllers were set that low.

Test-Flight Emergency

Before my next test flight, the Honeywell Maintenance Service Plan (MSP) insurance policy had replaced the fuel inlet sensors on both engines. Rob said everything was good, and he didn't think he needed to fly with me. "I prefer you come anyway," I said. We had this conversation twice in the days leading up to the flight, and another straightforward conversation before start-up in which he was more insistent. I couldn't blame him for not wanting to go. I didn't want to risk my life again either.

"Every time I fly in this plane, we have an in-flight emergency," he said, referring to a failed attempt to restart the left engine in flight several months before. I jokingly said, "Okay what's your point?" I knew what he was saying. I was scared too.

I remember looking over at Rob during that emergency. His eyes were closed like he was praying. What risk was I subjecting him to? Luckily, I was able to get the plane on the ground without damage using only one engine.

Still, I was not taking no for an answer. I pointed to the seat. "I insist, have a seat."

The third test flight of *Citizen* took place on my birthday, January 11, 2019. As we were climbing into the flight levels, the environmental system hiccupped. The gauges went crazy for an instant, reflecting what was happening internally, and then reset, a foreshadowing of what was soon to come.

As we continued to climb toward 35,000 feet, with the inlet heaters on, the fuel controllers froze up again. To make matters worse, the *Citizen* suddenly lost cabin pressure at 34,500 feet over Northern Arizona (-67 °C, ie –88 °F). Immediately we felt our ears pop, the cabin pressure warning horn blared, and the backup altitude sensor blinked and sounded off. Fifteen seconds of total confusion followed as things began failing all around us.

Our brains instantly shifted into panic mode. My old friend Fear was back, happy to resume its important role in my life. I instructed Rob to put on his oxygen mask. At this altitude, we had approximately 30 to 60 seconds of consciousness before blacking out. It only took us 10 to 15 seconds to get our oxygen masks on. Mine failed to stay in place so I was forced to use my left hand to secure it over my nose and mouth. It was an on-demand system allowing me to breathe in as I needed. Additionally, I could press a button to get extra air if necessary. Rob started hitting the supplemental oxygen button, receiving life-saving oxygen, and I did the same a few times. It sounded like a symphonic shit show with the *shhh shhhh shhhh shhhhh* of the oxygen masks, sirens, and buzzers, all complemented by the light show on the panel.

After a few seconds, we realized we were still conscious, and we got busy. Rob turned off the turbocharger that powered the environmental system and turned on the emergency pressurization, flooding the cabin with hot compressed air known as bleed air from the turboprop engines. I pushed the yoke forward and began an emergency descent, contacted the air traffic controller for the Scottsdale area, and declared an inflight emergency. I thought, "Aviate. Navigate. Communicate," a common expression

Robert testing his supplementary oxygen system

from aviation training that pilots can recite in their sleep. When things get complicated, returning to the fundamentals can be imperative, allowing the fog of confusion, to clear both in flight and in life.

Once we established descent, and I had done what I could, I glued my eyes to the altimeter. It ticked away slowly at first, then at a rate of 2,000 feet per minute, as fast as I dared to descend without possibly over-speeding the plane on the way down. The altimeter showed us moving closer and closer to breathable air at 14,000 feet, equaling the height of Pikes Peak and others worthy of the best mountaineers.

Once we were on the ground safely, I felt anger, fear, and frustration. The very system intended to make my trip so much safer, faster, and warmer over the poles had nearly killed me. Grasping for the oxygen masks as the system failed was terrifying. The added responsibility of having another soul onboard compounded my angst. The words of the mechanic who had flown in to complete the work on our brand new, high tech environmental system the day before kept running through my mind: "Good to go."

I felt betrayed and angry as everyone who had been paid was sitting fat on the ground while I had been dealing with this dangerous reality at flight level 345 (34,500 feet).

A Mistake and its Consequences

At that point, I made a really big mistake. I called up the system designer of the pressurization system and said, "You almost killed us." He hung up and refused to talk to us or look at the system for almost three months. This left the *Citizen of the World* unable to fly above 14,000 feet and delayed my departure for the South Pole for another six months.

While Rob would later say he never felt like his life was in danger, he admitted he felt like he was starting to black out.

On Facebook, I explained:

"The facility that installed the environmental system is having it examined, and the Honeywell MSP has agreed to bench-test the fuel controllers in a temperature-controlled climate before I become a Zen Test Pilot for a 4th time since the completion of the 150-hour inspection.

I wanted all of you to know we are still more than ever dedicated to preparing the plane for its Pole-to-Pole Flight this Summer but will, as always, put safety first. Your good thoughts and energy are always appreciated."

I reached out to the company that had refurbished the engines and explained that after two in-flight failures of the fuel controllers it would be reasonable to remove and bench-test them. Although the fuel controllers were rebuilt only 1500 hours ago, they failed to work properly during our test flight putting both myself and Robin in great danger. This was reason enough to pull and test them.

When my request was rejected for financial reasons, I suggested that those making the "financial" decision be present on the next test flight. That comment was enough to tip the scales and get the work done.

The solution would ultimately come when I started contacting executives and sharing the negative publicity created by the repeated failure of the engines and the slow response by their authorized representatives.

The difficulty I experienced getting my oxygen mask on at altitude led to the installation of Aerox oxygen masks, which can be put on quickly and inflated in a single movement.

I was losing faith in my refurbished engines. Everyone with whom I had talked said they engines were bulletproof and could run reliably at or above –60 °C. I heard that pilots were running them at –53 °C and below in Canada without issue, but mine were freezing up at –30 °C. I felt that the Universe was throwing me curve balls with issue after issue. I couldn't have left on time even if I wanted to.

Windshield Crack

To add insult to injury, when lifting off from the environmental install facility in Tennessee, I noticed that a small crack in the lower right corner of the pilot side windshield had developed during the installation. Then, en route to Gemini Air Group in Scottsdale, the window started to delaminate in flight. The installer of the environmental system had used a small gasoline blower to pressurize the plane on the ground, and I suspect that as the blower surged, it acted like an air hammer. The entire right side of the pilot window cracked at 31,000 feet, and as I flew at 350 mph I worried that the entire windshield would collapse on me.

As the cracking spread to the top of the window, it was as if the Universe were saying, "You aren't going anywhere." I slowed the plane to reduce the stress on the windshield and began my emergency descent. I later learned that the windshield consisted of two pieces of glass with a plastic centerpiece encasing a heating element. The cost of that part alone was $52,000 plus $4,400 to install—equivalent to half the cost of the fuel needed to travel around the world and a significant setback to the schedule and our limited budget. When the windshield broke it also broke my budget.

At what point does one start to recognize the writing on the wall and say this wasn't meant to be? I couldn't imagine that so close to my departure the Universe would take me this far only to pull the rug out from under me. The thought of letting down my sponsors and supporters by not following through on the great things we had promised for the planet and world peace was not even an option. Perhaps the Universe was looking out for me by allowing this to happen while I was here in the United States, where help was readily available, rather than over Antarctica, thousands of miles from home.

Financial Issues

Getting sponsorship had always been one of my most challenging tasks. I had never experienced rejection on this level (even in high school), and on most days it put me squarely outside my comfort zone. But I knew how important sponsorship was for generating resources and leveraging the support of other marketing organizations.

By the time the *Citizen* trip came around in 2019, finding sponsorship was getting easier since I could leverage my past success. This included a successful equatorial circumnavigation, a solid social media presence, an established battle-tested team, a ton of high-stress flying experience to provide lecture material, and a best-selling book on Amazon with endorsements from famous people in aviation including Mark Baker, President of the Airplane Owners and Pilots Association (AOPA), and Jack Pelton of the Experimental Aircraft Association (EAA). To add to that, I had done more than one hundred TV, radio, newspaper, magazine, and internet interviews.

Our relationships with cherished sponsors from the equatorial circumnavigation continued to deepen, and we grew from 35 sponsors in 2015 to 95

Robert DeLaurentis recording his Overcoming the Fear of Flying video for Gleim Aviation; and, signing books at the Avidyne booth during the NBAA 2018 (National Business Aviation Association) convention and exposition

sponsors for the circumnavigation over the poles. Without the support and strength of those wonderful organizations, an expedition like this would not have been possible.

To supplement the resources from my sponsors and supporters I dug deeply into my own pocket, making up for any cash shortfalls. My initial instructions to my property managers had been to "bleed the business," because sponsors mostly gave items like tires, batteries, and propellers, not funding required to finance the six months of preparation and the four to five months of the trip. That bloodletting would continue for the three years it took to eventually complete the trip. As successful as our efforts were, they were still not enough.

I raised funds from the sale of our innovative Zen Pilot branded products, which included Courage coins, One Planet decals, compression socks for pilots, key chains, and the *Overcoming Fear of Flying* videos, as well as from speaking engagements, and book sales. Contributions from our amazing "Angels" also helped. And despite what others thought, I never took a salary from the foundation, and to this day I remain its biggest sponsor. It is my great hope that one day soon we can bring in other professionals who can take the DeLaurentis Foundation to higher levels. *(See https://DeLaurentisFoundation.org)*

*Courage Coin developed by the DeLaurentis Foundation
intended to help aspiring pilots develop the Courage they
need to overcome the many challenges presented by flying.*

As my preparations continued, so did the bills. I had been using my credit cards to save the day, with the hope that a big sponsor would step in. I knew there was a distinct possibility that at some point during the trip, I would have to buy my way out of a bad situation, such as a major equipment failure. The loss of an engine, for example, would cost approximately $250,000 to $300,000 to refurbish.

My departure was only three months away and after two six-month delays, I realized I couldn't wait any longer. I needed a substantial cash infusion to cover the remaining liquidity needs of the polar expedition or else things would grind to a halt. In desperation, I asked my father for help. His response shocked me. He said, "If you had managed your money properly you would have enough." Clearly, he was not going to be a supporter or part of my solution. Going down that road would only create emotional challenges I didn't have the bandwidth to meet.

In the end, I decided that it was finally time to take a chance, and I took the equity out of one of my rental properties. It was time for that sort of calculated risk. I was not getting younger, but everything still worked, and my energy level was high. With the financial reserves in place, I could set personal issues aside and stay focused on my mission. As for potential equipment failure, I would leave that in God's hands.

I reasoned that the only way to move forward was by practicing surrender. I had to stay strong by not giving up, and having faith that I was being guided. The Universe had always taken care of me, and took comfort in that as I prepared for the days ahead.

One Last Detail: Insurance

Two months before departure, we still didn't have any insurance to cover the extra risk of flying over the poles. On the first circumnavigation along the equator in 2015, getting insurance proved quite easy, and the additional cost of $4,000 was split between my broker and the insurance provider resulting in no additional cost for me. Five years later, however, the industry had tightened up considerably due to the numerous claims filed as a result of the bushfires in Australia and the Boeing 737 Max failures.

The polar circumnavigation was also seen as a very different animal. It was uncommon to fly to the South Pole, and no one had done it nonstop in a single or twin-engine turboprop, because it was not thought possible. To make things even more challenging, the Antarctic Treaty required that any aircraft that crashed must have its wreckage removed. As you can imagine, the cost increased significantly based on the logistical issues associated with removing a plane the size of the *Citizen*, which would require renting a Russian Antonov cargo plane at enormous expense.

After scouring the planet for potential insurers and talking with ferry pilots who had flown over or near the poles, we found that many were self-insured, or their governments took on the financial responsibility for the bigger scientific projects. Eventually, I arranged a meeting in Las Vegas with Daniel Walker, an underwriter from the Great American Insurance Group, who specialized in insuring warbirds.

After a few drinks, Daniel and I got down to discussing the risks with my journey. First, I assured him that one of our team members, commercial pilot Mike Jesch, felt we had identified all the risks and mitigated what we could. Having logged 20,000 flight-hours since getting his license, he would know. Second, I said, even when a company insured a plane for open ocean legs, they would expect a total loss of the aircraft since it would sink. The same would be true for a plane lost in Antarctica which could not be recovered for logistical reasons

Third, I pointed out that we postponed the trip for twelve months because we had uncovered new risks that needed to be addressed. We were taking our time and not rushing anything. I assured him that I would not start the trip until we were ready. It would involve only about 150 hours of flight time spread over six months, which was just 50 percent more than most turboprop pilots fly in a year. I assured him we were in no hurry, would err on the side of caution, and only fly on fair weather days.

The policy ended up costing $30,000 with a $100,000 deductible. This seemed like a bargain since the plane with all its modifications was now valued at close to $1.5 million. Having the insurance gave me peace of mind.

By the time the trip started, there was not another dollar to spend as all of the systems that could improve the efficiency of the aircraft, make it more reliable, or give me peace of mind had been replaced. Leading experts on this subject had been contacted, contracted, and their wisdom and knowledge applied.

Would it be enough?

Peace Moment

What was clear to me now was that this trip was inspired. The forces of the Universe were working through me and my team for the greater good. The mission was meant to help others see what we can overcome when our passions and purpose align for peace. What often appear to be insurmountable obstacles can be overcome. With persistence and connection to Spirit, we can manifest something positive for the planet and our personal evolution.

Chapter 7

For Science, Education, and Exploration

We can't solve problems by using the same kind of thinking we used when we created them.

—Albert Einstein

Part of the plan for my flight involved conducting four scientific experiments, all cutting edge and offering many benefits to the scientific community as well as the planet. The flight would function as a bridge between aviation and space.

#1 Global Atmospheric Testing for Plastics/ Microfibers

To capture the plastics in the atmosphere while adding no more than a pound of weight to the *Citizen of the World*, marine biologist Dr. Dimitri Deheyn of the Scripps Institution of Oceanography devised a clever collection process. The *Citizen* would carry two pieces of duct tape on her nose and one on each wingtip, all with a piece of sticky double-sided 3M tape adding no more than a single ounce of additional weight to the aircraft.

The sticky tape would collect particles in the atmosphere, and then, after each flight I would carefully remove the pieces of sticky tape with tweezers, wrap them in wax paper, and place them in a small zip-lock bag. The bags would be labeled with the starting and finishing points of the leg, and the flight profiles would be recorded by one of two tracking websites. The sticky tape would then be dissolved in a solvent, after which the particles would be examined.

Dr. Deheyn explained that water flows through plants and animals, including humans, and also through the hydrological cycle from the oceans to the atmosphere, from the high clouds back down to land, lakes, and rivers. Pushed as vapor by wind, and precipitating as rain or snow here and there, water carries small organisms, molecules, and various contaminants across all ecosystems of the earth, spreading its load to even the most remote places.

Recently, plastics, particularly microfibers, have been found in bodies of water, as well as on land and snow, from the North Pole to Antarctica. Microfibers are generated by the textiles and garments we wear

Dr Dimitri Deheyn, the lead scientist for the Scripps Institution of Oceanography's plastic particle experiment, shows Robert how to place the double-sided tape used for collecting atmospheric microfibers on the leading edge of the wing

and wash. Those found on the earth's surface provide indications of their atmospheric origin, although a large-scale analysis of the number and type of microfibers in the atmosphere has not yet been done.

The *Citizen* was to provide an exact location of the air masses involved in each microfiber collection. We expected that flying downstream from large cities would show the most significant amounts of contamination. However, we also expected that there would be many exceptions to this scenario since, sadly, microfibers are found almost everywhere. Every leg of the trip would be analyzed for atmospheric microfiber content, which Dr Deheyn would compare to the number of microfibers found in equivalent studies monitoring microfibers in the air, waterways, along the coast, and in estuaries and rivers along the equator, allowing the scientists to determine the number of microfibers coming from the rivers and watersheds, and well as from airborne sources.

If all went well, *Citizen of the World* would be the first to provide global estimates of the microfiber load in the atmosphere, including over the North and South Poles.

#2 Wafer Scale Spacecraft Experiment

The Wafer Scale Spacecraft was affectionately named after my mother Frances. My mom was an adventurer

The NASA-funded Waferscale Spaceship was tested for the first time outside the UCSB campus

and it seemed right that she would ride along with me on this adventure as she had on others, including hot air balloon trips and motorcycle rides to Mexico.

The NASA Wafer Scale spacecraft experiment consisted of a tiny "spacecraft," just 10 centimeters in diameter and one centimeter thick. It would serve as a prototype for the NASA Starlight program, which is intended to replace future manned rocket missions involving heavy rocket motors, fuel, and astronauts that must be lifted above the earth's atmosphere. Instead, a spacecraft like Frances would be shot into space using an electromagnetic cannon and then propelled even further by lasers. The spacecraft was self-contained except for needing a small amount of power (less than one watt) and sat in a plexiglass box about 30 x 30 x 30 cm, mounted near a window. It had a GPS, optical communications devices, an ultra-low power radio (optional), inertial navigation, temperature, and optical imaging sensors. Data was recorded on-board on a Secure Digital (SD) memory card.

So far, the wafer scale spaceship had been tested only locally, at UC Santa Barbara, using a helium balloon. This expedition was her big chance to be tested by collecting data in the real world and over the poles. After we returned, she was next scheduled to fly on the Amazon-funded Blue Origin Rocket.

#3 Biofuels Over the Poles

As I prepared for the polar circumnavigation, biofuels, which are a blend of regular gas and plant or algae material were being used more often in aviation. The European Union had already mandated that 30 percent of Jet fuel sold had to be biofuel. It was just a matter of time until the mandate came to the United States, and some fuel providers were positioning themselves for easy compliance. The problem was the extra expense associated with their production and distribution.

GAMA, the General Aviation Manufacturers Association, was supporting the use of biofuels in the United States. United Airlines, and Gulfstream had contracted to buy everything being produced on the West Coast. The fuels could be made to the exact specifications for Jet A from several different sources. They burned cleaner with fewer particulates and gelled at a lower temperature, which meant they were of particular interest to me.

A lucky call to senior executives at Gulfstream reminding them that they had manufactured the *Citizen* years before resulted in 200 gallons of biofuel for the trip a few days before departure. So I flew up to Long Beach to a bit of fanfare and uploaded my precious fuel, making the *Citizen of the World* the first aircraft in history to fly over the South and North Poles using biofuel.

#4 Tracking Over the Poles Experiment

The *Citizen* was the first aircraft in history to use data from the sixty-six new Iridium NEXT Satellites processed by Aireon to display a track over the poles. This was a leap forward in the ability to track aircraft anywhere on the planet, including places as remote as the poles.

STEM Education

In recent years, the number of general aviation pilots has free-fallen despite the best efforts of all the major players. General aviation, simply put, includes charter and private (smaller) aircraft. The pilot population involved in general aviation has historically been composed primarily of privileged middle-aged white males like me and wasn't drawing in the requisite number of younger people or women, mostly because litigation in the industry had pushed costs way up and they couldn't afford to fly. I hoped to ignite new interest in general aviation by showing what could be done with aircraft that are readily available on the open market.

One of our sponsors, Redbird Flight Simulations, helped us create raw and chilling simulations of five key legs of the pole-to-pole circumnavigation so that young people could experience the conditions and dangers of these flights in a safe environment in order to develop their critical thinking skills and hopefully be inspired to pursue their dream of flight. Surprisingly, the fifth simulation, which included a departure from Mahajanga, Madagascar, during a cyclone was not used because it was determined too dangerous.

Our long-term intention was to use the *Citizen of the World* as a mobile science, technology, engineering and mathematics (STEM) lab. Using Redbird's

3800 simulators worldwide, people could experience—at no charge—virtual flights like mine over the South and North Poles. The simulations included problems like both engines failing from fuel gelling, whiteout conditions, loss of a magnetic compass, flight management systems, and autopilot, to name a few. Once the aspiring pilots had experienced flying over the poles, they would be able to see, feel, and smell the actual plane that had made history and maybe even push buttons on the best video game on the planet courtesy of L3Harris, Avidyne, and Genesys Aerosystems (STEC), the companies that sponsored my avionics.

The aspiring pilots would be able to select any simulated airplane and fly their own mission of global peace and adventure. Our hope was that they would realize that the impossible is possible with the help of others who share their vision, hard work, and determination. They would learn that life will throw you many challenges but the challenges are not insurmountable and are intended to make you a better pilot and person. These simulations are now in use in aviation schools, museums, and STEM-based programs across the country dedicated to flying.

The Explorers Club

The Explorers Club is an international multidisciplinary professional society dedicated to the advancement and promotion of the scientific exploration of land, sea, air, and space by supporting research and education in the physical, natural, and biological sciences.

Since its inception in 1904, the Club has been a meeting point and unifying force for explorers and scientists worldwide. Members include many of the greatest adventurers of the 20th and 21st centuries, including Mt. Everest explorer Sir Edmund Hillary, astronaut Neil Armstrong, marine biologist Sylvia Earle, and Scripps oceanographer Dr. Walter Munk.

Just a few months before departure, I connected with Mary and Walter Munk. Walter, at 101 years old, was the modern-day Jacques Cousteau. He was knighted—twice, and he's received many awards for his scientific achievements, including the prestigious Crawford Award, a list as long as both my arms. Though in a wheelchair, Walter didn't slow down a bit. He was delightful, engaging, funny, and mentally sharp, and his wife, Mary, was one of the strongest women I have ever met. She had a kind smile, quiet confidence, and absolutely wonderful spirit. I adored her and her energy immediately.

Explorers Club flag #44, the oldest in circulation, was entrusted to Robert to carry around the planet and over the Poles

Our first conversation was thirty minutes long, after which Mary said they wanted to support my trip. She and Walter had an amazing circle of friends that included dignitaries, Hollywood producers, and other influential people. When Mary and Walter took me under their wing, I knew that we could all do wonderful things for the planet using my plane. I spent several evenings at their place having dinner with them and Mary Marcdante, author/speaker/Director of Communications for the Center for Mindful Self-Compassion in San Diego, and one of my biggest supporters. Both Marys had a love for the oceans and neither of them would ever take "no" for an answer.

Prior to his passing, Dr. Munk nominated me for admission to the Explorers Club and lived to see my induction in 2018, which was a great honor.

To carry one of the Explorers Club flags, a Club member must show that his or her expedition holds the promise of scientific results. The flag must be exhibited at every suitable opportunity on the expedition, and it must be returned to the Club along with a written record of the expedition called the Flag Report.

As of this writing, 202 expeditions have carried flags. Some flags are retired when returned while others are assigned to future expeditions. With the help of Dr. Dimitri Deheyn and his Plastic Particle experiment, I was given Flag #44 to carry, one of the oldest used by the Club that had been on many epic global expeditions for the betterment of the planet since 1918.

World Citizen Passport

Just as the mission of the entire Flying Thru Life Team is to use aviation as a vehicle for spreading our global message, "One planet. One people. One plane. Oneness for humanity," back in the mid-1940s Garry Davis spearheaded a similar cause. He was an ex-Broadway actor and had been a bomber pilot during World War II who grew so displeased with the divisiveness of the planet that, in 1948, he walked into

A World Passport, carried by many refugees without documents to gain entry into neighboring countries and intended to break down the borders that divide humanity

the American Embassy in Paris and renounced his U.S. citizenship to become what he termed a Citizen of the World. His rationale, as stated in his *New York Times* obituary, was that "if there were no nation-states... there would be no wars" because boundaries keep people apart, and his "one World" model had the support of many intellectuals and celebrities including Albert Einstein, Albert Schweitzer, Jean-Paul Sartre, and E. B. White.

Garry's peace rallies filled stadiums with tens of thousands of people and he formed the World Service Authority, which issues "world government documents" such as the World Passport, which I carried on my trip along with my US Passport.

Peace Moment

Two of the important common threads of humanity are science and overcoming the global challenges we face as humans. Our natural curiosity leads us to discoveries in science and moves us forward, joining us in one common mission to relieve suffering and increase joy.

Chapter 8

The Power of Courage

Have the courage to follow your heart and intuition. They somehow already know what you truly want to become.

—Steve Jobs

With less than a week remaining until my departure from the continental United States, I began pulling away from my friends, family, home, car, and beautiful San Diego. The National Science Foundation, the Environmental Protection Agency, and the U.S. Department of State were now referring to the *Citizen of the World's* global journey as a "Polar Expedition."

It was time to shift to a different mindset: one of constant movement, challenge, lack of comfort, and facing the unknown. I remembered a thought I'd had in 2015 while flying in pitch darkness over the middle of the Pacific. I was heading toward American Samoa, an island that was fogged-in and surrounded by mountains, focusing on landing at their non-towered airport. I closed my eyes and turned my head toward the pilot-side window. When I opened them, it was dark, without any comforting visual reference or hint of humanity. At that moment, I realized I was totally on my own, with no support and a little voice in my head said, "What are you doing? You could be at home in San Diego on your comfortable sofa watching TV with your girlfriend!"

The realization that I was now doing another circumnavigation and that it was three times more difficult than my first, with a host of deadly new risks, now prompted similar panic attacks, waking me up at 3 a.m. most nights in a cold sweat.

And I wasn't the only one questioning my journey.

When people learned I would be flying a radically modified 1983 Turbo Commander 900 with damage history and dozens of upgrades including more plumbing than your house, a few referred to my plane as a "Frankenstein," (which, by the way, was a nasty way to refer to such a fine, fine lady).

Humor aside, their obvious concern didn't do anything to raise my comfort level. I knew I had the best people with hundreds of combined years of experience working on the airplane, but they had made mistakes along the way—and so did I. We were all still here, but fear of the unknown and what might happen next rode shotgun in my mind.

Where would I find the courage to do challenging things—things that honestly scare the piss out of us—while navigating my ever-present fear?

Courage comes from many sources, among them the people who believe in us and support us with their time, resources, words, and faith. Because of their belief in us, we tell ourselves, "If they believe in me, I can believe in myself as well." They see our abilities from a different and perhaps more accurate perspective than we often do.

Why Was I Doing This?

Twenty-four hours before departure, I began to question why I was doing this trip. Was it for ego? Was it truly for the planet or was it just the wildest adventure an adrenaline junkie could dream up? There was probably some truth to all those reasons. But, whatever the reason, it would not be easy to back out now, after two years, with so many promises made and so much support accepted. I felt as if I were about to take the biggest chance of my life. It was certainly the riskiest flight I'd ever made, with more opportunities for failure than I had ever experienced.

It was like that leap of faith you make when you parachute out of a plane. You have that last instant where you decide, "Do I stay, or do I go?" This was one of those moments when I realized I'd lived a good life, and if it ended on this flight I'd be doing something I was passionate about that also had a great impact on the planet. I felt that even in failure, there is success because you have tried. I don't think the successes that had gotten me to this moment in time were all just so that I'd back out now. I knew I was going through with it. I was in that moment of fear when I was questioning everything, and I knew that at some point if I went deep enough into that feeling, it would go away. I've found that, in situations like this, people respond in one of two ways. Either they freeze or they move ahead. I'd had my moment of panic, self-doubt, and fear and now it was just time to get it done!

A Mother's Love

Before my departure from Ushuaia, Argentina I had to deal with the emotions that had been bubbling up for months. The reality of what I was about to attempt could no longer be put off or ignored. I put on a brave face and told people that I was prepared. This was similar to what I had done many times before. Truthfully, though, I was seriously scared. I was risking my life by flying to the most remote place on the planet in extreme temperatures for peace. If this entire scheme went bust, I had no more than 24 to 36 hours to live on this planet.

I combed through my backpack to remove anything that wasn't essential. Feeling overwhelmed and insecure, wishing for comfort, I reached my hand blindly into the front pocket, where I carried my most important items, including *rudraksha mala* beads from the Dalai Lama, one of our beautiful courage coins, a meteor flake that a buddy had asked me to carry, a written prayer, and a few other things. When I pulled my hand out, it was covered with gray powder—my mother's ashes, which I was taking with me in a small glass vial.

Mom was the adventurous one in our family. She would have loved to fly along and would have trusted me 100 percent, no matter how dangerous my undertaking. She'd joined me on hot air balloon rides, horseback rides, and adventures on my minibike, which included getting stuck in a mud pit in Squaw Valley before I was old enough to drive legally. Later, we rode another motorcycle on sketchy dirt roads to Mexico for fresh lobster and shopping. I named the NASA experiment "Frances" to honor her sense of adventure.

At first I was shocked to see her ashes on my hand, but then it dawned on me that she was reaching out to comfort me in my time of need, touching my hand as if to say, "it's okay, you are okay," as a mother would. In my mind, I heard her say, "You are going to be fine." Tears flowed. I wept like a child as I was re-minded that hers was the only unconditional love in my life. What were the chances that the tightly sealed container would open at that exact moment after weeks of being bounced around?

I reached into my backpack again to remove what I expected would be a broken glass container. In-stead, I found the vial still almost full and the cap right next to it. Only the smallest amount had leaked out. I sat there in disbelief; this was beyond probabil-ity. Mom was with me in spirit for this trip.

Peace Moment

On a spiritual level, I believe that courage comes from within—deep within us—maybe even from our souls. On the other side of the fear, which takes courage to pass through, is the greatest freedom we will ever feel.

Chapter 9

Launch of the Pole-to-Pole Expedition

If your dream doesn't scare you, it's too small.
—Mark Batterson, *Chase the Lion*

As I departed San Diego to finally begin what some referred to as my bipolar journey, I prayed my plane would work perfectly for the entire polar circumnavigation. We'd invested thousands of hours and hundreds of thousands of dollars into this effort and prayed the Gods were with us. I knew my journey was going to be long and difficult. I hoped I had what it took. Time, of course, would tell.

Sidestepping a Country

Aviation offers us opportunities to learn lessons that go beyond improving our skills as pilots. While flying at flight level 310 (31,000 feet) and moving along at just over 266 knots (306 mph), I had a moment of clarity. As I was getting ready to pass over Nicaragua, I got my spiritual lesson for the day.

The air traffic controller for Central America (CENAMER) came on the radio. "Do you have permission to overfly Nicaragua?"

"Only the overflight permission that you at CENAMER issue for all of Central America countries," I replied. "Would you like the reference number?"

Considering CENAMER had issued the permission, it seemed like a strange conversation to be having. But flying internationally is always filled with surprises.

No response.

After a minute, I repeated myself.

"We need to reroute you," the controller said.

At this point, I lost my Zen mind. "How is it that the organization that issued the permission for my overflight is now asking me if I have permission?"

Again, no response.

I asked three more times before I got an answer: "I'm sorry. They (Nicaragua Air Traffic Control) are asking for it."

A brief time later I got the reference number from Eddie Gould, my trip coordinator, via satellite text and gave it to the controller, who agreed to call the air traffic controller in Nicaragua. A few minutes later, we got the same rejection. "I'm sorry, it's out of my hands," the controller said.

Then the Universe stepped in, and I heard myself say calmly, "You know, I'm on a World Peace flight trying to show the world the things that prevent us from being 'One planet. One people. One plane.' Borders that we as human beings create and that's what divides us."

No response.

I kept quiet but was silently thinking that this need to fly over another country was entirely a human thing. Our airplanes don't know boundaries, they just fly between waypoints. The weather moves unobstructed across the globe. So, then it must be people who keep us divided, right?

Our eighteen months of planning and preparation for the Pole-to-Pole Expedition had been chock full of rejection, roadblocks, and inconsistencies on a scale that could fill this and many other pages. But never by an entire country.

Certainly, this was the Universe telling me, "Hey, you seem to have missed the lesson that you can sidestep some issues that slow you down the first hundred times I sent it your way, so now I'm giving you the equivalent of a two-by-four cracking you across the forehead and your all-knowing third eye."

Realizing I was destined to repeat this situation unless I learned the lesson, I decided to take action. First of all, I accepted that maybe the sage words of wisdom—"What you resist persists!"—were in fact true. Second, I gave up needing to be right. Third, I asked for a spiritual solution.

Within a few seconds, the voice of reason spoke within me: "There will be those that try to stand in your way for reasons you may not ever know. You can stand and fight, and it's almost a sure bet you will lose focus, energy, and momentum, and risk injury or retribution. Or you can take one step to the left or right and then keep moving ahead. Your mission is greater than this obstacle or possibly any obstacle. If you know you are on the right path, this is just one more lesson you were meant to learn along the way."

Okay. There was no way I was going to change the air traffic controller's mind, and he had given me two new waypoints that would enable me to sidestep the entire country. In the span of about thirty minutes, I left Nicaragua behind at over 300 mph.

No question, I certainly could have gotten bogged down on that one. I could have chosen not to comply with the ATC's instruction to sidestep. I can only imagine how that would have played out with my license or what would have been waiting for me when I landed.

So, learning and understanding that resisting life lessons only causes them to come back stronger than before, over and over again, begs the question: "What other blocks are popping up in my life repeatedly and what is the lesson?"

It was during moments like this that I realized I was being tested. I also understood that it is through these tests that we progress in our personal evolution as humans, that our vibration increases, and that when one human on the planet moves ahead, the entire planet moves and increases its vibrations as well. These are our "Peace Moments."

Cartagena

I was a little nervous about taking the *Citizen* to Cartagena, Colombia, one of the drug capitals of the world. The Twin Commander, the piston predecessor of my aircraft, was one of the planes most widely used beginning in the early 1980s when the drug lords reigned supreme. It was one of the fastest twins of the day, and it could fly well on one engine because of its oversized tail, which counteracted the asymmetrical thrust created when one engine failed. Also, flying on one engine saved fuel so they wouldn't have to land and risk getting caught on the ground. This, combined with the fact that the plane could carry lots of payload and still fly into and out of the most remote and shortest runways in Central America, made it ideal for drug running. In fact, I found out that one of my mechanics used to take in these planes for annual inspection and then, for the next two weeks, use them to run drugs. After that he'd do an abbreviated inspection and return the planes later than he'd promised. He always had a valid excuse for the two-week delay.

The 690D model Turbo Commander that I was flying was that earlier plane on massive doses of steroids. The Panamanian and Colombian military both used the older models for counter-drug operations, so it was no surprise when the *policia* wanted to inspect the *Citizen of the World*.

The first things the police officer noticed were the ferry tanks just about falling out of the airplane. They ran halfway from the entry door to the back, and then continued into the unpressurized luggage compartment. Connecting each of these tanks was what seemed like miles of hose in every direction. I was concerned I would be called to explain to her in specific detail about a system I didn't fully understand. My worst fear was that someone would insist on seeing the ferry tanks inside the back of the plane or inside the tanks themselves. I would then be forced to take the tanks out, unraveling weeks of work.

It wasn't long before the police officer was snapping pictures of the tanks and talking in Spanish with someone on her cell phone at about 100 miles an hour. I knew that couldn't be good, so, rather than letting her imagination run wild and having the issue run up her chain of command, I smiled and signaled that I wanted to show her something. I knocked on the first tank, which was hollow, and empty, and said, "Nada" meaning nothing. Then I walked her to the baggage compartment and showed her the deflated bladder tank. She then pointed to the middle of the plane and put her hands up while shrugging, as if to say, "What is in here?"

I said, "*todo* aviation fuel," meaning "all" aviation fuel. I pointed to the fuel truck and then said it again: "*Todo.*" I walked her to the flag decals on the front of the plane and showed her the one for Colombia. Then I pointed to the one that said "South Pole." I spread my arms and said in my broken Spanish, "*Mucho milas ayi* (Many miles there) *y entoces aqui* (then here)," and pointed to the ground.

Her confused expression indicated that she didn't really understand my bad high-school Spanish. Then she looked down at her phone, where a picture of me wearing my Scheyden "Zen" sunglasses and standing by the plane was lighting up her screen. I was amused, because I knew at that moment that our website, PoleToPoleFlight.com, had been worth every ounce of energy we'd put into creating it.

The officer blushed, pointed at me, and smiled. I could see she was smitten, but I knew the person on the other end of the phone would definitely not be. Probably just the opposite. I knew there was nothing to be gained from staying on the tarmac a minute longer. I just wanted to get out of there, so I turned my attention to finalizing my bill.

The fixed base operator had handed me a $1,700 bill for some of the worst handling I'd experienced on the trip so far. I knew they could charge me anything they wanted, but I made it clear I felt overcharged. As the words flowed from my mouth, I realized too late that I was at the mercy of greedy Colombian bureaucrats who had been feeding off general aviation pilots for a long time and could make my life really miserable. I decided to shut up and fight this battle once I was out of there.

To further complicate matters, the transponder antenna on the bottom of the *Citizen* had nearly been scraped off during the test flights when the plane was heavy with fuel, and I was unsure if it was still working. I was unable to test it on the ground and was concerned that I would be ordered to return to Cartagena if it turned out to be faulty in the air. I didn't want to be stuck there, where the daily avionics rate was probably as high as the ground fees. The best thing I could do was put this country behind me at about 340 mph. I pushed the throttles forward as I was given clearance to take off. The nose wheel of the *Citizen of the World* lifted off the runway—followed by a deep sigh of relief lifting from me.

Avionics Failure over Panama

With hundreds of systems on the *Citizen* working in unison, it was asking a lot of the Universe to allow everything to work perfectly for all 150 hours of flight time it would take to complete the trip. Still, I prayed for ease and grace.

The last thing I expected to fail was any component of my avionics system. Most of it was solid state and reliable. When I was flying over Panama and lost the satellite connection to my GPS, I thought it was because there was so much moisture in the humid Central American air. It rained most of the time, and, inside the cabin, the windows were almost always dripping as I descended, and any ice that had developed started to melt. The problem was compounded by the fact that other components, such as the L3 NGT 9000 transponder, and the Avidyne Ex600 display screen, used that same satellite signal, which meant that when the satellite connection failed, I lost my ability to detect traffic, terrain, and my position on both GPS units. Luckily, I had an independently functioning GPS, and maybe the most bulletproof component of the entire setup—an Apple iPad mini.

I contemplated making the flight to the South Pole with a partially functioning avionics panel. The *Citizen* had enough redundancy that I could do it. If Lindbergh crossed the North Atlantic using a magnetic compass and not a lot more for navigation, surely, I should be able to do the South Pole with a single flight management system and a backup for redundancy.

Luckily, the issue turned out to be a bad connection on the back of the GPS unit, easily repaired by Aerotech's competent technician on the tarmac in Mendoza, Argentina.

Circumnavigation Diploma

To earn what the FAI (Fédération Aéronautique Internationale) called a "Circumnavigation Diploma," previous circumnavigators would go only as far as 75 degrees south, which still left them 1,500 miles short of the South Pole at 90 degrees south (and 3,450 fewer miles than what I was attempting). Going to 75 degrees south and north seemed like a half measure and a polar vacation to me.

I had seen other pilots take this route. One even took his friends along, videotaping what seemed like

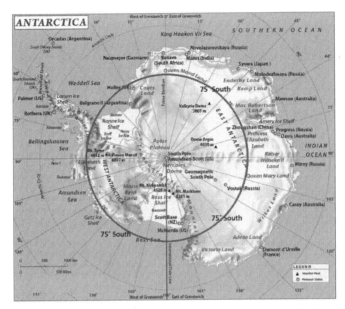

A map of Antarctica showing 75 south latitude, which the FAI (Fédération Aéronautique Internationale) considered far enough south to qualify for a Circumnavigation Diploma

a party inside the plane. I think they even had Champagne. My experience was radically different. I would be alone, strapped into a plane wearing a survival suit, the fuselage jammed with venting fuel tanks to stretch the range of the aircraft from 6 hours to more than 18.1, three times the limit for which it was designed, and I would be tasting Jet A-1 instead of Champagne in my throat while feeling my eyes and sinuses burning.

This was no vacation. I was going all the way. No excuses.

Determining the Departure Point

When I started planning the Polar Circumnavigation back in 2018, I gave the most reputable company in the industry the responsibility for getting me permission to fly from Punta Arenas, Chile, to the South Pole and back. Our challenge? The Chilean government kept changing its mind. At one point, our permit was expected in a few days, and then, without reason, all general aviation travel to King George Island (a Chilean military base at the northern tip of Antarctica that could potentially shorten the roundtrip by five hours) had been stopped. Two years before, the same flight planning company had successfully received permission for another flight to the 75th parallel in the Antarctic near the South Shetland Islands, 1,500 nautical miles short of the South Pole. In February 2019, two Chilean aircraft had been given permission to fly to 75 degrees south. When I contacted one of the pilots, he told me they had been trying to get a permit for three years when the approval unexpectedly came through, but he could not tell me why.

So I let the flight-planning company grind away and hoped for the best.

With my constant nudging, they worked on my project off and on for eighteen months. Then, a week before my scheduled departure, when I was led to believe we were ready to go, they told me they hadn't been able to get me the permit. They had called government officials, including politicians and generals, in a desperate last-minute attempt. They had stirred things up right to the head of the scientific community, which created a roadblock as wide as Antarctica. As a result, we would now need to submit an application to the Chilean scientific community for approval, and it would take six months.

I learned this as my ferry tanks were being installed. When I heard my rep say, "Sorry," I was standing on the 105 °F tarmac in Las Vegas, feeling utterly defeated and betrayed.

I called my crisis team, which consisted of my trip lead advisor Susan Gilbert, Michel Gordillo, a mentor and circumnavigator, and Eddie Gould, my trip coordinator. Together we came up with a four-phased plan:

- First, I would immediately terminate our relationship with the flight-planning company that had created the issue.

- Second, we would request that our lead scientist, Dr. Dimitri Deheyn, write a letter to the senior scientist in Chile explaining that our experiments were passive and would leave nothing behind. Never mind that I already had permission from the U.S. State Department, the Environmental Protection Agency, and the National Science Foundation. Further, he would ask if the Chilean scientist could quickly route our request. In return, we were willing to share the data obtained from our scientific experiments with them.

- Third, Michel Gordillo would help us get permission to fly out of Ushuaia, Argentina, located on Tierra Del Fuego. Michel had always encouraged me to depart from that point, but I preferred Punta Arenas because the runway was slightly longer, it was closer to the South Pole, and it had fewer mountains around it.

- Fourth, Eddie Gould and Ahmed Mohamed from General Aviation Support Egypt would try to secure permission for us to leave from a British military air base in the Falkland Islands, which had been quiet ever since 1980, when the British sent its renowned Royal fleet nearly eight thousand miles through the Atlantic and re-took the islands following a brief occupation by the Argentinian *junta* that ruled the country. Based on the rigid nature of the British Military, what I was asking seemed impossible. Eddie had assessed our chances of getting permission for this departure point at close to zero but agreed to give it a try anyway.

Another, more clever—and risky—option suggested by Michel was to take off under visual flight conditions from either the Falkland Islands or Ushuaia so that we would not be required to file any flight plan at all. Of course, this would have meant that nobody in the air traffic control system would know I was flying 18.1 hours to and from the South Pole unless I declared an emergency on the far side of the world.

Eventually, I went with Michel's suggestion to leave from Ushuaia, which, in hindsight, turned out to be my best option, given the efforts to find the Chilean C-130 that went down in the Drake Passage that was underway out of Punta Arenas.

As it turned out, Chile's refusal to allow me into their air space violated the Antarctic Treaty Article II, which ensured unrestricted exploration of Antarctica.

While Antarctica is claimed by many countries, it is owned by none. Even the land on which the U.S. post is headquartered is claimed by other countries.

The Antarctic Treaty was clear about not restricting flight over Antarctica. The 12 countries that had signed the treaty in 1959 and were granted the right to fly in Antarctica where and when they wanted.

Peace Moment

Obstacles become opportunities for growth. These obstacles push us beyond our comfort zones and allow us to move beyond what we think we are capable of achieving. We emerge from the experience more confident, more capable, and with a different perspective on ourselves and our world.

PART TWO

To the South Pole and Back

Chapter 10

To the Ends of the Earth: The South Pole

You don't concentrate on risks. You concentrate on results. No risk is too great to prevent the necessary job from getting done.

—Chuck Yeager

As I prepared to leave Ushuaia that Monday morning, December 16, 2019, I kept my self-talk as positive as I could, but underneath the bravado, a question lurked: was I coming back? I wasn't sure.

Given all the unknowns and "first-time it's been done" modifications to the aircraft, I'd never embarked on a journey with a higher probability of failure. I thought about all the people who had helped me and were counting on me, including the kind people at the local hotel who had graciously accepted the responsibility of returning my belongings to my family if I didn't make it back. This had been my

A map of Antarctica showing the size of the continent and its remoteness in relation to the other landmasses

dream—and now was my reality and, possibly, my demise.

I wanted to take off to the east to avoid having the mountains directly ahead of the runway. They were foreboding, snow-capped and jagged peaks, including some volcanoes

I planned to use the 50-mile Beagle Channel connecting the Atlantic and Pacific Oceans at the southern tip of Tierra del Fuego to climb slowly to altitude. I wanted to use Runway 07 so I could take advantage of the lift created by ground effect over the water if necessary. But on that Monday morning, it was not in

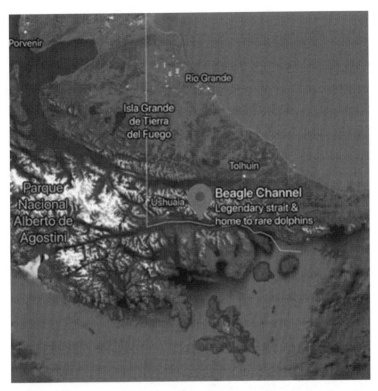

The Beagle Channel, from which the Citizen *departed and returned to Ushuaia, Argentina*

the cards. The Universe threw me another deadly challenge: 15- to 20-knot winds blowing in the opposite direction from what I had planned, so it looked like I would be making a Runway 25 departure. Runway 25 was uphill, requiring more power to build up speed and lift, and it pointed directly at the mountains.

I'd originally intended to do a rolling takeoff from the taxiway onto the runway, as had been recommended by Morris Kernic, a pilot who had flown

Commanders for more than 50 years before he passed. But then Super Fred told me a rolling takeoff would collapse the gear when the plane was almost fully loaded with fuel. That made me wonder if I were I making the departure deadlier with each questionable decision. Probably. This could end terribly for me.

The Haters and Doubters

I was careful not to miss a step on my checklist. The voices in my head, however, were brutal and going crazy. "Don't do it. You will certainly die! You aren't a good enough pilot. You will die! You are a foolish fame-seeker!"

I responded, "I'm going, so f—k you all."

As I admonished my mind and began to taxi for takeoff, the plane needed extra power to overcome the inertia created by ten heavy fuel tanks. I taxied to the end of the up-sloping runway to assure the longest takeoff run possible and sat there with the Predator B drone engines growling. I'd like to say that I then had my most enlightened "Peace Moment," but I was buried in absolute fear. I thought about the people who had told me they didn't think this plane could make it to the South Pole and back and couldn't fly as heavy as I wanted. I was reminded of the person from the organization that monitors aviation records who sent me an email saying, in effect,

Robert flashing his best poker face just before take-off from Ushuaia, Argentina, to the South Pole

"If you are so Zen, maybe you should listen to what the Universe is telling you and not do this flight."

Then there was the sponsor who told my mechanic I would never succeed. And another sponsor who told me to rip their decal off my plane because he didn't think I would do the trip. Hanging up on him was probably not a recommended play for building sponsorship, but then again, this flight was not out of any playbook I had ever read. At least he'd know I wasn't going to accept that kind of treatment from anyone. Ever.

I thought about all the articles that might be written about this flight if I failed—how I had ignored all the rules of flying a plane, turning it too tight in the air under load, modifying it too much, and being reckless. The naysayers were going to have a field day from the comfort of their reclining La-Z-Boy chairs!

The Takeoff

My one final thought as I pushed the torque levers forward to 100 percent was: *What you are doing is totally insane.*

As I released the brakes with the Predator B Drone engines pulling hard at full throttle and pounding out 2,300 thunderous horsepower on the edge of the runway threshold, the plane hesitated just a split second longer than usual, as if to take a deep breath and say, "Here we go!" before accelerating. By only halfway down the runway, I was at the normal rotation speed of 85 knots. "Yesss," I said. I had worried about the takeoff for two years and it was looking good at this point. I allowed the plane to accelerate to about 110 knots, and then pulled back ever so slightly to take the weight off the nose wheel and let her lift off on her own. I ran the risk that as the nose went up and the tail went down a bit I would scrape off what remained of the transponder antenna that had already been slightly damaged during the test flight in the Mojave Desert.

The plane built up speed, and, to my great amazement and relief, I saw the landing gear struts lengthening as the weight they had been carrying was relieved by the lift that the long Gulfstream 52-foot quarter-inch wing created. The plane was steady as it rolled down the runway as if it were on rails.

Finally, and magically, as if freed to be where she had always belonged, we were flying.

My first thought: *I grossly underestimated this plane.* People kept telling me I had really big brass balls, but at that moment, I realized the *Citizen's* were bigger. Once she was liberated from her earthly bonds, she responded nimbly and nicely to my control inputs. The *Citizen* was ready for this mission! She climbed at a surprising rate of 1,500 feet per minute, far exceeding my hope of just making it into ground effect for the first fifty miles. Her performance this heavy blew me away. I had never flown her this heavy before. At Mohave she was tested at 70 percent and then we projected her performance at full fuel. Super Fred had told me never to overload a wing spar more than you have to. For the first time, I felt like I had a fighting chance at success. At 1,000 feet, I started my 180-degree turn to the left to avoid the mountains, knowing the amount of lift the wings could create was greatly reduced. Considering the climb performance, though, I was no longer afraid.

Anyone who might have been hoping for a fiery end-over-end NASCAR-style crash, was going to be disappointed, at least for now.

The *Citizen of the World* climbed to 30,000 feet in just 58 minutes, despite being very overweight. I was in total awe. How she did it, I will never know.

On a long flight like the one to Antarctica, most of your fuel burns on the outbound leg, when the plane is full and flying slower with a high angle of attack. It's comparable to a speedboat that requires a huge amount of power to start planning across the water. Once there, it doesn't need as much power. For the *Citizen of the World*, there was a 30- to 50-knot difference in performance when she flew heavy rather than light.

My hope was to make up for the lost efficiency on the return leg, when we'd be flying lighter, higher, and faster, and we had more favorable winds.

Fuel Leak

About an hour into the flight, while transferring fuel, I thought I saw a light flicker, but by the time I rotated my head, it was gone. I started looking more closely. I stared at the valves for about five minutes—and then I saw what caught my attention, a drop of fuel fell from one of the fuel valves. I swiped my finger across the bottom of the fitting, hoping that maybe it was condensation in the cockpit, but it definitely smelled like jet fuel. The valve was leaking at the point where three fittings came together. To tighten one meant I would have to loosen another. As I worked on the problem, I realized that the leak only happened when I was transferring fuel using that valve. Further, it was a slow leak, so I would not take the chance of trying to fix it and inadvertently making things worse in flight. I jammed a dirty rag into the leak and continued flying.

But there was another issue. The smell of fuel in the plane continued to grow even stronger from all the leaks. Eventually, it would get so strong that I put my clothes in a plastic bag after each flight until I could wash them so that they wouldn't stink up my hotel room. One thing I had not expected of this expedition was to smell like a garbage can full of fuel-soaked dirty rags. I started making jokes about it. First I told people I had "created" a cologne called "Jah-tay", short for Jet A. Next, it was "aromatherapy for pilots."

Joking was a way to deal with the painful reality of tasting fuel in my throat, burning sinuses, and feeling my eyes water. The Universe was not giving up the South Pole without a fight.

Antarctica and the Antarctic Peninsula from 31,000 feet on the way to the South Pole

Faulty Fuel Gauge

I'd been anticipating problems with the copilot-side fuel gauge. It had acted up intermittently since leaving the U.S. and I'd spent hours thinking about it. To compensate if the gauge failed, I would need to fill up the main fuel tank on the pilot side with the working fuel gauge and then transfer Jet A to the copilot side. I'd have to supplement the fuel in the right-side tank without knowing exactly how much was already in it and, therefore, risk overfilling it. If I overfilled it, the fuel would dump out the vent. If I under-calculated, the copilot-side engine would run out of fuel and stop mid-flight. Either option would be disastrous.

About two hours into the flight, I struggled to decide if I should head off-course to the west of the Antarctic Peninsula to pick up a 100-knot tailwind that was showing on windy.com. I looked down at the copilot side fuel gauge. It sat at zero. *Here we go. Let the deadly game of fuel management begin.*

"You didn't think you would get off that easily did you?" the Universe responded.

I eventually decided to try and pick up that tailwind to the West. An hour later I was about 30 degrees off course and had not picked up a single knot of tailwind. Every passing minute made my situation worse. The weather was unpredictable at best, and I couldn't afford to play my hunch any further. I adjusted my course directly to the South Pole, which turned out to be a good thing, because I didn't pick up that needed push until I passed over the Pole.

Next, the fuel gauge. Both tanks were carrying about the same amount of fuel when the gauge went out, so I would wait until the pilot side indicated half full, and to minimize the possibility of underfilling or overfilling the tanks, I would fill the pilot side and transfer fuel until the gauge read three-fourths, a reasonable plan.

Suddenly, the co-pilot's gauge came back to life as quickly as it had plummeted to zero. It matched the pilot's fuel gauge. "Okay, you have that under control, but this isn't going to be fun. Let's get on with the really big issues; this is far from over," the Universe echoed in my head.

Thoughts in the Air

Antarctica is eerily quiet, far quieter than the voices in my head, which had eighteen hours on the South Pole leg of the journey to express their concerns, fears, and doubts as I surveyed the deeply frozen land below, where no human had ever walked before. Those voices had been well-rehearsed during the two years it took to plan this trip. They had played out the worst-case scenarios in excruciating detail: freezing to death, getting caught in an avalanche and suffocating, plummeting from mid-air—the night-marish list was long.

The mind is an interesting place to live-powerful enough to conceive an idea as bold and adventurous as a polar circumnavigation, but more than willing to pick the same idea apart. It is a form of cosmic torture to the untrained soul. In reality, the Universe was training and preparing me by tossing out an endless series of "what ifs" to ponder, plan for, and prevent.

The only thing left to work on was me. Was I truly ready for something like this? If the military or some other multi-billion-dollar organization made this flight, they would hire an astronaut or a pilot with twenty years' experience flying in Antarctica. Somebody who had proven themselves a hundred times under extreme stress. That person was not me. Still, I was as ready as I could be. I had attended four survival classes and flown the plane a lot in challenging situations, on days when nobody in their right mind would take off. I had flown to remote places like Dutch Harbor in the Aleutian Islands after just a few weeks' experience with this plane. In total I now had taken off and landed in 43 countries flying solo. In 2015, my single-engine plane failed at 14,000 feet over the Strait of Malacca while overloaded with 600 pounds of highly flammable aviation fuel. Could there be any real-life training or preparation better than that?

My most important characteristic in these circumstances was persistence, in addition to which I was hard-working, a detailed planner, and fierce in my desire to deliver on my promises to my ninety-five sponsors and supporters. I knew these skills made up for the many shortcomings others saw in me.

Then I started judging myself all over again: How foolish was I when I could be at home enjoying a comfortable retirement? Why would any rational person put it all at risk? Did I have a death wish? What a silly end to the story of my life. I could see the lede now: "This guy made it and then threw it all away for fame, records, and ego." My mind kicked in to defend the reasons I was doing it: to test the latest aviation safety and technology equipment; to advance STEM education; to inspire people to live their impossibly big dreams; to help me find peace within; and to do what others said couldn't be done. Maybe most importantly, to challenge myself in every way as a pilot and human being.

Another story funneled through my mind: *this plane can't possibly operate for 18 to 20 hours straight without failing.* Our preparation history seemed to indicate that. Over the past two years, I had hardly gone more than a few flight hours without a major system failing. Why would everything start working perfectly now? Even on the way down to Ushuaia, my primary GPS couldn't pick up the satellites it needed to provide an exact position. And who in their right mind would select a 36-year-old aircraft to outfit and retrofit for a trip like this?

I also wondered if I was too old. I was fifty-three, not a twenty-five-year-old who could take all kinds of physical abuse and stress while still operating at peak performance. How ironic, I thought: by the time you can acquire the resources to pull off a trip like this, your body struggles to make the journey. It reminded me of those elderly people who save their entire lives to travel and then find that they can barely get on and off the tour bus. Aging athletes certainly know the feeling as well. Life can be so cruel. I knew I was slowing down in terms of reflexes, vision, stamina, and strength, but I made up for it with grit, determination, and sheer force of will. I seemed to have boatloads of energy and inspiration. Nothing was going to stop me, especially the voices of self-doubt.

My father's words replayed in my mind. *You are just going to get yourself killed. Why not just join a country club, learn to play golf, and enjoy the rest of your life?* If anything, his doubts inspired me to do even more, to seek out even more danger. I didn't want to be the guy who settled into that country club lifestyle. I wanted to see the world and challenge myself.

Several months before my trip, Los Angeles Lakers legend Kobe Bryant died in a helicopter crash after a remarkable life of athletics, service, inspiration, and philanthropy. Would I too be snuffed out after years of preparation, money spent, and hard work? I prayed that it would not be my story, but I was powerless to control it. That said, however, my time in the Navy did train me to stand what we called a "vigilant watch," complete with navigation, communications, and the ability to function at all hours of the day and night.

I "saw" the occasional mental snapshot of the plane going down in Antarctica. I saw myself struggling to survive while rescuers located the crash debris field and did their best to save me. Would I be injured? Would I suffer, starve, and freeze? My brain was making quite a case against me, and yet, somehow, I persisted. In fact, the debate going on in my head was really nothing more than a distraction. This mission had become bigger than me, and while the enormity of it scared me beyond words, all I could do was put one foot in front of the other until I was physically unable to move another inch.

Meanwhile, unbeknownst to me, my satellite communicator, Garmin InReach Explorer, had abruptly stopped sending out my position every three minutes when I was about one-third of the way down the Antarctic Peninsula. My team, who were tracking me from the ground, initially thought I went down, and it wasn't until about six hours later, when I posted from that same satellite device that I was passing over the South Pole, that they knew I was still alive.

Peace Moment

The Universe was so closely tied to this trip that it was involved in every minute detail of the planning process. It clearly knew better than I did what would be required of me. It was like this had been planned long before I ever came into the picture. It was meant to be.

Chapter 11

Navigating the Zone of Confusion

You start to understand that by accepting the unknown, the doubts and question marks become extremely powerful stimulations for creativity and performance.

—Bertrand Picard, Solar Impulse Pilot

One of the most challenging parts of my nonstop flight was navigating the 50-nautical-mile "Zone of Confusion" airspace around the South Pole, where GPS does not work. Think of it like the eye of a hurricane, only this "eye" fouls up navigation. The problem is that whatever side of the South Pole you're on, you're facing north. I came to call the "Zone of Confusion" the "Time In-Between," because it caused not only my magnetic compasses but also my mind to run amok.

I suspected I would lose navigation over the South Pole after I learned of similar situations from other pilots who had flown in the area. I was testing an Avidyne flight management system that had never been used over the South Pole, so I needed a backup plan. I went back to basics and installed an old-school directional gyro to allow me to dead reckon by using a metal ball spinning at 15,000 rpm. My backup plan, as I said earlier, included taking a line of position on the sun by determining its angle in relation to the nose of the plane as I crossed the Pole and then reversing it on the way out—assuming it wasn't too cloudy and I could actually see the sun. As I crossed the Pole, I also installed waypoints on my Avidyne before and after the pole for reference. To create triple redundancy, I marked all these way-points for this leg on my iPad, which I incorrectly be-lieved was set to a magnetic reference, as opposed to the more sophisticated installed systems that I could set to a "true" reference.

When I was fifty miles out from the true South Pole, my GPS units dropped offline, then recovered several times before failing completely. I was in the "Time In-Between." I was clearly on my own, isolated in a hostile environment. And scared. I was entering a space and time into which no one had flown before using this particular aircraft configuration.

None of the other circumnavigators, aviation engineers, and mechanics I'd spoken to could tell me definitively what to expect while I was in the Time-In-Between" or how to handle it. I knew I would enter an unknown dimension and had considered the risk of taking on so many first-time modifications, but I had run the scenario in my head and on simulators many times, and I had written and followed a checklist. But that didn't stop me from second-guessing myself or wondering if all the doubters might be right after all. Had I set myself up for a perfect storm of confused avionics, a highly modified old airplane, and an unknown biofuel response at 32,000 feet and −67 °C over the pole?

While I felt panic and powerlessness at times, and wondered if the brass balls that Super Fred had referred to might not freeze at these temps, my spiritual training came flying back when I needed it most, reminding me to focus on what I could control. For the rest, I would trust the Universe to take care of everything else. I knew the avionics were the best in the industry, and since the system was intermittently responding in what seemed like a pattern, I could tell it was doing its best to navigate. When the GPS failed and recovered for a third time, I took a deep breath and decided to enjoy the journey and the lesson it presented. I had faith that eventually, the uncertainty would lift, and I would return to more familiar territory. I was also grateful for having installed the old-school directional gyro, because that's what I relied on until my system began working again.

Thoughts of Survival

As I got closer to the South Pole and farther from the landing strip in Ushuaia, I thought about the sorts of challenges I would experience if the aircraft went down in Antarctica. One pilot from the British Antarctic Survey said I was being foolish and setting myself up for "prolonged suffering." Sure, I'd taken Tim Kneeland's survival courses, but had never even spent a night outside in below zero conditions, let alone –20 °C to –40 °C. It's one thing to say, "If this happens, I will then do this or that," but it's another thing to survive a crash, sustain injuries, and somehow hold out alone until help comes, which could take up to two weeks. And that's assuming the ELT (Emergency Locator Transmitter) went off or I could successfully set off one of my two personal locator beacons.

The more I thought about the possibilities, the greater my fear. At that moment, it seemed ridiculous to have taken on such risks for peace or even for science. I remember thinking, "God, I hope this is worth it!"

Survival training at CAPS (Corporate Air Parts)
and Survival Systems

Crossing over the South Pole Talking with Cory

At a specific point on my navigation chart, based on conversations I'd had with the Avidyne engineers, I shifted from magnetic to true navigation on my flight management systems. Fifteen minutes before my fly-over, I shifted over to biofuels, which have a slightly lower gelling point than the Jet A-1. Both these maneuvers went off without a hitch.

Then matters became complicated. My two primary flight displays fell offline simultaneously, leaving me without navigation, and then switched back on at different times. This prompted me to set my directional gyro, which would allow me to dead-reckon on the course I had set for about 15 minutes, after which the course would degrade and need to be corrected.

Finally, I took a line of position on the sun at two o'clock and calculated that it should be 180 degrees opposite on my return flight.

As I neared the South Pole, I called the Amundsen-Scott Station on the plane's VHF radio. To my surprise, I got a prompt and cheerful response from Cory Allegue, an Antarctic Fire Department firefighter from Blue Pont, New York, who was working at the communications center that day. It gave me a sense of comfort that out here in the middle of literally nowhere, I was talking to a human being. We had a brief but enjoyable conversation during which I told

Cory Allegue talking on the radio to arriving and departing aircraft

him I was on a World Peace Flight, was carrying experiments for NASA and the Scripps Institution of Oceanography, and was flying on biofuels for the first time over the Poles. I also told him that one of my closest friends, Professor Brian Keating, had a microwave telescope called "BICEP" at the South Pole. My new friend seemed intrigued and willing to answer questions. He explained that the people working at the South Pole did six-month tours and said he absolutely loved it there.

Landing at the South Pole would have required adding skis to the plane—something that had never been done before on a Turbo Commander. The enormous amount of engineering and modification would have placed the plane in the experimental category,

Robert looks joyful as he flies over the South Pole while communicating with Cory Allegue, the air traffic controller at the Amundsen-Scott Station

resulting in the loss of half its value. My insurance carrier had been quite clear that this was a no-go. And even if I had pulled it off, the skis would have slowed the plane enough to reduce the range of the *Citizen* to the point where she would not be able to make the roundtrip flight.

When I was within ten miles of the South Pole, I asked Cory for permission to overfly.

A long pause followed. "Negative, Ghost Rider," he finally said. Was he really quoting the movie *Top Gun* at the South Pole?

We both started laughing. I told him that was extra-funny, because we were both so far away from a movie theater that neither of us would be seeing *Top Gun* anytime soon!

"Of course, two niner golf alpha. Permission for flyover," he finally responded.

I smiled for the next ten minutes, then did a ten-second countdown with Cory as I neared the Pole. That was a moment I will never forget. Truly magical.

The primary and secondary Avidyne GPS units showing the Citizen of the World *doing the first of two circles around the South Pole*

I did two laps over the South Pole. One was for the planet and the second for the people. When I finished and pointed the *Citizen* back toward Ushuaia, I thought of all the risks, suffering, obstacles, learning, world records, and I felt an incredible sense of joy and accomplishment.

What happened next was truly remarkable. "Rob, some people have gathered down here, and we just want to thank you for what you are doing for the planet and the people," Cory said. "It is truly remarkable."

Tears poured down my face as I struggled to regain my composure and form a response. Finally, I said, "I'd like to thank all of you for your courage and service to our country and the world. To isolate yourselves in such an extreme way for the betterment of man and womankind is truly remarkable!"

Experiencing the South Pole

Soon, I was so busy inside the plane that I didn't have much time to reflect on flying over one of the most remote parts on the planet. Had I also reached one of the most remote parts inside of myself? Few would ever see or experience this place. I had struggled and sacrificed for more than two years to satisfy my obsession. The South Pole was covered by clouds, but I was somewhere truly unique. I could feel the energy moving inside me in a way I had not experienced before. I felt connected to nature, and was having a deeper inner conversation with God than would have been possible anywhere else on the planet. I was looking for God on my journey and in some sense I felt like I was staring him/her right in the face. All this that I was seeing was a reflection of God in the real world that could not be seen until I was somehow open to it.

I hit "send" on a message I had composed on my InReach Explorer an hour before. My supporters around the world would soon be cheering with relief. I'd burned more than half my fuel to get there, and hoped my plane would now fly faster and more efficiently since it was lighter. I was betting everything, including my life, that the *Citizen* would get me home.

The clarity I had hoped would magically strike me like a lightning bolt did not happen in that precise moment. Maybe it was buried behind the mountains of fear, fatigue, and stress and would take time to work its way through. I felt like the traveler who reaches his destination but still feels in his restless soul an eerie emptiness inside. The expectation of that moment far exceeded reality. It certainly was not a place that could instantly fulfill me. It was as if I were looking for my inner peace out in the physical world when I should have been looking inside myself instead.

One of the psychics I consulted while planning this journey had said I'd been to Antarctica before in another life, but this place did not seem at all familiar to me. I hit the "Direct to" button on the flight management system and felt the digital autopilot turn slightly as it pointed me directly to Ushuaia from 2,200 nautical miles away.

The trip back seemed to take much longer. Fatigue set in during the straight shot over the eastern Antarctic Peninsula and the dreaded Drake Passage. I transferred the last of my ferry fuel into the main fuel tanks and watched the hours and minutes tick away as I looked out the window and tried to take in all the beauty around me.

The worst part of the flight was over. It was all downhill from here, or so I thought. If the plane were going to fail, it would have happened already.

Peace Moment

Thinking that reaching a place or goal can fulfill you is unrealistic. Our growth comes from what happens inside of us on our journey. The struggle and obstacles that we overcome help us to learn, grow, and evolve. While this process can be extremely difficult at times, it is well worth the effort.

Chapter 12

Returning to Earth

Use these tough times because they are tough times. They represent a possibility to be a stronger and better version of myself.
                    —Borge Ousland, Arctic Explorer

The Drake Passage, known for the worst weather in the world, had taken the lives of thirty-six souls just a week earlier. As I approached it, fatigue was catching up with me. I was struggling to stay awake, and my stomach was starting to knot up. I knew the Universe was warming up to throw me a series of new challenges. This flight was far from over.

I had been in the air for sixteen hours, and while I'd attempted to take micro naps, it wasn't working. I couldn't take my mind off the mission, and I woke up from my second micro nap only to feel and hear roughness in the left engine which I could not diagnose. It seemed to stop about five minutes later but still made the thought of closing my eyes again seem like a really bad idea.

The fuel gauges on most aircraft are notoriously inaccurate and are only required to be accurate when the tanks are empty. On the *Citizen*, the left tank would burn faster than the right and then slow a bit. Then both would slow as they dropped below half full. One of my biggest concerns was that the right fuel gauge would fail again and read empty. In the past, it had sometimes read zero for an entire flight, but at other times it would fluctuate on and off. The control box was located behind the five internal ferry tanks in the pressurized cabin. Getting to it was impossible, which left me to estimate how much fuel remained in the copilot-side wing tanks when the gauge went offline.

Was it enough to make it back?

The problem with having ten fuel tanks is that it's difficult to know exactly how much fuel was being added when the tanks were fueled over a period of several days and the fuel was being measured in liters rather than gallons. In addition, I had to factor in the amount of fuel that was spilled while being transferred among the six tanks in the passenger and luggage compartments as well as the fact that you can never get 100 percent of the fuel out of a tank.

But even assuming I knew exactly how much fuel I had left, I had to multiply that by the current air-speed, which changes constantly due to wind, weight, air density, and other factors, in order to determine how far I could go.

Next, I started doing fuel calculations at different reduced-power settings. As I continued to throttle back and reduce the drag that is induced with greater speed, I found that the plane would start to fall out of the sky when I throttled down from 62 percent to 39 percent torque. At 40 percent torque, the plane stayed at altitude. If my calculations were correct, I would land with about twenty gallons of fuel per side. This was cutting things close.

Paranoia set in as I flew low over the water. A mistake meant ditching in the near freezing Antarctic waters of the Drake Passage, where survival was unlikely. Plus, the tailwind speed kept falling, not what you want to see when you're in the 18th hour of a flight. On about the 41st time I calculated the remaining fuel, I realized something that scared me. The reserve tank that was supposed to have the Bio-fuel for the North Pole was actually empty.

Big mistake. I didn't believe I had enough fuel to make it back to Ushuaia.

In a panic, I sent Susan Gilbert a satellite text saying that I didn't believe I had enough fuel to make it back. That, of course, left her terrified, and I still regret sending it.

Suddenly, I lost contact with the Chilean air traffic controller who controlled the airspace and to whom I was reporting my position hourly via my satellite phone. When my call cut out suddenly, I tried to call back, but the phone number no longer worked. It seemed as if they hadn't paid their phone bill and needed to buy more minutes, which I was sure I would be billed for.

My options were to try and stretch my fuel even further by throttling down and staying high, landing at the Chilean military base at King George Island without permission, or landing on an Argentinean dirt landing strip in the middle of nowhere without services. If I landed at King George Island, where there wasn't any fuel, I would be violating my permits with the State Department, the National Science Foundation, and the EPA. It would create serious problems.

I decided to take yet another chance and avoid creating an international incident, or being stranded in the middle of nowhere. I headed back onto Ushuaia, my departure point, and prayed the Universe had my back.

Since the Chilean ATC didn't have a VHF frequency and I was out of range of Ushuaia tower control, I had two choices:

1. Fly the instrument approach with mountains on all sides in zero visibility while fatigued, using the flight instruments with no visual references, and potentially colliding with larger, faster aircraft that were in communication with ATC. Or,

2. I could descend at sea through the solid cloud deck without the aid of the air traffic controller, not being able to see other traffic below, and running the risk of hitting the water.

With tears running down my face, wondering how hard the Universe was going to make this, I opted for the illegal descent through the clouds at sea rather than using the published approach. After watching the weather for the past week, I knew that the clouds generally hovered no lower than about 500 feet above the water. *Generally.*

From 80 miles at sea, I saw nothing but overcast. The chances of hitting another aircraft or structure were low as I descended through the clouds. What concerned me was the height of the clouds above the water. Since I was not talking with the controller, I didn't have a current altimeter setting, so there was no way of knowing. To conserve fuel, I throttled all the way back to 8 percent torque and allowed gravity to take me down to what I believed to be approximately 500 feet above the water. At that moment, I broke out of the clouds. It was foggy, raining, and dark. After spending the past seventeen hours and thirty minutes in high-altitude sunshine, it was as if I had entered a darker and more foreboding world.

I remembered how Charles Lindbergh described flying over the Atlantic:

> It's a fierce, unfriendly sea—a sea that would batter the largest ocean liner. I feel naked above it, as though stripped of all protection, conscious of the terrific strength of the waves, of the thinness of cloth on my wings, of the dark turbulence of the storm clouds. This would be a hellish place to land if the engine failed.
>
> —Charles Lindbergh, The Spirit of St. Louis

I intended to fly along the Beagle Channel into Ushuaia, avoiding the islands and mountains on either side. My mind started popping with doubt: "Hasn't this damn leg been hard enough? When will the lessons stop? When will I have endured enough? Must the Universe try to take this from me at the last minute? How many times must I be tested? Wasn't it enough that I had just completed a round trip to the South Pole?" I wondered what God had in store for me that required me to be this strong.

This part of the trip broke me open emotionally, physically, and spiritually, so the true learning could begin.

Those following on the flight profile now being reported by my InReach Explorer had no idea what was really going on. My plane was descending from a GPS altitude of 30,000 feet to only 500 feet, at glide rate, without power. My Swiss friend André Müller, the former VP of Pilatus Aircraft, thought I had run out of fuel and that he was watching his friend about to ditch into the Drake Passage. People were living this nightmare with me minute by minute, which must have been terrifying for them.

Below the cloud deck, closer to the water than I had ever flown the *Citizen*, I worried about birds flying into my huge Honeywell turboprop engines. And also, down low, where all turboprop engines are fuel pigs, I was burning 300 pounds of Jet A per side per hour. My remaining safety margin was just sixty minutes. The place looked prehistoric, with huge, jagged, snow-capped mountains jutting out of the ocean as if they had been ripped from the earth during the world's formation. There was nothing gentle about it. The name "Tierra del Fuego", Land of Fire, said it all. There had been violent volcanic activity here in the not-so-distant past.

I was scared and just wanted to be back in my hotel room, covered with warm blankets and curled up in the fetal position as I hid from the world.

I checked my fuel gauges and realized I could slow the plane down even further to visually navigate the last fifty miles back to Ushuaia. Rather than flying at 250 plus knots, I could slow to 120 and fly as I had with my instructor in a Cessna 172. Sure enough, as I slowed, the plane maintained altitude. I had to dodge little islands at the mouth of the channel, but otherwise the *Citizen* was running well.

When I finally established radio communication with Ushuaia, the tower operator was surprised to hear that a plane was flying according to visual flight rules (i.e., VFR low) from the open ocean in such miserable weather. I had just appeared mysteriously from out at sea, and I'm sure he was wondering, *where did this guy come from?* As the airport came into sight after such a challenging flight, I had such a new appreciation for how much beauty there was all around me that I could barely comprehend it. I set up to land with 30-knot winds. I again felt tears dropping from my face. The confidence I had gained on this flight was invaluable and something I could draw upon for the rest of my flying career. I had earned my way into the record books.

Arriving in Glorious Ushuaia

As the overinflated 16 ply tires of the *Citizen of the World* touched down on terra firma with that characteristic *chirp* followed by the jerk backward, I put the massive engines into reverse thrust and the plane slowed. "Oh my God! I did it! I'm alive! I made it! Yesss!" I shouted loudly with a fist pump! I had learned that I was capable of preparing for, going after, and accomplishing something bigger than I ever thought possible.

Landing at Ushuaia (aka Tierra Del Fuego, the Land of Fire) after a grueling 18.1 hour nonstop solo flight to the South Pole and back

My relief was beyond words, and I felt a sense of pride and calmness exceeding anything I had experienced before. I had accepted this epic challenge for myself and all the people to whom I had promised so much. I had prepared for two years for this day. Now it was over. For a moment I felt lost, and it would be months before I could process it completely. But a tremendous burden of responsibility had been lifted from my shoulders, and the feeling of lightness was indescribable. I was safe, on the ground. Worry, fear, and self-doubt were replaced by inner peace. It was as if a turbulent wave had rolled through, churned up sand and debris, hit the beach, and then turned silent as it skimmed across the beach, smoothing out everything in its white foamy path.

After I landed, the tower operator directed me to the commercial side of the airport. I explained that the airport manager wanted me with the other GA traffic, and the airport handlers would have no way of towing the *Citizen* to the general aviation ramp afterward. I would have to start the plane up again to taxi. When I turned toward the GA ramp, however, the tower operator forcefully ordered me to position 4 at the commercial terminal. I told him I was going with the prior instructions of the airport manager, I had been in that spot before takeoff, and it was still open.

As I began the shut-down process, I heard the tower operator screaming at the top of his lungs. Less than a minute later, I spotted the airport's senior police officer walking quickly and purposefully toward me, gun and vest on. I had dealt with this same man the week before, and I knew that, like me, he was an ex-military officer. I thought I was going to be taken into custody for ignoring the tower operator's instructions, for returning to the country before the 24-hour time restriction was up, for my lack of communication with the Chilean air traffic controller, or any other number of infractions real or imagined.

As I unstrapped my seatbelt and began to move my body in ways I hadn't for almost twenty hours, I felt like I was waking up from a really bad dream. Stiffly, I moved slowly and deliberately to avoid getting tangled up in the many wires and hoses that crisscrossed the cabin like a spider web designed to ensnare anyone who tried to pass. I worked my way to the door, swung the big silver latch open from right to left, and breathed the cool air of civilization and life.

I made eye contact with the officer with whom I'd spoken with briefly before I departed. He looked very serious. We stared at each other in silence for a long moment as I thought, *this is how it feels just be-*

fore you get handcuffed and marched to jail in front of a lot of people aiming their iPhone cameras at you.

After what seemed like forever, the officer's serious countenance lit up with a smile. *"Bienvenidos."* He pointed at the plane and said, "I used to fly one of these!"

My response was typically American. "Awesome!"

It turned out he had flown an older version of the Turbo Commander for three years. He was part of the brother- and sisterhood of pilots. I had been calling

Avoiding arrest and getting escorted back to the passenger terminal by security after completing the South Pole leg

him "Senor," and he told me his nickname was "Mig." I wondered if he'd ever shot down a Russian MiG fighter jet, but I was too tired and overwhelmed to ask.

Mig marveled at the aircraft as I prepared her for her time on the ground. She was in all her glory, dirty with black dust the starter generators had blown back along the nacelles, waves of heat radiating off her engines. Mig examined the props, which were irresistible to anybody who got close to the plane. He reached out and gently touched them as if wanting to connect with this miracle of modern technology that had just accomplished what so many said was impossible and reckless.

As we walked the quarter mile to the terminal building, I struggled to put one foot in front of the other. In the distance, I heard Jeremy La Zelle yell, "Yahhhh, you did it!" As my eyes connected with his, he thrust his fist into the air in a victory salute as he stood on a staircase overlooking the field. His camera was set up with a long lens, and Kristin was at street level behind a fence, going for the second angle. Both of them were smiling broadly, and it was wonderful to see their familiar faces and feel their energy at this defining moment. They had been tracking my flight on FlightAware and FlightRadar24 until it stopped working at the northern tip of Antarctica, and they were scared I had gone down. I put my right hand up in victory and could not resist smiling ear to ear, even though I was exhausted and tears were once again running down my face. Our worldwide team had just emerged victorious from one of the greatest challenges of my life.

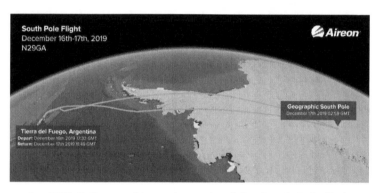

An ADS-B Out tracking schematic of the South Pole flight provided by Aireon

The South Pole flight was a total success. I'd achieved a number of firsts:

- First use of biofuels over the South Pole
- The greatest distance (approximately 4457 nm) and flight time (18.1 hours) in a single or twin-engine turboprop.
- First time testing for microfibers in the atmosphere over the South Pole.
- First time flying a NASA Wafer Scale Spacecraft over the South Pole—or anywhere be-

yond the University of California-Santa Barbara campus.

- First time flying AOPA's 80th Anniversary Year logo over the South Pole
- First time being tracked using ADS-B Out over the South Pole.

While this leg had broken me open, it had also allowed me to recognize my limits, heal, grow, and accomplish many things in the process.

Celebrating being alive by eating a delicious crab dinner recommended by mentor Michel Gordillo

Peace Moment

This was the point of total acceptance. This was the Universe breaking me wide open. Taking me beyond my absolute and total limits. Stripping away all my defenses and showing me that I couldn't do it all on my own. Preparing me for the lessons that were ahead on the trip and in life. I would not have been able to receive this wisdom unless I was raw and broken open to the learning that each of these challenges would bring me. The tears dripping off my face indicated that all these lessons were in motion and could not be stopped.

Chapter 13

The New Me

*As we let our own light shine, we unconsciously
give other people permission to do the same.*
—Marianne Williamson

For the month that followed the South Pole leg of my journey, I floated in the clouds. My feet were not planted firmly on the ground. I really did not believe I had done it—and on my first attempt, no less. I was afraid that I'd wake up one morning and realize it was all just a dream. I'd find myself belted down in a psychiatric hospital or doing meaningless repetitive work somewhere. Sometimes, when I told people what I'd done, they would just stare blankly at me, as if they simply couldn't comprehend what I'd said. Or they'd just keep on talking as if I hadn't said anything.

Our interactions reminded me of the story of the natives in the New World who couldn't see the early European and Spanish explorers arriving off the coast like ominous hurricane clouds, because it was totally beyond their comprehension.

People of the World

One of the most meaningful and joyful aspects of my journey was the enormous respect I gained for the people I met around the world. Citizens from all parts of the planet had shown compassion and respect for my dedication to completing what seemed at times like an impossible mission.

Prior to my departure for the South Pole, Michel Gordillo was translating rules and regulations into

Ushuaia Flight Planning Team who helped me get my permit from Chile at the last-minute

English so I could avoid pitfalls and blocks, and a group of four young people in the flight-planning office in Ushuaia helped me push my flight plan through the system when it was rejected. At the eleventh hour a Chilean scientist helped me get permission to fly over Antarctica, I made contact with Cory and his colleagues, who praised and encouraged me for flying the experiments that were designed for the betterment of the planet. My list of friends and supporters was growing as well as my faith in my mission.

The Change in Me

I came to realize that change begins in our hearts and minds and is reflected in the world around us. If we can find inner peace wherever we are, we can share that peace with others, wherever they are.

We are all tasked with taking peaceful action and not waiting for others to do our work. It's up to each of us to do something positive for our community, for humanity, and for the planet. As the International Children's Choir from nations around the world has been singing every year since I was a child, "Let there be peace on earth and let it begin with me."

On a global scale, I believe we will come to learn the value of peace on our planet and the importance of cooperation versus competition between countries that is required to achieve it.

Robert standing next to a painted quay wall is Greece on his earlier Equatorial Circumnavigation, getting clarity on his mission of One Planet, One People, One Plane.

The Emotional Aftermath

I think many people had underestimated my ability to complete the trip because I had been talking about it for so long that it gave doubters an opportunity to emerge. They assumed that because I was often calm and soft-spoken, I must be weak, which was the furthest thing from the truth.

I made the South Pole flight at great risk. Now it was over, I was very much alive, and thankful for that. At the same time, however, completing the flight left a void inside me, a vacuum that had once held the energy of preparing, anticipating, and hoping. I had talked about it until I was blue in the face, leveraged it, made promises about it, and lost sleep night after night worrying about it. It had become a part of me.

At this point, after thirty hours of adrenaline-infused effort, I was numb. I had engaged in a fierce struggle for my survival and won, fulfilling a major part of my life's purpose, probably what I was placed on this planet to accomplish.

The phone calls, text messages, and emails of congratulations rolled in. My supporters told me I had secured a place in the history books. They were proud of the impact I was making on the world. I hoped the rest of the trip would be much less stressful, a global victory lap of sorts, since we had completed the most difficult leg of the polar circumnavigation. Jeremy would later remind me of the moment when I said this, followed by a deep belly laugh—and a reference to all the hell that came after it.

After a few days, my body released some of the energy I had been holding onto so tightly for years. The emotional energy released as sobbing tears with snot coming out my nose, and I remember saying, "Oh my God, I did it." It felt like the flu. My head was about to explode. The level of emotion would well up in me each time I saw the two-minute video our cinematographer had put together to serve as the trailer for the *Citizen of the World* documentary. I watched it at least twenty times.

Documenting and Decompressing

I spent that Christmas in the Falkland Islands, watching penguins and exploring shipwrecks with the film crew before moving on to Rio De Janeiro, Brazil, for New Year's. Rio was the perfect place to blow off some steam, get reacclimatized to civilization, and celebrate life.

Jeremy suggested I take a paraglider ride, which he would film for the documentary. The colorful kites were visually spectacular, the flight was exciting, and it introduced me to a new kind of flying. After I landed on the picture-perfect beach, it seemed like a great opportunity to film my first interview asking what someone thought it meant to be a "Citizen of the World."

We found a pilot named Flavio who spoke English and was willing to be interviewed. At the last minute, however, he decided that while he was okay with me asking my questions in English, he wanted to respond in Portuguese with his buddy acting as translator. I expected the interview to be pretty generic given that Flavio spent the bulk of his time flying tourists around. But when I asked him, "How do you find peace in the world?" he thought for a second and then responded, "I must first find peace in my heart; only then can I share it with the world"

What Flavio said changed the course of the documentary and my life. We had been operating on the premise that we were just going to go around and ask people how they found peace. Now I was going to have to find my own inner peace in the midst of the chaos of life before I could share it with the world.

I had no idea how I could do that given everything I was dealing with: equipment failures in the plane, fuel leaks, logistical issues getting the film crew from place to place, budgeting issues, interviews, social media comments, and much more. I thought that the world would literally have to stand still in order for me to find inner peace. How was I going to do that on a trip with so many moving parts? Was it even possible? It took some people a lifetime to find their inner peace, and I would have to do it before this trip was over so that I could resume finding peace in the world. That seemed like an even more challenging task than a Polar Circumnavigation. As it turned out, however, I would eventually find peace on the ground and not in the air.

Processing and Reflecting

I had attempted to create the perfect vehicle to take me on this wondrous adventure. Along the way, I learned there is no such thing. Is the pursuit of perfection an aphrodisiac? Do we think that hidden in every machine and person is someone or something trying to reveal their true potential? Maybe it's a way to define ourselves free from outside influences? Who am I when I'm not being nudged, pushed, judged, and controlled by others?

Intuitive doctor and bestselling author Caroline Myss says, "silence is oxygen for the soul." Maybe it was a matter of trying to return to the primordial place I inhabited before I landed here on planet Earth? It is said we are all souls having a human existence. Maybe we just need a break from our lives?

The Universe didn't make it easy. I had spent years preparing, hitting every conceivable wall, barrier, naysayer, and blocker. And as I got closer to reaching my goal, obstacles started coming at me even faster. The issues accelerated.

Along the way there were three groups of people circling my wagon. It became crystal clear who my supporters were—they encouraged and pushed me harder than I could have imagined. Then there were the naysayers spreading information that was untrue, while still others seemed to get their entertainment from sitting on the sidelines and wondering, "Will he live? Or die?"

One thing is certain: I learned what I am made of. I discovered that I'm much stronger, physically and mentally, than I ever imagined, so don't get in my way, because I'm moving forward, I'm reaching my goals for me, for the planet, and for you.

I had also searched for God on this flight, thinking that maybe I would see and experience him or her in a new, more defining way. Flying was always about reaching my hand up toward the heavens. Maybe I would finally touch the hand of God? Would I even recognize it if it were stretched out in front of me?

Maybe achievements are the way we prove to ourselves that we are unique. Go somewhere, do something that has never been done. That would certainly prove our uniqueness. Are we not enough just as we are? Do we not believe that? This bold way of being in the world could be how we exceed our boundaries and the limits we find constraining.

On some level, I wanted an indication that other humans had been in Antarctica long before me, a civilization that perhaps flourished during another, warmer time on the continent. I did not receive any indication of that, even though I spent hours looking out the window for signs. I thought, if I ever return to this place, it would be fun to do aerial archeology.

In the process of flying the polar mission, I felt as if I were, like it or not, becoming a pilot ambassador for the world. This was an opportunity for me to have real impact. Each time I took off, landed or stepped out of the *Citizen* I couldn't help thinking that my remarkable flying machine was the vehicle that allowed me to become a living example of our message: peace and connection among all of humanity.

Peace Moment

We are the sum total of all of our experiences. These experiences are not good or bad, they just exist and define us in the most personal way. We prove to ourselves who we are through struggle and by overcoming hardship. These experiences build our confidence for what is to come and define the essence of who we are.

PART THREE

To Africa, Asia, and Europe

Chapter 14

On to Africa, the Cradle of Civilization

"The most effective way to do it, is to do it."
—Amelia Earhart, first female aviator to fly solo across the Atlantic Ocean

After filming and celebrating New Year's Eve and ringing in 2020 in Rio de Janeiro, I headed on to Africa, the cradle of civilization and, for me, one of the most truly magical places on earth. It is rugged and teeming with wildlife, and I was excited to return. My previous trip there, in a Cessna 182 in 2013, was one of the best experiences of my life in terms of exploring, flying, viewing animals, seeing the country, and meeting wonderful and inspiring people.

Flying into Dakar, Senegal, was interesting on many levels. I had heard about the exotic-sounding Dakar Rally, an off-road endurance auto race that until 2008 had run from Paris to Dakar. But, beyond that, because it is located on the western tip of the continent, Dakar also happened to be the shortest distance from South America. Little did I know that most of northwestern Africa would be covered by a sandstorm when I arrived.

As I descended from a bright clear sky off the coast of Senegal, I got a sinking feeling as it grew darker and darker, even though it was relatively early in the day. I quickly realized this was going to be an instrument approach. The weather report said 2,000 feet RVR (Runway Visual Range), which meant seeing the runway would be difficult, but, luckily, the Citizen had been outfitted with a Max-Viz 1400 infrared camera, which made spotting it much easier. My stomach sank, however, as daylight turned into dirty brown pitch darkness. I saw the eerie glow of the runway lights on my display screen first, then up close, and I had a foreboding sense of something very dark about this place. My next thought was, "God, get me the f—k out of here."

My concern diminished somewhat when the fueler greeted me with a wonderful, kind, giant smile. Was my intuition failing me for once?

I had just flown more than a thousand miles over the Atlantic Ocean, crossed the equator, and was alone on the tarmac in the middle of a sandstorm and feeling a very human connection with a total stranger from a very different culture.

Fueling the four wing tanks in the dark went relatively well, considering that the fueling guy actually had the proper nozzle, a rubber protective cover for the wing, a flashlight, and a flat-head screwdriver, which rarely happened in Africa—or anywhere, for that matter. You are lucky if the fueling crew shows up with even a rag or a screwdriver. They usually dump fuel all over the wing and the deicing boot, for which they, of course, charge you.

Since the fueling was going well, and my fueler demonstrated competence and confidence, I asked him to help me fuel the number one ferry tank as well since I'd be flying to the island of San Tome the next day. Maybe things would be easier from here on out. Maybe I finally had this trip under control.

Hours before I landed at Dakar, I had misaligned one of the twenty valves used to vent the tanks inside the cabin. The tanks had started making loud contraction sounds and moaning like they were in pain. The changing pressurization as I descended was exerting stress on this delicate system. The sounds didn't make sense to me, but I knew that what was happening was not good for the tanks or for me. I immediately closed all the valves, took a deep breath, and asked myself, "What the f—k is happening?"

I pulled out Super Fred's twenty-page instruction manual complete with idiot-resistant pictures and realized I had opened one wrong valve. When I eventually saw my mistake, I opened the pressure-relief valve, which relieved the stress on the first two tanks, and vowed to be more careful in the future. I did not realize I had taken both the tanks and myself to the breaking point.

Now, however, as I began to fuel the #1 ferry tank, I was fueling more quickly than I had previously done because I was using a high-capacity fuel truck that was generally used to fuel bigger planes. As a result, the tank was expanding and popping faster than expected. Then something shocking happened. The front tank, which fed all five behind it, made an explosive "POP" sound and, a millisecond later, Jet A-1 sprayed forcefully all over my face, into my eyes, on my legs, arms, groin, and all over the interior of the plane. The tank had split apart about a third of the way up at the back pilot-side seam. About half of the fuel was going out the door and the other half into the floorboards. I fell backward out and away from the plane while the fueling guy kept yelling, "Oh my God, Oh my God, I'm sorry, I'm sorry," in his African accent. At that moment, as I was falling to the ground and the plane was about to burst into flames and smoke, I thought, *thank God this is finally over*. For a

grueling two years and two months I had been struggling with rejection, frustration, and getting my ass
cosmically kicked day after day.

My father was right, I was just going to get myself
killed. A deep sense of relief came over me.

Then, as my body hit the ground I felt something
change inside me. It was as if the Universe were
snapping me out of my dream saying, "It's not your
time yet. Get back in there and fight."

I yelled for water. It had been a direct hit into my
eyes. My hands instantly went to my face. My entire
front side was wet with Jet A fuel dripping off my
clothes and skin. My face, chest, arms, legs, and gen-
itals started to burn immediately.

One of the handlers ran up with a big bottle of
water, and I tilted my head back as I poured it over
my eyes, left to right, and then back again. Surprisingly, it seemed to work. Even though my vision was
blurry, I could see the dark brown, dirty, and dusty
day-night of Dakar. Then I looked at the plane. The
fuel was exploding out of the hatch in a fast-moving
spray. Was my trip over? I thought so. A deep sense
of relief came over me. As I poured more water over
my eyes, I thought that if it weren't for the water, everyone would see the tears running off my face.

An ever-expanding puddle of fuel quickly covered the surrounding area. Fortunately, before the fu-

eling I had moved my bags and most important gear to the airport shuttle. I was happy about that.

The handlers and fueling guy wanted nothing to do with this developing mess, and, honestly, I couldn't blame them. I had just created a huge issue for all of them.

My pity party quickly ended when I realized that the mission had become bigger than me. Somehow, I found the courage and jumped back into the plane—danger be damned—to try and save her. I grabbed plastic bags intended to pass solids in flight, to deflect the fuel out onto the tarmac. It was a futile effort, and the cabin was getting drenched, as were some maps of Antarctica that I had hoped to frame someday and sell to raise money for aviation scholarships.

I grabbed a blade intended to cut my way out of my seatbelt if I crashed and cut the clear plastic fuel line on the front of the tank that indicated the fuel level inside the tank. I pointed that clear line outside the plane. I also grabbed a wrench, disconnected the supply line from the bottom copilot corner of the tank, and directed it onto the ground as well. With the mess developing outside, another ten gallons would not matter to the people who stood staring in disbelief all around the plane. I felt like I was polluting the very planet I had set out to save, but Dakar was so dirty that I didn't think anyone would even notice or care. I was thankful it wasn't the U.S. They would have erected containment barriers, fined me God knows what, and forced me to fill out paperwork for the rest of my life.

About five minutes after the fuel leak started, the fire truck arrived, but the firefighters just stood there and watched the gusher with their mouths open. They had nothing for fuel containment. Had they ever trained for this? Doubtful. Eventually, they decided to use their water hose to spread the fuel even further, making an even bigger mess. It was a real shit show, with fuel flowing out of the plane and dripping from a hole in the belly of the fuselage.

By this time the jet fuel was beginning to severely burn my legs, arms, chest, and private parts. I grabbed the remaining water, opened my pants, and poured it on my testicles, but this provided only temporary relief as my clothes were still covered with jet fuel. I stripped naked on the tarmac next to my shuttle, tossed my clothes into a pile to be disposed of, and grabbed new ones from my bag.

After almost an hour, most of the fuel had drained from the bottom third of the tank; it would continue to drip from the bottom of the plane for hours and intermittently for days. The handler said he had a family and was anxious to leave. He suggested I close the hatch and said, "We go."

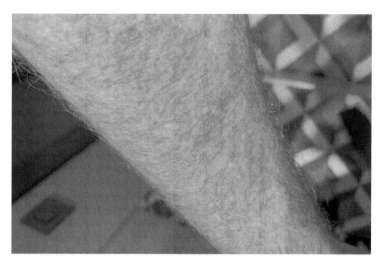

The Jet A fuel burns on Robert's arm reflect those on his back, stomach, legs, and groin after ferry tank #1 burst on the ground in Dakar while refueling

The white spots are chemical fuel burns on Robert's flight suit after ferry tank #1 burst inside the cabin in Dakar

I knew that the rest of this trip was going to be a living hell. I'd be living inside a fuel tank rather than sitting next to it. The smell would be unbearable, and I was concerned it would damage my lungs.

I was already exhausted after the long flight from Brazil, and the stress of thinking I could burn to death in a puddle of fuel only made things worse. Defeated, I turned to the handler and confirmed. "We go."

He nodded. I would deal with the plane the next day. I locked the hatch, because I knew that if I didn't secure the plane, my entire avionics panel would be gone by the next day and sold for pennies on the dollar in the local open-air market. The problem was that, because the plane was closed up tight, the oily fuel that had just spilled inside would not evaporate even slightly overnight. Approximately seventy-five gallons of fuel and fumes would soak the inside of the plane. It was like putting an angry skunk in a sealed tank over-night and hoping to come back and breathe the air.

I walked through the airport still reeking of oily jet fuel. My taxi driver asked me to roll down the window because I smelled like hell. When I got to my room, I put my clothes, belt and shoes into a plastic laundry bag and tossed them in the garbage. I showered, try-ing to scrub the fuel off my bright red skin, put on clean clothes, and went to the restaurant before it closed. All I could think about was how that spill could have ended in a terrible fire, either on the ground, or worse, in the air if the tank had burst in flight. How was I still alive—again—when all these catastrophic things were happening to me and my beautiful lady, the *Citizen of the World*?

In the restaurant, I ordered my signature vacation drink, a Pina Colada. I needed a drink. I was shaking and my skin still burned. For a second time, I wished the plane had burned so that it would all be over.

After a painful and restless night, I arrived at the plane early the next morning expecting to see an ocean of Jet A fuel and a bill the size of Africa. But somehow the tarmac was perfectly dry except for small patches under the front and rear fuselage drain holes. Amazingly, when the fire department sprayed the area with water, that, in combination with the heat, evaporated what was on the ground.

When I opened the hatch, however, as I had anticipated, the smell of Jet A-1 nearly knocked me over. The inside of the plane was damp, and I knew I would be flying inside a fuel tank. The fuel had pooled under the floorboards, in the many spaces between the internal ribs of the fuselage. Over time, with the pressurization and movement of the plane, some of it would work its way out, but the Universe had drawn a line in the sand and was asking me, "Do you have the brass balls for this? How much do you want this?"

The answers to those two questions were easy. I got in the plane and flew.

The plane would continue to leak for the next five stops as fuel got pushed around below the floorboards during takeoff and landing. My sinuses, eyes, and throat burned continually, and I could taste Jet A-1 in the back of my throat when I swallowed or yawned. People would continue to complain about how I smelled at each place I visited. I was like a child in a dirty diaper. Everything seemed normal until you caught that first whiff; then someone would say, "Oh God, what is that smell?" and back away.

Jeremy, my cinematographer, said the stench was both unbearable and a testament to my determination to get this mission done and meet my commitments at all costs. He was right. Failure was not an option.

Meanwhile, my team back home was researching the effects of jet fuel on my lungs, eyes, and sinuses. Long-term exposure was catastrophic, to be sure, but I was nearly halfway done with my flight and had only about seventy flight hours left. I was not going to let the Jet A-1 smell or fumes slow me down. My mission of peace was bigger than me, bigger than a fuel spill, and bigger than the Citizen of the World. It would impact the entire planet.

Corruption in Africa

What I didn't like about Africa was the massive corruption that permeated aviation. Because the *Citizen of the World* was a big, impressive plane, it drew attention. Eddie Gould from General Aviation Support Egypt summed it up best when he said, "Africa is known for outright thievery."

One of the many examples of this came when I was opening the hatch in Accra, Ghana, during an unplanned stop. I had realized en route to the island of San Tome that I didn't have permission to land, and the island airport was likely closed at night. So I had to put down in Accra. As I opened the hatch, the first airport worker ran to the plane and called in an excited tone, "Cash, cash, you have cash?" This was typical in Africa and a reflection of the corruption and inequity that existed in the world

Other challenges later in my journey included not being able to fly within Ethiopia once I landed in Addis Ababa, because the country only allowed intra-country flights by regional carriers who, I'm sure, paid dearly for the privilege. Europeans seemed to be treated differently than Americans. In the end, Susan Gilbert—who was with me from South Africa to Ethiopia—and I flew commercially in Ethiopia and, therefore, ended up spending much less money in-country.

As I flew through Africa, I recalled experiencing some of my best low-level flying ever above the plains of Namibia, Botswana, South Africa, Zambia, and Zimbabwe seven years earlier.

On that earlier trip, one of the most important lessons I learned came from watching the animals. It was interesting to see how the lions, monkeys, and cheetahs helped take care of each other. When two brothers became separated, for example, because a fence had been erected between neighboring game preserves, they would cry out to one another. I first thought it was interesting that animals acted like humans. But then I realized the animals had been around for a lot longer than we humans had, and, therefore, our behavior must mirror theirs. Taking this one step further, it became clear that in the same way predators and disease would cull the herd to keep them stronger, the same thing was about to happen in our human world with the pandemic.

Peace Moment

God puts obstacles in our way to teach us our most critically important life lessons. At first glance, they seem impossible and overwhelming. With the help of others, we go on to tackle these problems to learn and grow together.

Chapter 15

Animals as Teachers

The place, the challenge, and the human endurance experience ... sometimes we need to return to our original home in the wild, to reconnect with where we've come from.

—Anonymous

From Dakar, I flew south to Accra, Ghana, then to Maun, Botswana, and La Mercy, South Africa, about 17 miles north of Durban. It is the location of Durban's King Shaka International Airport. It has four distinct areas—the airport precinct, the main residential area, a shanty town, and a beach-front strip of apartments along South Beach Road.

Susan along with Jeremy and Kristen had arrived a day prior and was already at KwaZulu-Natal where we would spend the next week or so. We would be speaking with indigenous Zulu inhabitants, going on game drives with guides and connect with Wild Tomorrow Fund representatives to observe and discuss what they were doing to protect nature and our environment.

After the stress at Dakar I was looking forward to being on the ground for some recovery time and meeting with people from such a different environment that being in the sky. The people we would be meeting were all grounded by jungles, animals, and nature.

One of our first guides was a man named Welcome. Even though he liked to joke a lot and made us laugh, we knew he had much more depth than simply to entertain us when he said, "Everything is connected. We need each other. We need the vegetation. After that, the vegetation needs us, it's a chain. Everybody is depending on nature all over the

Robert at the Zulu Nyala Game Reserve with Welcome as guide

world. Keep connected. That common thread connects us all over the world."

A stop to a Zulu village was a step back in time. We asked Mzamo, a Zulu Artist, what his favorite thing was about his culture. He replied, "My favorite thing about the Zulu culture is the respect. We respect every people. First, when we are young, we learn to respect ourselves. Next, we learn to respect other people. Everything is about respect and it helps us accept differences between cultures."

We spent several days at Wild Tomorrow Fund's location learning how they had acquired land which had been razed of all native vegetation in order to plant pinapple crops, and rehabilitated it to a natural habitat or as they say, 're-wilding the preserves'. From their work, key mammals like giraffes, elephants, rhinos, leopards and antelopes will be be protected along with key birds and healthy habitats. Clinton, a Wild Tomorrow Fund Conservation Manager, had much to offer as we walked and talked. He said, "We see ourselves as caretakers. We want to protect the land so that my kids, my grandkids can come here and both the land and the wildlife can still be here. In the western way of thought, we always separate things into categories, but it all is one. These systems have to be managed as one thing including people and animals and plants and water systems. It's all linked."

Helicopters are used to oversee the property, and I was fortunate to join them in the air for about an hour. Jason Fischer, Helicopter Pilot at Heligistix, explained their helicopter choice—the Robinson R44. The R44 is a single-engined helicopter with a semi-rigid two-bladed main rotor, a two-bladed tail rotor and a skid landing gear. It has an enclosed cabin with two rows of side-by-side seating for a pilot and three passengers.

Jason explained, "The Robinson R44 is our machine of choice. 95% of our work is conservation work. Aviation has become so important in conservation around the world and specifically in Africa. You look at the terrain we are working in and before the Wild Tomorrow Fund, there was no wildlife here. There is no point in reintroducing wildlife without taking care of it. Aircrafts make this possible. I get to protect the rhino. The biggest reward in our work comes from relocating animals to areas where they will be safe. Areas where they can exist and be protected from poachers. Every time I fly over and see them, that is really satisfying."

The day before leaving this area we spent time on another game preserve drive with a new guide—Sandiso, a Zulu Nyala tour guide. We were in an open-sided 4×4 Land Cruiser with open tiered seating allowing us to feel closer to the wildlife and nature

Robert with Sandiso, our Zulu Nyala Tour Guide

while offering great visibility and awesome photography opportunities. After viewing many elephants and zebras we stopped at a viewpoint to stretch our legs Sandiso shared, "I have to do more than this" as he spread our his arms to the views. "I want to make you understand that you, coming all the way from the States to here, is not only about game viewing. It's also about preserving what we have for next generations. We need to teach, we need to educate. I am hoping that after your trip, you tell more people about South Africa. If they come, like you did, by the time they leave, they will have a better understanding. It's not about looking at the stripes on a zebra. It's about what role a zebra plays in the ecosystem. Each and every one of us fits in the ecosystem. If you feel you are outside the ecosystem, then that is where you get it wrong. You need to be there your-self. You can explain to the person next to you that they are a part of the ecosystem and we all need to play our parts."

Passionately he continued, "We need each other. No one is disparate because we belong. We all be-long in this world. This is home. Let us educate. Cre-ate that awareness. Let everyone understand what is happening. Educate. That is my message.

To see a bird hopping from one branch to another, that bird is not hopping around aimlessly. Each movement has a reason out here. Seeing an impala walking around, snorting and sniffing, there is always a purpose behind it. We need to find that purpose."

We were blessed by the experience at Zululand's unique cultural heritage sites and by having such a great teacher in Sandiso.

Time to Leave South Africa

Now it was time get back in the *Citizen of the World* again for a brief stop at the island of Mauritius, a hop over to Madagascar, and then we'd meet back up with Jeremy and Kristen in Nairobi, Kenya.

Chapter 16

Cyclone Madagascar

There are times when life is happening so quickly that our souls struggle to stay in sync with our bodies. This often happens when we accelerate ourselves in the physical world. And while the separation is temporary, our souls must catch up with our bodies.

—Robert DeLaurentis, Peace Pilot

Susan was with me now as my next flight took us over the Indian Ocean to the island of Mauritius off the southeastern coast of Africa, and then to the island of Madagascar. We had learned when visting Mauritius that there are four levels of cyclones, common at this time of they year. Level one—Tropical Depression, Level two—Tropical Storm, Level three—Typhoon, Level four—Super Typhoon. We had arrived on the heels of a Level two, Tropical Storm that had passed by the following morning.

Madagascar was not the tropical Disney paradise we expected. Our second-hand reports did not reflect what we saw on the ground, which was a very poor third-world country with a host of problems that made travel challenging. In fact, it was considered the poorest island on the planet.

Our planned three day stop at this northwestern port city of Mahajanga provided numerous unusual challenges. The motel where we were staying did not take credit cards or US money. Cash payment with their currency was required daily, not at checkout. Each meal we ate at the motel required an immediate cash payment, no accrued billing. We called for a taxi to take us to a bank in town where we waited in line for almost an hour to exchange our US bills into the only accepted form of exchanges, the Malagasy Ariary. When we finally made it to the teller, we pulled out every bill we had—100 dollar bills, a few 50's, many 20's as well as smaller bills but were told no bills smaller than 100 dollar bills could be exchanged. Then of the 100 bills we had, each were heavily examined with some rejected. By the time we left the bank it was apparent that we would barely have enough funds to cover our short visit.

Tropical storms were rolling through the area daily, knocking out power and therefore internet resulting in lack of communication most importantly with Eddie.

We spent our day driving around the bumpy dirt roads on the island, sightseeing in three-wheeled taxis, and looking for lemurs. Mealtime was always an adventure and felt like we were living out an episode of Fear Factor armed with our flyswatters. With time, we became adept at swatting flies off our food. I showed Susan that creating a diversion and approaching the flies from behind was essential if one was to become a world-class fly swatter. The chickens we ate at almost every meal were likely the same scrawny and forlorn birds that always seemed to be darting off the road at the last possible instant.

It was on Day 2 after another power outage we learned that a huge tropical cyclone categorized as a Level 3 with wind speeds of at least 130 knots was barreling down directly on our position.

We couldn't stay and wait out the storm due to the currency issue and we weren't sure what damage would happen to the *Citizen of the World* sitting out on the tarmac during the cyclone. It was clear we needed to get out rather than risk damage. The first problem was getting our permit for an early departure to Nairobi, Kenya. Eddie Gould was able to do that in less than twenty-four hours. However, the local police and flight-plan office didn't receive the update and initially denied us permission to leave.

Then our fueling was delayed, because the local company wasn't familiar with my fueling card, and the increasing rainfall only slowed their already relaxed effort. In addition, we were required to pay fees to the police, customs, visa, health, flight plan office, and other agencies that magically appeared to collect again after we had already paid them on arrival. By the time we finished paying everyone who could produce a hand-written invoice on paper, the winds had picked up. Rain turned into a downpour, lightning flashed, and the weather continued to worsen. In between power outages, windy.com reported that conditions would remain constant for the next two hours, with a brief reprieve, but that's not what we saw.

My anticipated window of opportunity never materialized. We sat and waited for an hour, and despite the weather reports on my cell phone, the only change was increasing rain, lightning, and thunder. Nature was clearly in control, not me.

I made the decision: The longer we waited, the worse things would get. I was quite concerned for our safety and did not want to subject Susan to such intense risk. I told her I thought my decision to fly was questionable, and I was risking a lot. I told her I would make sure she got home commercially and we would figure out the funding issue if she wanted to wait out the storm on the ground. If I were her, I would have taken that option, but Susan made it clear she wanted to go with me. She had always been my biggest supporter, and once again, she would stick by my side. Without wasting another second, and drenched from head to toe, we got into the plane and put on our life jackets, packed our survival raft and gear, and belted up. I started the detailed checklist.

By the time I turned on the starter generator on the copilot side engine, the windows were completely fogged because of moisture in the cabin. Susan and I kept wiping the windows with our hands. The smell of Jet A-1 continued to permeate the plane, and Susan's eyes were burning before I even got the first engine started. The silence of a sealed cabin was broken only by her coughing to clear the taste of Jet A from her throat. What with the weather, lack of visibility, and the stress of this remote corrupt airport, we were both scared, although neither of us would admit it.

As I taxied to the takeoff point, I supplemented what I could see out the window with my geo-referenced position on the iPad and then cross-referenced that with the synthetic vision on my Avidyne flight management system, which also showed the runway centerline. For the first time, I experienced what it meant to literally taxi in instrument flight conditions.

Meanwhile, questions flew through my mind:

- How much moisture could these big Predator B drone engines ingest without risking a flameout on takeoff?
- How much precipitation would we have when the temperatures reached freezing in the climb?
- Would I have to deal with icing conditions?
- Would the Citizen experience a lightning strike on departure?

For the first time ever, I lit off all the Citizen's deicing equipment on the ground, which included the engine air inlets, igniters, pitot tubes, static ports, windshields, rudder cap, prop, and generator inlets. I also lit off the onboard radar and set it to twenty nautical miles. As I throttled up to 100 percent torque, I looked down the runway and saw how the centerline disappeared into the weather and threatened to swallow us up in six to ten feet. It was as if we were flying into what South Americans call "La Garganta del Diablo," the throat of the devil.

With one last wipe of the windshield, the Citizen accelerated as if she wanted out just as much as we did. We were thrown back in our seats as I struggled to see the centerline. I watched my ground speed in-

Windy.com weather map showing a cyclone barreling down on Robert and Susan's position in Mahajanga, Madagascar

crease on the digital display and kept an eye on how much runway we had left. I pulled back on the yoke as we passed 85 knots and felt the nose begin to lift. It seemed like the plane was so strong and determined she wouldn't let up, even for a second.

It was terrifying to see so much water hitting the windshield, as well as the force of its impact. When we first hit the heavy precipitation, it slowed the plane, causing me to lunge forward slightly. I had never heard precipitation hammer the front windshield like a water cannon. What I didn't know then was that the rain was ripping the decals off the front of the plane and the edges of the prop de-icing boots. The decals had been applied with painstaking care and were so thin that I wouldn't think the edge on them could be pulled up, in addition to which the edges had also been sealed, and a ceramic coating applied. Honestly, they were the last part of the plane I expected to show wear.

I remembered that windshield had cracked a year earlier at 31,000 feet, and for a second, I thought it was a blessing that we'd had to replace it, because the older, weaker windshield would never have survived this level of stress.

Susan and I stared at the storm scope, flight instruments, and windshield, waiting for something to fail. Time slowed, and I questioned my decision again. Was this worth risking our lives? I felt I should have been more forceful and insisted that Susan stay behind to catch a commercial flight. There was no reason for both of us to be subjected to this extreme risk.

When the rain slowed a bit, it was time to deal with the next—potentially worse—risk, icing. We were climbing through 10,000 feet, and the outside air temp was dropping toward 0 degrees Celsius, at which point ice would form. As a plane climbs, air temps typically drop way below freezing. This is called the lapse rate, and it was just a matter of time until the ice began appearing. I reported to Mahajanga Control that I was deviating fifteen degrees to the left for weather, which showed as a big red patch on my radar. We watched our altitude indicator continue to climb, and the temperature drop. By the time we reached 14,000 feet, trace ice was forming on the wings. I reported "Trace Ice" to Mahajanga Control and then laughed. What could they do about it? I was lucky to even have communication with them.

All the deicing equipment had been turned on and appeared to be working, so there was nothing more to do but wait, watch, and see what our fate would be. I took shallow breaths of Jet A-1 infused air, wondering what the Universe planned for us. Ice hit the windshield, but it was quite light. I kept looking out the side window at the leading edge of the wing for the real-world story, wondering what's next?, silently thanking the Citizen for her heroic performance, and thinking, this plane is f__king amazing.

Everything seemed to be working, and the mood lightened in the cockpit. We were getting closer to the top of the cloud layer. As quickly as the bad weather had started, it cleared. The worst was behind us and the radar confirmed it. We could finally see blue skies for more than 50 miles. We had left the wrath of Mother Nature and Madagascar behind us at almost 300 mph. I looked over at Susan. "It's over, we made it!" We celebrated with a series of high-fives and "Yeses" and then took deep breaths of Jet A-1.

We landed in Nairobi, Kenya, a few hours later, thankful to be alive.

Peace Moment

Our behavior as humans mirrors that of the animals that have been on the planet for millions more years than we have. The behavior/herd mentality that has kept us strong evolved from the animals and how they function.

Chapter 17

Discussing the Planet in Kenya

We are one people, one planet. There is no other planet for any one of us to go to. Our actions in Nature Kenya are locally based but globally relevant. We recognize the need to see the planet as a village. It boils down to the simplicity of life. We are all one. We might have the privilege of resources others don't have but our actions impact all of us.

—Paul Matiku, Executive Director, Nature Kenya

In Nairobi, we'd be staying at the Aero Club of East Africa, home to aviation in Kenya since 1927. The club had played an important role in opening up the country, and its members were the world's greatest aviation pioneers, including Beryl Markham, who was the first person to fly across the Atlantic from East to

West and Tom Campbell Black, who won the London to Melbourne Air Race in 1934.

As Susan and I touched down, it struck me how expansive my mission was becoming. We were promoting global peace by:

1. Flying between the poles, the two places peace has always existed, and metaphorically connecting everyone in between on our mission of peace.

2. Interviewing people from many different countries about what it means to be a Citizen of the World and how they found peace in their world. In the process, we were demonstrating that people all want the same things: Safety, financial security, health, peace, joy, and happiness for their families and themselves. In the end, we are more similar than different.

3. Moving science ahead for the good of the planet by testing for plastics in the air, using biofuels, promoting technology that could track aircraft anywhere on the planet, and testing a new platform for NASA that could eliminate the need for manned space missions. In the end, we were helping to achieve sustainable living and calling attention to the environmental and climate challenges throughout the world.

One of my hopes for this mission was to get people to work together instead of competing with one another to solve the problems that affect us all. And that cooperation, I think, was clearly at work in Kenya. I was looking forward to the meetings I had scheduled with two of the nation's leaders.

Our first meeting was with Dr. Paul Matiku, director of Nature Kenya, along with his assistant, Paul Gacheru. When I asked them to describe their mission, I was struck by how much it resembled our own.

Dr. Matiku started the conversation by saying, "I believe that locally driven solutions are the best way to address many challenges in this world. The energy of the small steps we make at the grassroots level radiates from that nucleus of change and impacts not just our entire country but the entire world. At Mount Kenya, one of Nature Kenya's biodiversity areas for example, we work with local groups to carry out forest restoration. In 2019, with community groups and help from partners around the world, we were able to plant more than a million trees on the mountain. Those small steps build up to solutions that affect the world by reducing carbon emissions and providing carbon sinks that remove carbon dioxide from the atmosphere. With those small solutions we work toward making the world a better place.

"Mount Kenya is a forest," he continued, "and it is the source of the largest river in Kenya, the Tan River. A lot of the electricity in Kenya is hydropower, and Nairobi itself is dependent on Mount Kenya for water. Water comes from the forest to provide electricity. One thing is very clear. The world is perfectly connected by water and the world is perfectly connected by air, and the atmosphere. We are all one. Most Kenyans believe that a sustainably managed environment is the best avenue for peace-building. Imagine a world without carbon dioxide, a world without climate change, and a world without hunger. Imagine a world where all people have access to energy, a world where there are no inequities because of the way resources are being used. It will be a peaceful world. There will be no need for conflict.

"The more people there are thinking about nature conservation, thinking about peaceful coexistence, thinking about taking from nature only what is needed, the more peace there will be in the world, the more peace of mind we will have from knowing that we are ensuring intergenerational equity. The world has only one planet and so we have to take care of it like a baby. Globally, we lack the commitment to nature conservation. Economies are about capitalism. The resources needed to take care of nature are limited. If humans could prioritize nature just for a day, a week, a year, and if the leaders of the world could truly engage with a commitment to save nature, the planet would be a better place. Let's increase those efforts."

I was more than impressed. "That's very close to our mission of One Planet, One People, One Citizen of the World," I replied. "And it's inspiring to see that it's being done efficiently and that many people are winning. Your work is based on the premise that we want people to thrive on this one planet; there is no other planet."

Dr. Matiku nodded and smiled. "For example, in the recent past, the ability of local communities to plant crops in their local environment has been put into serious jeopardy because of the effects of climate change. Local people must be able to plant at the right time. They do not know when rain will come because patterns have changed the predictability of rain. Some days they experience floods when they ought not to be having any rain at all. Nature Kenya sees the world as one planet, too. We are trying to restore our people's past, when people all over the world lived in harmony with nature."

"At that point, I asked Dr. Matiku, "What does it mean to you to be a citizen of the world?"

"For me," he answered quickly, "being a citizen of the world means using local, indigenous knowledge or citizen science to provide solutions. Citizen science provides the opportunity to find locally-driven solutions. Being a citizen of the world is recognizing the usefulness of the local person on the ground who uses what he or she has learned in order to provide small solutions that, when taken cumulatively, can have a global impact."

We learned from Dr. Matiku Nature Kenya, an organization since 1909, focused on taking care of the environment, and that their policy was all about biodiversity – saving and protecting species. For eighty-seven years they worked to create awareness and, moving forward, their strategic plan is to embrace traditional beliefs, and encourage ecological sustainability by empowering people. A pillar Nature Kenya uses to create a sustainable environment is to ensure that people are part of the action, removing barriers that prevent them from saving nature so that all people can then take charge of their own conservation and development objectives.

Having said all that, he then turned to me and said, "What you are doing is unique. I never imagined it could be done. I wish you success. Hopefully, the outcome of your effort will reach the people who matter. If the world could have a few other people like you, if we had a few more of us in the world asking,

'Can you make the planet, as our home, habitable?' it would be a much better place."

Wow!

Knowing that our time together was coming to a close, I added, "You know, I think that along the way we're upsetting and disrupting a few people and some ways of thinking. But ultimately, I think our goal is good and our motives are noble."

Energized by our "green" conversation, we were looking forward to continuing the dialogue with Director General Mamo Boru, who worked closely with Kenya's president.

After taking out seats and exchanging pleasantries, I got right to the point. "Part of the reason we are here," I said," is because you're doing such a great job. In the United States, we are making inroads on a state-by-state basis but we have not banned single use plastic bags across the entire country. We come here and find that you have already passed the law and you're now enforcing it. You have been very successful in getting the people to cooperate. And a lot of the environmental programs that you're supporting actually end up benefiting people because they are profitable and sensible for many different groups. I think that if every person did something responsible for the planet every day, even if it were just recycling their water bottle, we would be light years ahead."

General Mamo nodded his head. "Absolutely," he agreed. "Our planet is the common home for all of humanity. So it takes a concerted effort from each and every individual to care for the planet. We must enhance the life, the biodiversity, the ecosystems on this planet, and we can do that both individually and collectively. You can do small things at your local level, but the impact could be felt at the global level. I think this is what we need to start teaching even our children in primary school. In our country, we have started providing environmental education for the children and ensuring that we inculcate these values so that, as they grow up, they will be able to appreciate the importance of the environment and God's creation. That connectivity is very important. I want to say this: This is our environment. It's our life and our responsibility. That is the message that needs to go out.

I think the biggest challenge is getting people to take responsibility at the individual level, the family level, and the community level. If all of us can take responsibility for our environment and responsibility for our waste, we can live on a clean, healthy planet that can provide the ecological services we require. These initiatives can add to bigger initiatives. We are a global family working to protect the planet."

I quickly agreed. "Yes, that is our mission as well." And as we wrapped up our wonderful conservation,

I had one final question: "What does it mean to be a citizen of the world?"

Director General Mamo didn't hesitate. "Being a citizen of the world," he said, "is using our local knowledge in local political institutions. We rely so much on scientists seeking some sort of solution for all, but science, while certainly necessary, can also dependent to some extent on the political situation."

While it would be impossible for me to reproduce a verbatim account of everything we discussed with these two gentlemen, I have tried to capture the message and meaning of what they both said. There were many common themes in both interviews:

1. We can make changes at the local level – take small steps that have a great impact.
2. We must care for the planet as one people. Our environment has no borders.
3. Think locally, act globally. We are a global family.

Plastics in Kenya—Solving Problems in Kenya as Citizens of the World

Since I was collecting plastic particles in the air for the Scripps Institution of Oceanography, Kenya's attention to the environmental dangers of plastics was particularly fascinating to me. In August 2017 they banned the use of plastic bags everywhere in the entire country. Their law is the strictest in the world, with fines nearing $50,000 US, as well as up to four years in prison. I was eager to learn how the ban had affected wildlife, wildlife habitats, and the human population.

I found that not only were Kenyans on board with the single-use plastics ban but they were also trying to reduce or get rid of plastics altogether. Now I could see why: with groups like Nature Kenya and NEMA leading the way, how could they not want to do their part? However, Nature Kenya and NEMA kept running into headwinds with the private sector, which continued producing plastics by saying there was going to be a shortage of packaging materials when, in fact, they were just trying to save their businesses. As a result, there are still tons of plastics in the sewage systems and on the roads.

Director General Mamo told us about the Flip-flopi Project, a movement whose mission is to end the use of single use plastic once and for all. To do that, they built the world's first recycled-plastic dhow (a traditional sailing vessel with one or more masts), using traditional boatbuilding techniques, and covered it with 30,000 multicolored flip-flop sandals. In 2019, they sailed 500 km from the Kenyan island of Lamu to Zanzibar, Tanzania, stopping at twelve communities and garnering significant attention among the media, policy-makers, communities, artists, and plastics manufacturers.

While clearing out plastics is one thing, maintaining a cleaner environment is important as well. In addition, conservation initiatives like the United Nations Environmental Program, among others, will continue to raise awareness, and more projects like Flipflopi will call even more attention to this huge problem.

There are common threads that connect all people, but in Africa we also discovered the magical connection between people and nature that is known and practiced by all aboriginal or indigenous peoples. Sadly, in our industrialized world, nature is often seen as a business commodity, and much of the population has disconnected from the land.

Another environmental issue we discussed with Dr. Matiku and Director Mamo was Kenya's water situation. Right now, they pointed out, the majority of the country is dependent on water supplied by traditional hydroelectric power, but the rural population relies on the water coming from springs—some of the same water being tapped by the hydroelectric plants. In addition, however, the Kenyans are building wind farms to provide electricity. So, hopefully, this will increase the supply of running water rural citizens can depend upon.

Dr. Matiku had pointed out that on land we often see ourselves as a nation, or a state, a town, or even a household, separate from everyone else in the world. But when you fly above the world, and around it, those perceived divisions vanish. First, the world is connected by water. Second, you don't see boundary lines as you do on a map; you see land rolling into more land, spilling into the sea, and then more land. It becomes clear that what we do in America—or anywhere in the world—to protect or destroy the environment also deeply affects the villagers in Kenya we were visiting.

During the course of our interviews, I was also asked for my take on solutions, for which I felt honored yet again. Anytime someone from another culture, especially an indigenous culture, asks me to brainstorm and create solutions, it's deeply honoring and not something I take lightly.

I said that, like them, I believed that taking small steps makes it easier for people to see what is possible, because if you look at the lofty goal of world peace or connecting people around the planet, it might seem unattainable. But showing people what is possible, that we are more similar than different, sets the foundation for peace and cooperation.

I continued by saying that we wanted to go out into the world and take one step every day, maybe arrive at one small solution, some positive progress. So, for example, we wanted clean air for the planet just like everyone else. And for that reason, we decided to burn biofuels rather than regular aviation fuel for a portion of our journey. We know it's a step in the right direction. And we know that persistence will get us there.

The most important thing is that the planet is reaching a tipping point, and our ability to satisfy human needs is in danger of collapse. While it is very late in the game, it's not too late to take action, not too late for both you and your neighbor to do something to save humanity, which is what we've been trying to do on this mission.

I told them that the last place we visited before coming to Kenya was Madagascar, and when we were driving into town, we saw a lot of different colored plastic barrels that were actually on fire. They were burning the barrels as trash, and I thought to myself, *well, there's one of the reasons for all the plastic particles in the air.*

And, I added, with you here it's been exactly the opposite. We've seen first-hand how sustainability, climate, and the environment affect individual African villages and nations—and the great things people, from the poorest citizens to those in the highest levels of government—are doing about it.

Saving Wildlife in Kenya

After learning so much about the ways Kenya is working to preserve and expand its natural resources as well as the ways that Kenyans respect and bond with nature, we were very excited to visit the "Nairobi Nursery," which is located in the Nairobi National Park. The first and most successful elephant orphan rescue and rehabilitation program in the world is run by The Sheldrick Wildlife Trust, a pioneering conservation organization, dedicated to the protection of wildlife and the preservation of habitats in East Africa. In addition to its rescue and rehabilitation work, the Trust is dedicated to safeguarding these magnificent creatures from being poached for their

An elephant and his overseer at the Nairobi Nursery

tusks and to protecting and preserving Kenya's wildlife habitats.

Because one way they protect the elephants in their charge is to limit the number of visitors to the Nursery, we were fortunate to be among the lucky few. We lined up with the other visitors on a patch of land with a scattering of water pools and waited. Soon a bunch of beautiful, playful baby elephants came bouncing through the forest with their over-seers, and it hit us that these incredible creatures would not be there if they hadn't been protected and nurtured to health and well-being. They frolicked in the dirt, came over to check us out, and rolled around in the mud. We were awestruck. By saving these orphaned babies and eventually returning them to the wild, the Trust was ensuring that there would be future generations of elephants.

To me, one of the most fascinating and personally gratifying aspects of their work was that, in addition to Kenya Wildlife Service rangers and tracker dogs, they use aerial surveillance to monitor wildlife and deter illegal activity from the sky.

You've heard the saying, "It takes a village," and it is becoming clearer every day that we must work together to save our beautiful planet, resources, and all living things.

Peace Moment

There are no boundaries when generosity, gratitude, and appreciation are present. This creates a time of spiritual growth for our souls that stays with us forever. We evolve together and the growth of a single individual influences the growth of the entire planet.

Chapter 18

Ethiopia:
Finding Peace Within

If you have the capacity to quit the world, quit the activity, quit the noise, then you can be nearer to God or at least be at peace with yourself.

We do not think about nationalities; we think about human beings without taking into consideration whether one is from east or west or north or south. We feel like we belong to the world. To not have boundaries around you.

—Luigi Contamessa, Korkor Lodge, Ethiopia

From Kenya, Susan and I flew north to Ethiopia. It seemed a great place to stop for a few days to recharge. It turned out to be one of the biggest surprises of the entire trip—a country rich in history and natural beauty, filled with wonderful, joyful people.

Morning view from Robert's room at the Korkor Lodge looking out at Korkor Mountain

My mornings started at the Korkor Lodge in the Tigray region of northern Ethiopia, sipping local tea, starting to write down my experiences and thoughts for this book and looking out at breathtaking Mt. Korkor through floor-to-ceiling windows. The stillness of the morning was punctuated by the music of birds chirping and other sounds of nature, and, in the midst of all this beauty, I was reminded of what Flavio, the paraglider pilot from Rio De Janeiro, had shared during our interview for the documentary we were filming: I must first find peace in myself; only then can I share it with the world.

I knew that if I was going to embody inner peace on my mission of Global Peace and bring it into the world, I needed to pull myself out of my "get it done" mindset and reconnect with the magical energy so present at Korkor. I came to understand that we have to be the change we want to see in this world. I knew some people worked a lifetime to get to this place of connectivity, and I thought it was a lot to ask of myself on a trip that involved so many responsibilities and challenges. I also knew that change could happen in an instant once I arrived at a place of balance, calm, and clarity. For some, it happens in an instant, while for others it takes a lifetime of suffering. For Eckhart Tolle, a living master, it took two years sitting on a park bench as a vagrant to reach that point in his personal evolution.

Ethiopia, often considered the cradle of civilization, was a great place to embark on such a lofty goal. It is said that the Ark of the Covenant was located somewhere in the mountains of the Tigray region, which contains many churches hidden away in caves.

I had reached this level of peace for brief periods a few times in my life, but never could maintain it. It was elusive. Circumstances would place me there and each time I had a powerful feeling of contentment. During these heightened states even strangers would approach and make conversation, saying they could sense something special about me. They could feel that I was at peace and wanted to achieve that as well. That "something special" was a connection with the Universe, God, or the Collective Conscience; call it what you want. It was about channeling the energy available to all of us.

As Susan and I hiked up Korkor Mountain, using our hands and at times the help of our guides and other hikers, I thought about what changes I could bring about in my life and my mind to find lasting peace within.

Nothing came to me.

At the top of the mountain, our guide led us into a dark cave. Living inside was a very old monk. On the floor were special woven carpets and a shrine with candles and other religious artifacts. The monk had spent seventy years living in isolation and praying, in the hope that he could move on to a better place after this lifetime. He seemed to be in a deep state of meditation but delighted to take a picture with me. While amazed at his commitment, I didn't want to live in a cave for seventy years. I preferred the space and comfort of my "badass" Turbo Commander 900 and its terrible Jet A fuel smell and taste.

I knew, however, that I needed silence to focus on the beauty and feel gratitude for the amazing things around me. I needed to see and feel the wonder it all

The monk that lived in a cave for 70 years on Mt Korkor

provided for my evolution here on the planet, and that included acknowledging my body, which had brought me to this place in life and, as I turned fifty-four, continued to work well. I also needed to release the judgments and chatter going through my mind at light speed from minute-to-minute as it interpreted the world around me.

This was also when Susan expressed her understanding of the "Peace Moments" I share throughout this book. While similar to the "Zen Moments" I had experienced and written about in *Zen Pilot: Flight of Passion and the Journey Within*, these were also realizations that would help bring the planet together in peace.

A "Peace Moment" is a time when all eight of these conditions are present:

1. Release judgments and chatter
2. Be in silence
3. Focus on the beauty around you
4. Feel gratitude
5. See the wonder in what had been provided
6. Acknowledge your body
7. Remain in the present
8. Do not dwell on the past

Peace Moments would move me toward an elevated state where all living things were connected and at peace—moments that could serve as examples for others and be repeated when needed in a divided world.

As a reminder of these lessons, I vowed to wear or carry something special each day to keep me focused on this goal of sharing what I learned with the world. These items could be beads blessed by the Dalai Lama, one of our courage coins, or a simple but special good luck bracelet that had been drenched in Jet A fuel when ferry tank number one burst in Dakar.

Each morning, I would set the following intention:

"Please allow me to see the best in all living creatures including myself, and to speak and act with compassion, love, and kindness. Help me elevate myself above those things I cannot control and accept my own humanity. Guide me in learning my lessons with grace and ease and assist me in finding the peace that exists within me so that I may be an example for others."

Finding Joy: The tale of a restless soul

I was now three months into my polar circumnavigation and had met hundreds of people from ten countries, but the happiest and most joyful people by far were those I was meeting in rural northern Ethiopia where they were removed from the culture, technology, and consumerism of our first-world life. How removed were they? Well, I flew Citizen of the World to Addis Ababa, caught a regional airline to the Tigray region, and then took a two-hour car ride into the remote northern Gheralta Mountains, where I felt transported into another time. The people were happy and smiling, even joyful. One of my most memorable

Korkor Lodge and the surrounding countryside

experiences was seeing three little boys, all about six or seven years old, lined up next to each other on the side of the road with big smiles on their sweet faces and their thumbs out to hitch a ride. They had their routine down and knew from experience that some passerby would stop and give them a ride. Over the next few days, I learned that these boys, their families, and their community had very little in the way of material possessions. Their houses had no furniture—at least, the way I think of furniture. They slept on straw mats on the dirt floor. They ate while sitting on the floor. They would bring their animals inside to protect them from the weather and prowling hyenas. Yet, their houses and land were all well cared for. They took pride in their ownership.

The land around them was beautiful, with the Gheralta Mountains singing out the grandeur of God and nature. It was the sort of beauty that made me stop to watch the sunset and get up early to watch the sunrise. The people were nourished by the land, the river a direct source of drinking water. Young boys herded their goats, cows, and donkeys that fed on the vegetation. One day, a boy sitting in a nearby tree called out, "These are my goats! I take care of them, and then I go to school in the afternoon." His smile was so big that the delight and pride he took in his responsibility were hard to miss.

Small groups of children were playing and singing and waving everywhere we passed. They weren't worried about what had happened in the past or would happen in the future. They lived rock-solid present in the moment. In fact, all of the people were living in their joy, not searching for happiness. In the so-called civilized world, many of us equate the pursuit of happiness with new possessions: new clothes, a new car, a new job, a new house, etc. After a while, these things don't make us happy anymore, so we replace them with newer things. Happiness is fleeting. Joy is actually with us from the day we are born, but it's difficult to access because we build walls and create distractions that prevent us from feeling it.

When Susan and I first arrived at Korkor Lodge for our weeklong stay, I sat and talked with the owner, Luigi. I felt as if I were in the presence of a sage, an old soul, and what he told me became a Peace Moment: "Robert, maybe these people are onto something. They may be more evolved than us. Have our modern lives really made us happier or just created more problems for us?"

"I'm not sure they have made us happier," I replied.

My mind wandered back to my mission: "One planet. One people. One plane. Oneness for humanity." All our responsibilities. All our possessions. All the products we consume. All the silly things we do to be better than the next person. I thought about how important our clothes, cameras, cars, dishes, cell phones, sunglasses, shoes, and other items were to us and wondered, "Why?"

Realizing I was beginning to go down the rabbit hole, I brought myself back to the moment. "We must have something as valuable as the simple joys of these 'evolved' people—at least modern medicine is something we can be proud of," I said. "What about our ability to use radiation and lasers to prevent disease, improve our vision, and perform surgery? Surely that counts?"

"The locals live to be very old, and when they get sick, they go and drink water from a special well," Luigi replied.

I wondered if the issues that modern medicine fixed were those we created from our lifestyles: stress, chemicals, ambition, worry, lack of movement, improper eating, and plastic everything. Clearly, I had more thinking to do about what it means to be a Citizen in the World for the World.

During a two-hour walk through the countryside with Susan, I was most impressed by a little girl who set up a small display when she saw us approaching. She had carved emblems into small stones, and she showed us a piece of paper with her original design for the artwork she had created—a budding entrepreneur, for sure.

We continued on to a 2,000-year-old church about a quarter of a mile away. When we came out of the sacred building, the little girl relocated her display to another spot we would pass. She was all smiles when we met her eyes a second time. As a gesture of goodwill, Susan gave her some local currency. The little girl reached down into her basket and gave her the biggest stone carving. Susan asked if she could have one more for a friend. The little girl smiled joyfully and handed her the next biggest stones Susan gave her a few more coins. We ended our time with the little girl with Susan telling her how beautiful she was and how wonderful her stones were. I could feel their souls bonding as they both smiled from ear to ear. We later learned that the amount of money Susan had given the girl was more than her father made in a week.

I felt that the little girl knew more about business than most people with whom I'd gone to business school…and maybe even more about the "School of Life" that was currently in session for me. She and Susan showed me that there are no boundaries when generosity, gratitude, and appreciation are present.

After a few days at the Korkor Lodge, it seemed to me that those of us living in first-world countries have totally missed this thing called "joy." Joy is available to all of us, just as it was for the little girl with her stones, the little boy with his goats, and the three boys attempting to hitch a ride. We don't need to wait until we get that promotion to be happy. We don't need to wait until we have that dream house or car. We don't have to wait until we lose those ten extra pounds to decide that we are whole, complete, and a success.

Peace Moment

We don't need to wait until everything is perfect for joy to happen in our lives. Life will rarely be perfect. Maybe we are enough just as we are. Maybe we don't have to keep postponing our joy. Maybe interactions with our earthbound angels are meant to teach us that we already have what we need to be happy. Maybe slowing down and taking the time to notice—with gratitude and appreciation—what is already available to us will help us remove these self-created limitations so that we can live a fully joyful life.

Chapter 19

On the Way to Europe

It was easier to find inner peace when I was isolated in the country without another soul around, immersed in the beauty of nature, listening to birds, feeling the cool breeze and sunshine on my face. But to make our mission and desires known and realize them, we must be in the world.

—Robert DeLaurentis, Peace Pilot

Leaving the peace of the Tigray region behind, we flew back to Addis Ababa Bole International Airport. From there, Susan returned to the United States and I flew on to Cairo, Egypt, for a few days of sightseeing before I continued on to Tbilisi, Georgia, where I reconnected with the film crew. Situated at the intersection of Eastern Europe and Western Asia, Georgia is a country in the Caucasus region, on the coast of the Black Sea, It is generally considered a kind of transcontinental country.

*At the Gergeti Trinity Church, looking out at the
Caucasus Mountains*

The people didn't really identify completely with either culture, and somehow that seemed to work well. The city had been thriving for hundreds of years. There was no judgment. It was not about us or them. Instead, they saw everyone as part of a big melting pot. Tbilisi had achieved something that much of the world had not.

One of the places the film crew and I visited was the Gergeti Trinity Church, a monastery high atop the Caucasus mountains with some of the most beautiful and inspired views I would see on the entire polar circumnavigation. The monks sought out these "elevated" places in order to connect with God, but for us, getting there required a four-wheel-drive vehicle and an experienced driver.

At the monastery, in the bitter cold, I could feel the opening-up inside me that had started on the South Pole flight. I felt as if I could just reach up and touch the heavens. I remember leaning against a door to get out of the wind and cold when the door swung open and I saw a monk whose peace I had disturbed. Looking distressed, he was rushing toward me to shut the door. Apparently, it was easier to maintain one's peace when not confronted by the realities of the outside world and an unforgiving, sometimes brutal Mother Nature. This was the same struggle I was facing trying to make sense of all that had happened on the South Pole leg of my journey. It was a slow process and achieving that understanding would require the patience I had always struggled to find inside me.

By now, it was February 2020, and rather than return to the U.S., I planned to make Europe my home for the next several months while waiting for the North Pole to warm up. Talk of a virus spreading from China already had governments warning against travel. Would that affect my expedition?

From Tbilisi I flew to Sofia, Bulgaria, where I stayed for a few days before moving on to Genoa, Italy, then to Madrid, Spain, where I met with my fellow circumnavigator, Michel Gordillo. Michel is a seasoned commercial and general aviation pilot, and to me, a philosopher. With extensive experience flying in Antarctica since landing his RV-8 there in 2016, Michel had coached and advised me about flying over the South Pole

When I had to delay my polar expedition twice because of problems with my plane, Michel told me that the Citizen was talking to me and telling me she wasn't ready. He advised me that until the problems were resolved, I had to continue working on the aircraft. When I complained that preparations were becoming difficult, perhaps a sign that I shouldn't go, he reminded me that "If it were easy, no one would care. You'll have to overcome countless obstacles before this is done."

Mentor and friend Michel Gordillo at the South Pole with his heavily modified RV-8 aircraft on skis

Michel sent an early version of the Antarctic Flight Information Manual (AFIM) to help prepare me for a potential emergency stop en route to the South Pole. Further, he encouraged me to contact the four established bases representing different countries and business ventures ahead of my initial departure so I would have a better chance of survival. He's also the one who facilitated my getting the necessary permits and approvals and helped to determine my take-off point before the very fraught South Pole leg of the expedition.

Then, during the flight itself, he sent me satellite text messages concerning the weather he was tracking online, and when I was low on fuel and concerned for my life, he texted me words of encouragement.

Michel was clearly one of the angels sent to help me on my very difficult journey. He appeared at exactly the right time with all of the knowledge I needed to get past some very difficult hurdles the Universe was presenting to me.

Michel has never asked me for anything except cheesecake—his favorite. He has given help unconditionally. When you have great people like him behind you, how can you not succeed? I am thankful that he has become a part of my life.

In Madrid, he helped to facilitate repairs to the *Citizen's* ferry system, as well as a minor leak from the copilot-side brake caliper. He showed me around Madrid and Segovia, previewed the documentary-in-progress about his trip around the world, and introduced me to various Spanish delicacies including pig, which seemed to be very popular. Based on its climate, native vegetation, and lack of predators, Spain is an ideal environment for pigs, and pork found its way into many of our meals.

Michel also took me up in his plane, Sky Polaris, where I got to experience the speed and maneuverability of his much smaller RV-8 experimental aircraft as he did high bank turns and a roll. The plane that had landed at the South Pole several years before was still in great shape, and it was relatively fast for a small piston plane at about 150 knots, half the speed of the *Citizen of the World*. It was as nimble as a ping-pong ball on the water, bouncing with each air current, and strong enough to handle the large loads that aerobatic flight required, which meant that it could also handle the big fuel load for his trip. The maneuvers, however, were too much for my stomach, I felt like I was going to barf all over the back seat. "I feel like I'm going to barf" are the last words a pilot wants to hear, because it takes hours to clean the plane and, just like Jet A fuel, the smell is a lasting memory. We returned to his home base, Robledillo de Mohernando Airport, just in time. I had confirmed that I didn't have the stomach to be a fighter pilot and was thankful for the smooth flight conditions of my heavier aircraft.

Michel shared some of the challenges he had, which were an entirely different set of issues because his plane flew lower, at 14,000 feet compared to the 35,000-foot RVSM (Reduced Vertical Separation Minima) of which the Citizen was capable. Since Antarctica had 10,000 feet of snow and ice, Michel was often only 4,000 feet above the snow and ice and only 3,000 feet if he was heavy with fuel. His plane was uniquely equipped with a fuel tank below the fuselage that he could drop once the fuel was used up, as well as another ferry tank from which he could jettison fuel in case he needed to return to base or climb over a mountain.

Our visit came at a welcome time. When I reached Madrid, I was burnt out from three months on the road, and I still had the North Pole to conquer. I really wanted to know what internal changes Michel had experienced while flying over Antarctica, and he told me that he had seen parts of the earth no other human had seen. But he couldn't really help me understand what I personally had felt, and I came to realize that this would take time, that what each of us experiences is deeply personal, and that our curriculums are different.

I was surprised when Michel told me he hadn't done any distance flying at all after his trip because he felt he needed a break. He had been to most of the places he wanted to see. He told me it would take a year or two for him to regain his drive to fly. After the South Pole leg, I could understand how he felt. I was exhausted and burnt out—kind of how you feel after a long drive. You don't even want to look at a car for a while. Besides, I felt I could never top the South Pole flight.

Peace Moment

The Universe will continue to teach me with progressively more intense opportunities to change my thinking or behavior until I finally get it.

Chapter 20

Seeing Spain

Each person's curriculum is unique. We experience what we must to further our personal evolution. These spiritual moments have an impact on everyone in the world, and each step forward we personally experience is a step forward in the evolution of the planet.
　　　　　　—Robert DeLaurentis, Peace Pilot

By the time I got to Spain, life had been happening much faster and more intensely than I had ever experienced before. It was life on steroids, and I had begun to feel some separation between my physical body and my soul.

After a few days, I left Michel in Madrid and took the bullet train to Granada. We were speeding along at a cool 172 mph, and I was impressed, even though I'd moved as fast as 410 mph in the *Citizen*, a blistering speed for a turboprop plane. After trips at that speed, it takes time for my soul to catch up with my body. It feels like I need to catch my breath, because life is happening faster than I can process it. I often feel a little "off" or in a bit of a daze. Adjusting to a different, slower reality takes a few hours.

What I was learning is that people who maintain that pace for an extended period of time need to make changes in their lives, because the soul and the body can't exist apart from one another for long periods. We all long to be one.

Realizing this truth, I knew I needed to slow down. I was missing opportunities to experience more of life. From a practical perspective, it's hard to snap a good picture from the window of an airplane speeding along at 410 mph at 35,000 feet in the air, on a bullet train, or in a speeding car on the freeway. Everything starts to blur, including reality. The problem is that if you don't slow down on your own, the Universe will do it for you, and sometimes not in the most graceful manner. It's sometimes called "Hitting the Wall" and often comes at the worst time possible, along with other issues, just to make sure you don't skip or miss an epic learning opportunity.

I knew "the wall" well, and thought that this time I would avoid hitting it by slowing down on my own. To do this, I rented a small car that wasn't very fast, and set the cruise control—or as we pilots like to call it, the "autopilot"—to 60 mph. After flying in my plane, that felt like standing still. As other cars drove by at close to twice the speed, taunting me to get back in the "game," I felt the urge to open it up, as I often do with the *Citizen*, to see what the car could do. But I resisted, turned on relaxing music, and settled into my new slower-paced reality. This really feels good, I thought. No crowds, no screaming kids, no barking dogs, no cell phones, nothing that was out of balance.

I held my ground and took a deep breath of fresh Spanish countryside air complemented by the fragrance of olive trees and grapevines. I noticed that I was breathing more deeply, not the rapid, shallow

Sitting in a field in Spain taking in nature and working toward inner peace

breaths that do me little good. This new, slower pace felt great. I even pulled over a few times to snap pictures of the beauty around me. I felt grateful to be alive and experiencing so much inspiration when so many people around the world suffered.

As I noticed the fields of yellow flowers divided by waist-high walls, with olive trees everywhere, I got a sudden hit of intuition, a "spiritual download." I needed to slow down even more. This place was so inviting that I just wanted to sit under a tree. I found my spot and started taking deep breaths, filling my lungs with as much fragrant flower-filled air as I could. I felt that I was reconnecting to the essence of life and being nurtured by the earth from which I had come.

During the time I sat there in silence, I was visited by bees, birds, rabbits, and dancing butterflies. What looked like a bull in the distance kept an eye on me for most of the time, but I wasn't scared; I was in the right place at the right time. I was where I was supposed to be.

As I emerged from what felt like a meditation, I was grateful to be doing this on my own, with ease and grace, rather than having the Universe stop me with a broken aircraft, injury, illness, or some other crisis I couldn't ignore.

A moment after I had that thought, I felt the urge to leave. A strong inner voice said, "Okay, checked that box. Next! Now it's time to go." Clearly, my ego was talking to me. The first thing I saw when I looked up? A giant red stop sign just down the road. It was as if Spirit were foreshadowing what was to come. I smiled as I realized I was again being led to stop and relax. I sat back down and continued to breathe deeply, listening to the symphony of chirping birds and watching the butterflies flutter through the air. I sat there for two hours, receiving what nature had for me, focusing only on what I was experiencing in that precise moment. I could feel the cool breeze on my face and the warm sun on my neck. It was heaven on earth. So peaceful and so calm.

As I reflected, I realized that my entire life to that point had been dictated by deadlines and moving ahead at warp speed. I had been achieving goals, some of my own, and some belonging to others. I had achieved a lot. I had reached my financial goals and had been recognized for having a positive impact on the world. But in the end, what I had been doing was putting my body through a spiritual shock treatment and demanding it respond to my egotistical desire to find the peace within me—on my schedule. What I now realized was that things happened on God's time. Everything I'd been doing so far merely led me to a place where my real purpose could begin to emerge.

After a time, I bid farewell to my enchanting place, thanking it for all it had taught me. As I continued on my drive, I kept thinking about the beauty of the rolling hills and grassy fields all around me. From this space of gratitude, I was clearly at peace, and I was ready to go back into the world to share what I had found inside of me.

I returned to Madrid, spent some more time with Michel, and then flew on to the island of Menorca.

Peace Moment

The soul and the body can't exist apart from one another for long periods of time. We all long to be one.

Chapter 21

Seeking Myself

Sometimes what adventure, what exploration gives you is the chance to drop away the baggage, the infrastructure that you normally take some meaning along and purpose from and go to that deeper space, and look at yourself, and look at life, and look at the context of life at very different scales, at slower scales, at more close-up scales.

—Kathy Sullivan, Astronaut

One unexpected consequence of being alone with nature for long periods of time was that I found myself becoming agitated by loud sounds, voices, and other noises. Kids crying or dogs barking would create more stress than I had felt before, and I began to withdraw from the world for fear of developing a painful headache. I realized that this was a problem. Wasn't it my mission to connect with people globally, not withdraw from them?

I thought about the monk in the cave. But I didn't want to live in a cage and, in any case, I couldn't accomplish what I'd set out to do by retreating from the world. I knew there must be a way to deflect this unwanted noise rather than internalize it.

An Angel, a Monk, and Encountering COVID

One stumbling block to achieving global connection turned out to be beyond my control. By the spring of 2020 COVID was sweeping across Europe on its way to the United States, leaving fear, confusion, and mistrust in its wake. The first signs of trouble came when Italy shut its borders just a few days after I left Genoa. I certainly was not in any of the high-risk categories identified by the World Health Organization, but the virus was having a powerful effect on everyone around me. Fear showed in people's eyes as they scurried from place to place, avoiding the very humanity with whom they so desperately needed to connect. When COVID was declared a global pandemic, politicians feared they would be accused of not doing enough, so they reacted by shutting down sporting events, gatherings, and eventually schools. By then I was concerned that it would force me to cancel the rest of my mission.

At that point, the Universe intervened yet again by introducing me to another one of my trip angels.

Meritxell Asensio was a police officer I met in Barcelona. She helped move me along on my spiritual journey by taking me to the monastery at Montserrat and convincing the monks that I should be allowed to live with them for a while, as she had done sometime earlier. Staying at Montserrat with the monks became one of the most defining and magical times of my life.

Meritxell Asensio, the Spanish Police Officer who assisted Robert during COVID in Spain

Montserrat had been established in 1025, almost 1,000 years before, and to me it was like heaven. The monastery offered daily opportunities to dine and pray with the monks. Food and lodging were free.

And what I loved most was its access to the most beautiful gardens, complete with old statues, fountains, winding walkways, ancient pillars, and many of the loveliest plants and trees I had seen in this part of the country. The place was also fully stocked and built like a fortress. It was exactly where you would want to be if the world fell apart. Since it had been around for ten centuries, the pandemic was merely a minor blip in its distinguished history.

The guest quarters at the monastery were perfect. My critical eye could not find a single imperfection. No expense had been spared. I could not find a

Robert with the Monserat Monastery in the background

missing screw, a dirty window, or a wooden door that showed any signs of neglect. Nothing that would cause the slightest distraction or stress. The linen closet was perfectly stacked to the top with fresh white sheets. I was blown away because, as a pilot and landlord, my eye constantly searched for something, anything that looked wrong, dangerous, or didn't make sense.

The rooms were basic but pleasant, with a bed, small desk, closet, and a nicely appointed bathroom. Beyond its ancient stone walls were stunning views of the courtyard and surrounding mountains. I spent my time, both before entering the monastery and while I was there, hiking the surrounding mountains, riding the funicular to the top of the mountain, exploring the thousand-year-old structures, sleeping on mountain tops, breathing fresh air, and listening to glorious bird songs.

This place was exactly what my restless soul had been yearning for since crossing the South Pole. Aside from the church bells that rang on the half hour and hour, peaceful quiet reigned. Guests were encouraged not to talk to anyone because they might disturb others who were in a deep meditative state.

In fact, the gardens were so enchanting that I could fall into a deep meditative trance in minutes. According to my advanced spiritual psychology studies, I was "blissing out." In the past, I would go over to Balboa Park in San Diego, walk, and sit for hours by the fountains in the Alcazar Garden, enjoying the spiritual high that, I was told, was better than what the strongest drugs could ever provide.

My plan was to hole up there for as long as they would have me, which I heard was about a month, before I would need permission from the Abbot to stay longer. I thought I could work on my spiritual practice, immerse myself in the lifestyle of the monks, and see how deep inside myself I could go while everything outside was falling apart.

As the world debated whether the virus had been created by China, and estimated how many would die terrible untimely deaths, I worked on writing this

The garden, courtyard, and the room where Robert stayed at the Montserrat Monastery

book and sat down with a monk who spoke English to explore my quest for inner peace. When I asked him what it meant to be a "Citizen of the World for the world," he didn't even have to stop and think before he said, "It means we are all children of God."

I told him that my peace of mind was deeply disturbed by the coronavirus and that it was causing me a lot of stress. The things I had heard in the media and online, including massive amounts of misinformation and speculation, affected all of us mentally, emotionally, socially, financially, and spiritually, and created a generalized disruptive panic.

"Why is the coronavirus happening?" I asked. "For what purpose?"

"First, let's look at what the virus isn't," he said. "The virus is not God punishing humanity."

His response surprised me, but also calmed me. I blurted out, "Why is it happening?"

"It's just part of the human experience. Everyone eventually dies."

I added, "Our souls are eternal but not our bodies. I knew this to be true when my Mom passed. I could see she was no longer in her body, but I still felt her energy and have several times since she died."

The Monk nodded again.

Another question formed in my mind. "So why do you think everyone is so afraid?

"People think that with technology and medicine, they will live forever—this is not true," the monk answered.

The monk's comments made it clear that things were unfolding as they naturally should for the world and for me. Understanding that allowed me to increase my ability to slow down and savor life instead of rushing through it. That came with an increased ability to listen more deeply to Spirit and practice acceptance, flexibility, adaptability, and creative thinking.

I decided to adopt that mindset for the rest of my expedition.

Peace Moment

To feel at peace in your heart, mind, body, and soul, you have to slow down and receive it at the pace of nature.

Chapter 22

Seeking Safety

If you are happy, you can spread that to the world.
—Giorgi Evgenidze, International Relations
Manager, Georgian Aviation University,
Tbilisi, Georgia

Unfortunately, my stay in heavenly Montserrat abruptly ended a few days after I arrived at the monastery when I was told that all nonresidents would have to leave because of the pandemic. I understood their position. All but two of the monks were old, and I was sure the virus could do some serious damage there.

By that time, all the general aviation airports in Europe were shut down, and I was not permitted to fly my own plane anywhere in Spain. I was either going to have to wait it out in Europe, adhering to the quarantine enforced by the police, or fly back commercially to the United States and deal with a mandatory two-week quarantine there.

I wasn't sure that flying back to the States would do much for me anyway, since things were gradually getting worse there as well. It would simply be trading bad for future bad, and I wanted to stay on mission. I felt as if the Universe was providing me with these circumstances as an opportunity to further our peace mission. I believed that I could help the planet deal with some of the fear and panic by being a living example of calm in the midst of the extreme chaos. I could show what was possible even when others were withdrawing in fear. Over the last several years, I had become a reluctant expert on the topic of fear.

Eddie Gould was sending me information on flights back to the United States, Michel Gordillo was strongly encouraging me to leave the *Citizen* in Spain and go back to the U.S. while I could still easily get out, and Meritxel was urging me to head to the northeastern coast of Spain, which had very few cases of the virus. I was on my way there, hoping to arrive before the roads closed down, but still not entirely sure I was doing the right thing.

I felt conflicted and missed the comforts of home after so many months on the road and cosmically getting my ass kicked across the world. So I did what I often do in situations of extreme stress, I called Susan and asked for help.

Susan was as clear and strong with me as she had ever. Her confidence helped calm me a bit. She is a rational thinker in crisis situations, and her rationality is complemented by her strong intuition and the spiritual downloads she receives. She strongly encouraged me to stay with our plan and not retreat in fear. This was, as Super Fred would say, a "grab yourself by your brass balls moment," an opportunity to have an even greater impact on the world and to get our message of Oneness out by being a living example in the most uncertain of times. Susan made it clear that I would be alone and isolated and would struggle considerably, but it was the right thing to do. I would be honoring the commitments I had made to my sponsors, supporters, team, myself, and our belief in pursuing the impossibly big dream. As she said it, I knew she was right, that holding our course would be a demonstration of the courageous action I often wrote about. The mission would not stop. I would continue working on this book, getting the word out by blogging, vlogging, social media posts, magazine articles, and doing internet interviews. Susan was always right, and that was why I sought her advice in the most critical moments of my life.

So, with that clarity, I stayed on the road and, with Meritxel's help, found a nice hotel with an ocean view in Vilanova, where I waited to see what opportunities would present themselves next. I was open to whatever the Universe had in store for me.

Vilanova

Vilanova was a pleasant port city and I figured there would not be any virus blowing in from the open ocean. It was a beach town with few residents in the off season, and now it was basically locked down with lots of restaurants that were now closed. On my daily walk to the supermarket, I generally saw three to five police cars and usually got stopped. I always took two shopping bags with me, whether I needed groceries or not, and like everyone else, I got used to wearing my mask. I could have driven to the market, but I wanted the exercise and to leave my small hotel room. But after I'd been there about a week, the president of Spain extended the quarantine another two weeks and shut down all hotels to tourists. Services were reduced, and it was clear that staying in this tiny hotel was not a long-term solution to wait out the pandemic.

Fear and Chaos in the Pandemic

As things were getting worse, I noticed that people were struggling and often had uncontrolled moments of fear and anger. One night when I was on the way back from a trip to the grocery store, I was stopped twice by policemen asking, "Why are you out?" In my broken Spanish, I explained that I needed to buy food. Then, before going back to my hotel, I recorded a minute-long video showing how tightly things were locked down. Before I could finish it, I heard someone slam their window shut behind me, as if to say "How dare you make videos during the pandemic!" My response was also caught on the video, and the shock and disbelief in my face showed how bad things had become.

I came up with a strategy for dealing with the increasing frequency of moments like that. In a way, it reminded me of the "upset training" I'd taken as a pilot. I was taught that when things get out of control, knowing what you need to do to recover can save your life. For example, if you get yourself into a stall spin situation, pull the power back, apply the opposite rudder, level the wings… and pray that it works.

During the lockdown, I found many opportunities to practice upset training right on the ground. We have all experienced it. You go about your day, minding your own business with a smile on your face, and somebody goes off on you in a big way for no apparent reason, leaving you to wonder, what just happened? How did things get so bad so fast? But the fact is, that person is afraid and out of control.

In the moment, it's always awkward, uncomfortable, or maddening. You can either take your gloves off and bare-knuckle it to the death or, by the grace of God, maintain your "Zen" composure and practice your high-level spiritual skills. In the past, I've tried to let people talk themselves out, but I quickly realized they might have way more to say than I could handle at this point in my evolution.

As Americans, we believe it's our God-given right to speak our piece, so it's extra-hard not to say anything. Your blood is boiling, and you have more energy than you can handle bouncing around in your brain. It's overwhelming. What you have just experienced is what some call another person's "pain body." The pain body is a pent-up hurt that someone has been carrying around for ages. When it rears its ugly head, you may not even recognize the person in front of you because you are dealing with a wounded part that lives deep inside them.

The Zen Villa Sitges, Spain

When I found out I had to leave Vilanova, Meritxell helped me to find a place on Airbnb. Legally, nobody was supposed to rent their properties, certainly not to someone from another country, but we were able to find a few people willing to break the rules. The place that caught my eye was a villa described as a

"Zen Villa," and, being that I was the "Zen Pilot," it sounded like a perfect fit. It was high atop a mountain in the coastal city of Sitges and featured a pool, an expansive and inspiring view, a main house with six bedrooms and a small apartment beneath it. In a word, it was paradise, but the owner was asking 11,000 Euros a month, which was more than five times what I was willing to pay.

Meritxell turned out to be a masterful negotiator. She offered 2,500 Euros and let them know that I was a pilot who would take good care of their place. After years of negotiating multi-million-dollar real estate deals, I would never have been so bold as to make such a low offer. And when the landlord tried to get me to pay for utilities and cleaning, Meritxell told him we were about to put money down on another place, so take it or leave it. Reluctantly, he agreed.

For the first time, I felt as if I were starting to get the upper hand on the virus. I had a rental car and a nice, comfortable place to stay on a hill with an ocean breeze, isolated from others. My workouts included a walk to the bottom of the hill for essentials and then carrying up to forty pounds of groceries the mile and a half back up. One of the neighbors had a rooster, but it apparently slept until about 9:30 before it would crow, whereas every other rooster I'd ever met crowed at sun-up.

This place was perfect.

My routine was to get up at 8:00 a.m. and prepare a healthy breakfast of organic fruit, nuts, and greens. Then I would sit by the window and listen to spiritual podcasts while I stared at the ocean and drank herbal tea. After that, I relocated to the dining room table to work on this book or a blog, or sometimes do voice-over work for the documentary or interviews via Skype. Like the monks of Montserrat, nothing about my existence was stressful, and I began to see how the remainder of my trip would play out if I lived in peace. Like the monks who did not want to be disturbed as they walked around the monastery deep in their meditation, I found that the silence was oxygen for my soul.

The beach in Sitges, Spain, with the old city in the background

I realized I could wait out the virus for as long as it took. The longer I was in the Zen Villa sanctuary, the more in control of the situation I felt. Until now, whenever I was in a foreign country I was just moving from one tourist site to the next. This was the first time I could actually live like a local: unpack my bags, go to the market, walk on a daily basis, and interact with people who were simply living their lives. The whole experience felt as if it were meant to be, and the times I spent meditating in the mountains of Spain were some of the most peaceful in my life.

While the world fell apart around me, I found myself comparing the risk presented by the coronavirus with that I had experienced over the South Pole. I had assessed my chance for survival on that polar leg at fifty percent. The coronavirus death rate was right around one percent at the time. In other words, my risk of dying on the South Pole leg was fifty times greater than my risk of dying from the virus. Meritxell gave me updates on closures within Spain and provided accurate information on the spread of the virus, which gave me peace of mind.

I began to look at COVID as just another hurdle to overcome. I didn't want to give it more energy than that. I knew the Universe would not stop me forever, but the timing was interesting. It arrived just when I needed the world to stop in order to find my inner peace and when people needed to come together to overcome the pandemic. Like it or not, this illness would move us a step closer to Oneness—or so I hoped.

Peace Moment

The peace I was seeking was inside of me the entire time, blocked only by the artificial creations of my life. Noise, technology, misdirection, ego, and mental pollution to name a few—everything that this magical place was not. I had been chasing global peace to the farthest points of the planet, like the South Pole and soon the North Pole, but it was within me all the time.

Chapter 23

Finding Peace in Turbulent Times

Where there is silence, there is meditation and peace.

—Robert DeLaurentis, Peace Pilot

As more and more chaos ensued, my situation surprisingly stabilized. I had as much food as I needed, I had access to laundry, and, when I got tired of being in my room, I was able to go outside for trips to the supermarket or to sit by the pool. At the same time, I realized that I could share what I had learned about overcoming fear and panic over the past several years, and I came up with a blueprint for people to follow to find their own inner peace.

One of the most profound questions being forced upon us by COVID was simply, "Who am I?" As ego-driven humans, that's scary, because it means we have to question our own identity, quite possibly for the first time in our life.

As I began to let go of my own ego, I came to realize that my inner journey was as frightening as flying over the South Pole. Was inner peace just one of life's potentially broken promises, or could it be the hero's journey that Joseph Campbell wrote about? Someone goes out into the world on an adventure, overcomes adversity, and comes home transformed to share what he/she has learned.

If anyone had told me that I would ultimately find inner peace during quarantine while in the epicenter of a pandemic in Europe, with a broken plane while stuck in a foreign country, I would have laughed. Spain registered almost 600 deaths a day in Spring of 2020 as healthcare workers struggled to save lives, politicians preached social distancing while not wearing their own masks, and scientists raced to find a vaccine while hoping for herd immunity to kick in. Meanwhile, the virus itself continued to "cull the herd" with brutal efficiency.

Quite surprisingly, during my two-month quarantine, I experienced extended periods of inner peace. For the first time in my life, I could say I feel truly happy, even joyful. At first, I also felt guilty that so many people were suffering and dying while I was not. But as I posed the question, "What are you feeling?" to many of my friends and followers on Facebook from all walks of life, I heard others share the same feelings—in particular, an unexpected sense of calm, even in the face of extreme hardship. I discovered a pattern and some key elements of this inner peace that I want to share with you: I felt more gratitude, I became more connected with nature, I surrendered to the situation, I slowed down, I began to live without expections, I cultivated a simpler life, I developed a deeper relationship with spirit that included meditation and self care, along with a deeper connection to nature. Ultimately releasing my ego, letting go of fear and accepted what is. Here's what each of these looked like for me:

Feeling Gratitude

I practiced a mindset of gratitude every day. Opening my refrigerator brings me the joy of knowing that I have food to eat. Starting the washer and dryer, I knew I had daily access to clean clothes. After living out of a suitcase for four months, having a closet in which to hang my clothes made me happy. I was even thankful for every sheet of toilet paper.

What are you grateful for?

Being Silent and Connecting with Nature

After being asked to leave a monastery and then a hotel when they closed to comply with social distancing, I worried for several days that I wouldn't find housing. The beautiful home I found in the mountains overlooking the ocean, town, and harbor of Sitges felt like a Zen monastery. With green trees and billowing clouds as far as I could see, I was alone and away from the sounds of the city. I could hear a pin drop. I breathed it all in as deeply as I could, meditating to bird songs and occasionally sipping a glass of Sangria with dinner. This was not 99 percent of humanity's experience. I yearn for it to be the same for everyone, which drives my mission now more than ever.

Where can you reconnect with nature?

Surrendering Control

It didn't take long to figure out that I had no control over what was happening around me, and I quickly came to understand that, in fact, we have only the illusion of control over about 99 percent of our daily lives and that worrying about what we can't control isn't going to help us or anyone else. Dr. Ron Hulnick, one of my spiritual teachers from the University of Santa Monica, reminded me that guilt and worry don't serve us, help diminish other people's suffering, or change what the world is going through. The more peaceful choice is to give people the dignity of their process while staying lovingly present as they work through their struggles.

What stresses are you carrying that need to be turned over to God?

Slowing Your Pace

I had been slowing down in the course of my journey around the planet. When I left San Diego in November 2019 and flew over the South Pole a month later, I was traveling at 340 mph in *Citizen of the World*. After I landed in Spain in January 2020, I slowed to 172 mph on the bullet train, followed by 60 mph in a Hertz rental car—and then I came to a full stop, with once-a-week mile-long walks to the grocery store in Sitges. I realized how much I had been missing, and for the first time, I was enjoying life on a micro-scale. Clichés like "stop and smell the roses," lyrics like "slow down, you move too fast" and "let it be" began to resonate more fully as I moved through my days.

In what ways can you slow your pace to find peace?

Living Without Expectations

The virus wiped away many of my expectations about the world and my life. I really am not expecting much of anyone, including myself. Since, in most cases, we are physically interacting with fewer people during the pandemic, we can work on our relationship with ourselves. Are we kinder and gentler with ourselves? Researchers have confirmed that self-compassion is not selfish. It makes us more compassionate with others.

By default, there is no one to disappoint me, because I'm living alone, buying my own food, preparing my own meals, and doing my own laundry and cleaning. I realize this is a unique and privileged life compared to most of the world and I do not take it for granted. I give back where I can. Yes, my single, living-alone, child-free, mobile life is 180 degrees different from the lives of families suddenly faced with parental unemployment or working from home while homeschooling their children. Yet we meet where we are similar.

What expectations do you place on yourself or others? What are ways you can ease up on these to bring more peace into your life?

Settling into a Simpler Life

When I was quarantined, I stopped interacting with contractors, mechanics, sponsors, tenants, or any other professional service people. Thus, I did not experience the usual stress of sustaining these relationships. I didn't operate a vehicle or make repairs on my plane or home. I was thousands of miles away

The view from the Zen Villa overlooking the small seaside town of Sitges, Spain

from my professionally-managed property business—and I noticed how little I really needed in order to be happy and at peace.

In what ways can you simplify your life to find more peace?

Cultivating a Relationship with Your Creative Spirit
My workload is greatly reduced, and I find myself doing the things I love the most, like writing this book, producing video blogs, and recording voice-overs for our documentary. What relationship do you have with your creative self? Do you like the person you are becoming? How do you see yourself? Are you encourag-

ing your imagination and vision by journaling, putting together puzzles, coloring, painting, gardening, or cooking? Are you proud of yourself for the home projects you are starting or for finishing those already started? Quite possibly, those walks to the grocery store and your home yoga sessions and workouts are making you look, feel, and think even better.

Do you have a creative hobby or outlet that you haven't found time to enjoy? Can you set aside time to nurture your creative side?

Meditating

I often find myself looking out the window at the ocean waves in an almost hypnotic trance. If it's raining or the wind is blowing, I'm even happier. I think we are so often busy talking or worrying about money that we rarely take the time to listen to what the Universe is offering us for free. Meditation begins anytime there is silence.

Have you tried meditation to find peace?

Practicing Self-Care

I've found myself more aware of my body and practicing better self-care. I prepared every meal at home, which is much healthier and less expensive than eating out. I'm doing more personal grooming. I'm exercising more. All these things, along with slowing down and meditating, seem to be having a positive effect. When I do Skype or Zoom interviews, I've been told how bright my face looks, that I look younger and more at ease. Having inner peace has its advantages, and noticing beauty in ourselves is one of them. I'm also learning that we must know what it feels like to love ourselves before we can truly love others.

Have we forgotten that our bodies are the vehicles for our souls and that we must love them unconditionally on our journey through life?

Enjoying Fresh Air and a Cleaner Planet

Never before have I enjoyed so much fresh air. Without the billions of vehicles polluting the air, water, and land, my temporary Spanish home next to the ocean has been a total joy. I took deeper breaths and felt my chest and heart expand as I breathed deeper than I could ever recall. It seemed that the entire ecosystem was getting a much-needed reprieve from the abuse of humans. Based on all the photos and reports from around the world showing clear skies, resting animals, and quiet freeways, the earth appeared to be vibrating happily for the first time in our lifetime. Can we keep this up?

How much time do you spend outdoors?

Releasing the Ego

How I define myself is changing. When we're not out in the work world, it is hard to define ourselves based on our job, clothes, car, etc. Instead, what really matters are the things we do to help others, and I find that when I let go of my ego, I'm able to experience myself as a more compassionate, caring, and loving person.

In what ways can you become more selfless?

Letting Go of Fear

You can only be afraid for so long...and then you realize that most of the horrible things predicted by politicians, media, pundits, scientists, naysayers, and others trapped by fear are just not true. Their fears do not need to be yours. The more you focus on what is working and take courageous action, the better the future will be.

How much energy do you waste on frightening possibilities you cannot control?

Accepting What Is

Start to accept your situation and realize that this is happening for your highest good. Accept that you have lessons to learn during this particular experience and as a human on the planet. This is the natural order of things. You are blessed by your time here in the Earth School as a soul having a human experience. It actually starts to sound divine when you can see how amazing it is to be alive and breathing in these extraordinary times.

Have you been able to appreciate the learning experiences the Universe is providing for you?

Collaborating Instead of Competing

Contemporary spiritual teachers remind us that our survival and growth are dependent on our ability to create and collaborate. Competition is in the past. The Dalai Lama puts it in perspective: "True happiness comes from having a sense of inner peace and contentment, which in turn must be achieved by cultivating altruism, love, and compassion, and by eliminating anger, selfishness, and greed."

Have you thought about finding ways to live a more collaborative life?

Finding Comfort Living in the Moment

Extremes have a way of bringing about change in the world. Sometimes this is what it takes to break down the old patterns that have defined us for years or generations. We need to be broken open to find the best version of ourselves. I'm excited to see this transformation unfolding. This is a time of rebirth and new beginnings for those who have felt trapped or stagnant. It is a global reset—not just for the planet, but for ourselves as well—and will bring us all together as One Planet and One People in Oneness for Humanity.

How often do you live in the past or focus on the future without living in the moment?

The Man in the Cave

As I was getting ready to leave Sitges, I stuck my head out into what seemed to be a scary place. The metaphoric cave where I had lived for the better part of two months had provided me with safety, but now I needed to leave. I had been taught a lesson: the world was not a safe place. It was filled with dangers that could hurt me. It would be safer to stay home. But as the weeks turned into months, it became obvious that hiding was not a long-term solution. Even if we could eradicate the present danger, there would be another around the corner.

I planned to go to Sweden, where they were practicing "Herd Immunity." I had to give myself a little nudge to get out the door, because the little voices in my head kept saying, "What are you doing?" My father's response to my first planned circumnavigation rang in my inner ear: "You are just going to get yourself killed." Pilots know this feeling. It's that little twinge down your spine you get every time you open the hatch or door on a plane, and you hesitate, if only for a split second, telling yourself, "I'm taking a risk. Life is full of them. We know that there is no adventure without risk."

I had dodged a cyclone in Madagascar that ripped paint and decals off the outside of the Citizen. A ferry tank had burst inside the airplane, dumping more than 75 gallons of fuel into the cabin. I had flown over Antarctica for 18.1 hours through the atmosphere at −60 °C, knowing that my fuel gelled at −47C. Life can be terrifying.

How then do we find what we need inside us to go out into the world and make a difference? Courageous action is called for, regardless of what your gut tells you. Courage is the price we pay for our freedom.

Peace Moment

It was as if my life had been defined by the past 4 to 5 months, moving from country to country, and meeting so many different types of people. I was exploring, having adventures, trying to get clear on what inner peace meant to me and how I could bring it into the world.

Chapter 24

Escaping Spain

We pilots know that at some point, it becomes dangerous *not* to fly because we start to get rusty and our skills diminish. Normally, I would fly every week to keep my skill-set as sharp as possible, honoring a promise I made to myself, which was to stay alive. But during the pandemic, almost eight weeks passed without my even starting the engines on the *Citizen of the World*, much less lifting off. That scared me.

Spain was locked down tight, and getting out of the country with my plane was going to be complicated. Spain had been the hardest-hit European nation, and people were terrified that COVID was going to claim every last one of them. I received a text from Meritxell saying that the Spanish government was not going to open the country to tourism until September at the absolute earliest, and considering that they generally collected $200 billion in tourist revenue every year, shutting down everything showed just how scared the government and the people really were. But it was just the beginning of May, and I couldn't wait until September, not only because I was afraid that by then I wouldn't be safe to fly, but also because it would be too cold for the *Citizen* to cross over the North Pole without risking fuel gelling which could cause both her engines to fail.

I had planned to go to Switzerland and do an aerial photo shoot over the Matterhorn with my Swiss friend André Müller; in addition to which, Switzerland had great mechanics whom I could trust to fix my ferry tanks and leaking brake caliper. But that was no longer realistic. Assuming I could even collect the required documents in the middle of a pandemic, I would have to get a special visa, which would take months to approve.

Another possibility was to go to Biggin Hill Airport, which was an hour and 20 minutes from London, but there was no ground transportation available at the airport and nowhere to stay once I arrived. In any case, at the last minute, the British government enacted a mandatory two-week self-quarantine for anyone entering the country, so that was the end of that idea.

The only remaining option was Malmo, Sweden. The Swedish had been practicing herd immunity, and their COVID numbers were closely aligned with those of neighboring countries that had enforced strict quarantines to limit the spread of the coronavirus. The death curve had flattened, and, given the size of the population, I calculated a .000095 percent risk of death. Compared to the 50 percent risk I experienced over the South Pole, I would take those odds all day long. And in Sweden, I would be able to fly my plane as much as I wanted, get some maintenance work done, and wait out the pandemic. The word was that the country would be open to the outside world (and my camera crew) on June 15. Making my escape happen, however, required a number of steps and the help of several generous, persistent, and inspired people. I laid out a plan.

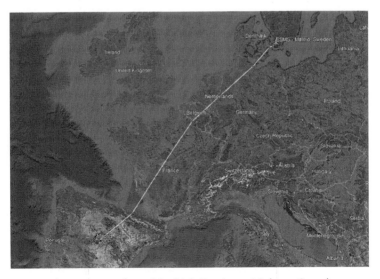

Robert's route from Madrid, Spain to Malmo, Sweden

Step 1: Get to Madrid… and the Airport

First, I needed to get to the aircraft in Madrid, 372 miles away from my "Zen Villa" in Sitges. The U.S. Embassy informed me via email that I could travel, so long as I was leaving the country.

> *The exception that most often applies to the U.S. citizens that we are assisting is: "to return to one's place of residence." The Ministry of Interior of Spain has specified that third-country citizens returning to their country of habitual residence are exempted from the movement restrictions.*
>
> *Determining which activities fall under the above exceptions or any subsequent expanded exceptions is entirely up to the Spanish authorities. We do not have the authority to grant permission to travel within Spain or grant waivers of Spanish laws.*

As a backup, I found that Spanish citizens could travel with written permission from their employers, so I had the DeLaurentis Foundation issue a letter indicating that I was a pilot and an employee supporting the expedition.

The U.S. Embassy also directed me to the front cover of my passport, where it said, "The Secretary of the United States of America hereby requests all that it may concern to permit the Citizen/National of the United States named herein to pass without delay or hindrance and in the case of need to give all lawful aid and protection."

As luck would have it, there were no checkpoints between Sitges and Madrid. I drove to the airport without issue while Meritxell followed in another car just in case the police tried to stop me at a checkpoint. If so, I hoped that, as a fellow police officer, she could convince them to let me proceed. An aspiring helicopter pilot herself, she was also very helpful at the airport, running interference, translating, and helping me get last-minute services for the *Citizen of the World*.

Step 2: Get to the airplane

With the help of Michel Gordillo, we emailed the Assistant Airport Manager at Cuatro Vientos Airport to plead my case and ask for access. He said it was possible, so long as I was escorted onto the field by someone with access. When, after days of trying, I was unable to find anyone willing to do that, I decided to just show up and see if I could do it on my own. I talked to a helpful man in the flight-plan office who then spoke to police security. I mentioned I had an email from the airport manager, and, to my delight, security waved me through.

Step 3: Get permission to fly out of Spain

The genius and science of Dr. Dimitri Deheyn came to my aid once again when I let him know I was being blocked from leaving. Dimitri suggested that his experiment could determine if COVID was being transferred on the plastic particles for which we were already testing the atmosphere. He provided a letter stating that my departure flight would be a critical opportunity to test the air for the virus over Madrid and the rest of the country during the pandemic's height. That apparently was encouragement enough for them to let me leave.

Again with the help of Michel Gordillo, who called the Spanish Police, the Flight-Plan Office, and Customs and Immigration, I was allowed to go. From Spain's perspective, I would be one less American to worry about. Translation: less possible coronavirus risk. Besides, Michel would not stop calling them every 30 minutes, and I'm sure they were tired of hearing from him as well as dealing with me.

Step 4: Get permission to fly into Sweden

Johan Wiklund, an Airbus A320 Flight Commander at Scandinavian Airlines, helped my flight handlers from General Aviation Support Egypt (G.A.S.E.) get in touch with a fixed-base operator in Sweden called Aviator Airport Services, which secured permission for me to fly into Sweden.

Step 5: Come up with a flight plan Eurocontrol will accept

The genius of Ahmed Hassan Mohamed, Eddie's partner at GASE (General Aviation Support Egypt) helped save the day. Normally, I would use the autoroute function on RocketRoute to find my way through the airspaces of Europe. But, on this four-hour, 1,200-nm flight, I needed to go through Spain, France, Belgium, the Netherlands, and Germany to get to Sweden, so I contacted Ahmed for help and after a couple of hours, he came back via email with an approved route that he had filed with Eurocontrol. It had more than forty waypoints and airways, but it worked!

Step 6: Don't get quarantined on arrival

With the rules changing daily, I was concerned about getting stuck in quarantine upon my arrival in Sweden. Michel had suggested a plan, and with the help of Meritxell, I was able to get two tests for the COVID virus in Barcelona while I was still in Spain. The first test involved taking swabs of my mouth and sinuses that would indicate if I currently had the coronavirus. The second required a sample of my blood and would indicate if I'd already had the virus. If that one came out positive, based on the belief at the time that you couldn't get COVID twice, my movements around Sweden and other countries would not be restricted. In three days, I got the results—both negative. Having documentation that showed I didn't have the virus (as of a certain date) would help make my case against having to quarantine.

Step 7: Last-minute servicing

Upon examination, I determined that the *Citizen* needed both the emergency oxygen for breathing and the nitrogen for the landing gear charged up. The mechanics from Aircraft Total Service, an aviation service center on the field at Quatro Vientes Airport in Madrid, were able to help with this, and I was ready to go.

We all know that no great plan ever goes off without a hitch—so, as luck would have it, the police rolled up to do a ramp check on my aircraft just as I was preparing to start the engines. They asked where I intended to go, and Meritxell let them know that nothing had changed since the week before, when I was granted permission to leave, as well as the reasons why they should let me go. They asked some questions, checked the registration number on the aircraft, and took off, wishing me luck on my trip. Meritxell was clearly one of my angels. It was a sad moment in many ways when I left Spain because I had become very close to her. She wanted to come with me to Sweden, but we both knew that wasn't possible.

With no other planes in the sky, I was granted permission to depart without delay. I was about to accelerate to the speed of life once again. The flight was busy as I got reacquainted with the many complex systems on the *Citizen*, uploading databases and relaxing into what I have always believed aviation to be—one of the deepest meditations available to a soul.

Peace Moment

When everything is in constant flux, we can choose to be focused on what is happening from moment to moment because there is no future to focus on. We are forced, like it or not, to be a part of the here and now whether we are in the air or on the ground. Perhaps in this process, we give up a little bit of our ambition in order to move into this space of simply being.

Chapter 25

Sweden

*Cooperation, that's the only way we can sur-
vive. If we don't listen to nature and each
other there will always be conflicts over natural resources because that's what most people
are fighting for—the land to survive. Nobody
owns it, really. We must share it; of course, and
there must be some rules on how to share.*

*But most importantly, we must have respect
for nature and each other. The pandemic is a
good warning at least for us. It has shown how
bad it can be for all of us, no matter how much
money you have. it doesn't save you from the
pandemic.*

—Nils Torbjorn, Sami Indigenous People,
Kiruna Sweden

I expected that when I landed in Malmo, I would be
met by security, a handler, and medical personnel to
take my temperature and assess my physical condi-

tion. There was, however, only one female security officer who gave me a ride from the *Citizen* to the terminal. From there, I walked through the empty terminal building to the taxi stand and, within minutes, was headed to my hotel.

It felt as if a well-executed plan and a team of professionals had executed a well-rehearsed plan and sprung me from prison. The following day, I found myself sitting with Johan Wiklund, the SAS commander who had helped me get permission to land in Sweden, along with his wife, kids, and his tower operator, pilot, and friend Axel Leonhardt, eating carrot cake Johan's daughter had made and talking about our aviation adventures past, present, and future. After my experience of being locked down in Spain, it felt like paradise.

Bursting Ferry Tank #2

Ever since I misaligned one of the 20 valves on the ferry system, which resulted in the #1 tank bursting while refueling in Dakar and dumping 75 gallons of Jet A-1 fuel inside the cabin, I'd been carrying that useless tank around with me. I needed to remove it and reposition the 20 valves to tank #2.

I'd hoped to remove it in Spain. Still COVID derailed that plan, so I decided to do it in Malmo, where I had the support of MTS Aviation, a Fixed

Based Operator (FBO) that provided support, including fuel, maintenance, food, deicing and flight planning assistance, for smaller aircraft. Its owner, Helmet Gross, a happy and generous Austrian with a great sense of humor and a well-established business, offered to cover all my expenses, including handling, parking, and airport fees, while I visited. To make the situation even better, I had the help of Johan Wiklund and Axel Leonhardt to get the tanks in and out. Without a properly working ferry system, I would not be able to cross the North Pole on my way back to the United States.

Johan and Axel showed up in their coveralls ready to work. We worked for about four hours draining fuel, disconnecting and reconnecting the valves, the HF radio, vent and fuel lines, the pressure relief valve, grounding cables, and much more. It was dirty, smelly, and hard work, but they didn't seem to mind.

After removing the defective tank #1, we set the fuel lines up so that the #2 tank would function as #1. We labeled the many fuel lines that connected the 20 fuel valves only to have the ink partially washed off by the oily Jet A-1 fuel that seemed to get on everything. That made it difficult to trace the fuel lines back to their sources at the rear of the plane behind all the tanks, but eventually, we figured it out by tracing what we could see, reading the indentations on the labels, and by process of elimination. Any mistake could prove fatal, and I would be the person paying the price.

Once the valves and tanks were back in place, we needed to fill the tank and test the system first on the ground and then in the air. I decided to save testing for the next day when I would be less tired and feeling mentally sharper. I also felt anxious about another tank exploding.

The next day, with the help of a fuel line guy, we filled what now was the first ferry tank. We did it slowly; since the #1 tank we had just removed had burst when filled too quickly. We fueled past the one-third mark. At two-thirds full, the second tank burst with an explosive "POP" just like the one in Senegal. Here we go again. This time, though, the fuel came out with less force, spraying only about six inches and splashing on the upholstery on the copilot side of the cabin. I squeezed the seam to slow the spray, which seemed to work so long as I maintained the pressure. Now that I was a quasi-expert on fuel spills inside plane cabins, I grabbed a plastic bag and container to deflect the fuel outside. Then I immediately aligned the fuel valves and turned on two electric pumps to move the fuel into aluminum tank #3. Turning on electric pumps seemed like insanity with fuel spraying around the cabin, but Fred had mentioned it before as a casualty-control measure.

In about five minutes, the fuel was below the cracked seam. I heard the remainder of it going into tank three, which I assumed by now would be just as likely to burst. It did not. I placed a plastic container underneath the plane to catch fuel as it began to drain out of a small hole in the bottom of the pressurized aluminum skin.

I was shaken up and having flashbacks to my earlier traumatic experience in Dakar, Senegal, when fuel covered my body and I thought I was going to burn to death. This was the third major fuel spill since the ferry system was installed. By now, between 100 to 150 gallons had been dumped into the *Citizen's* cabin. I left the FBO feeling defeated, depressed, and shaking. I had no faith in the ferry system, and I needed to assume that if two of the four aluminum ferry tanks had burst under pressure, the other two would as well. I had hoped that the last part of the trip would be a bit more predictable and that I would feel safer in the plane. Not the case now. Thinking of it as my "victory lap" was beginning to feel like the ramblings of a madman. I would have to struggle and strain for every remaining inch of the Polar Circumnavigation as much as I had on the prior legs. *Again*, I asked myself, *how hard does this have to be?* What was the Universe preparing me for? What lesson was I intended to learn on this journey? And who would intentionally sign up for a trip like this anyway?

Over the next few days, I regained my confidence and determination and forged ahead with a new plan. I talked at length with Fred Sorenson, Johan Wiklund, and Michel Gordillo, and leaned on their more than 100 years of combined flying experience. We came up with the following plan: Johan's ferry tank repairman would sand the brittle and stressed seams off the sides of the tank we had removed and reweld them. I would fill the repaired tank and partially fill the two behind it to one-third capacity, since everything else had burst at the two-thirds level. I would also fill the rubber bladder inside the pressurized cabin. We would reinforce repaired aluminum tank #1 with straps one-third and two-thirds of the way up. This would give me the familiarity of a rebuilt metal tank functioning as the #1 and the flexibility of the rubber bladder which had been tested en route to the South Pole, to carry the lion's share of the ferry fuel.

This time, while shifting valves, I didn't just follow a checklist. I traced the flow of the fuel in and out of the remaining five interior tanks. I wished I had spent more time learning the system. I could have prevented the #1 and #2 ferry tanks from bursting and greatly reduced my stress level and risk from Jet A inhalation and exposure.

Theoretically, with reasonable winds, using these tanks in combination would give me the extra hours of flight time needed to cross the North Pole and deal with any remaining surprises the Universe had to throw my way.

By the time we got the rebuilt tank back in the plane and had all the fuel lines, vent lines, electric transfer pumps, grounding straps, transfer valves, by-pass, pressure relief valve, and cargo straps installed, I truly felt like I understood the system. Someone had suggested I take a second person along just to oper-ate it, but I didn't want the extra weight, especially during such a risky flight. In addition, on a deeper level, I thought my learning would be greatest over the most remote parts of the planet, when I was alone and most open to what the Universe had in store for me.

I intended to apply for a permit to leave for the North Pole from Svalbard, Norway, which was the closest European landmass to Alaska. Svalbard was closed to regular international traffic, but, according to Axel, because I was already in the EU, carrying four scientific experiments, intending to meet my camera crew, I stood a good chance of getting an exemp-tion. Leaving from Svalbard would allow me to fly an almost straight line across the three poles (Magnetic, True, and North Pole of Inaccessibility) directly into Prudhoe Bay, Alaska, also known as "Dead Horse." The distance was just under 2,000 nm, less than half the length of the round-trip flight to the South Pole. The *Citizen of the World* could theoretically fly that distance without ferry tanks, but she would land without the FAA required reserves, and there would be no added fuel to allow for headwinds.

Svalbard consisted of just a few buildings and not much more. By now it was July, the warmest month of the year with the most daylight. If all went according to plan, the higher temps would ensure my fuel didn't gel and stop both engines in mid-flight. I had intentionally stacked the deck in my favor to minimize the risk and give me a better chance of dealing with anything the Universe might come up with to challenge me on the North Pole leg. I felt that the experience I gained from my South Pole leg would be enormously helpful and that this leg would be routine.

Where is Home?

After almost seven months away from home moving from safe harbor to safe harbor, I was starting to feel totally disconnected from San Diego. "Where's home?" I often asked myself, and I would eventually come to realize that home was in every country I visited. I was becoming a Citizen of the World.

My new life was defining me, and I was living in the present. My experiences were no longer defined with reference to my past. I was building new relationships, getting stimulation from the people I met, and seeing life through a lens of peace, the experiments I carried, aviation safety and technology, pilot decision-making, and discussing what it meant to be a Citizen of the World. I was exploring distant lands, being repeatedly in awe of what I was seeing and experiencing, and flying more than I ever imagined possible. I had entered a magic place of gratitude, a wonderful space where my heart was full of excitement and wonder.

Gotland Island

While I was waiting for possible points of entry into Iceland, Svalbard, or Norway to open up for the film crew, I found my way to Gotland Island, off the east coast of Sweden in the Baltic Sea. I had initially planned to stay just a few days, but it turned out to be an ideal place to prepare both mentally and physically for the North Pole leg of the journey, and I wound up staying more than two weeks. Johan Wiklund had suggested that I land and stay at a private airport on the north coast at Bunge, a WWII military airbase purchased twenty years earlier by Inger Martinsson, a CFI (Certified Flight Instructor), her late husband, and their son, Claes, a SAS pilot. The Martinssons ran the airport and had converted the main hangar into a museum.

Gotland Island is often described as a paradise, and I would have to agree. The history and beauty gave me a chance to calm down, recharge, and rediscover the peace inside me. The nights were spent visiting with the Martinssons' friends, who flew in to stay on the island, and the days I spent exploring Cold War bunkers, flower fields, churches, the historic city of Visby, and the neighboring island of Faro. For me, it was a sanctuary and instrumental in my preparation for what still lay ahead.

When I first arrived, Claes and Inger suggested I wash the *Citizen of the World*, since she had seven months' worth of hard miles on her. They provided me with supplies and a facility so that I could remove the dirt and dust of twenty countries off her ceramic coating and make some repairs. They also made room to store her in the museum hangar, where the *Citizen* could be enjoyed by many local residents and a few who flew in to see her.

The Martinssons made me feel like family, introducing me to their friends and family. We shared many meals and stories about this historic airfield,

Swedish culture, and aviation, and they endured my frequent references to the Viking lifestyle of old and accessing one's inner Viking."

Peace Moment

The strange thing is that when I'm traveling this much, I don't feel like any single place is really home. In fact, my home seems to be every country I visit. My world is expanding, and it seems clear that the entire planet is where I belong. I am a citizen of the world. I'm seeing more similarities than differences between people and places. My particular hometown, religion, race, and ethnicity are not as important as my desire for joy, happiness, health, freedom, adventure, and peace. These are things that connect me to all the wonderful people I have been meeting and calling family.

PART FOUR

The North Pole Trip

Chapter 26

Mortality and Momentum

The bottom line is that we have all the tools we need to handle challenging situations so that we can level out, both in the air and on the ground.

—Robert DeLaurentis, Peace Pilot

As I spoke with local people in the cities I visited about what it means to be a "Citizen of the World for the World," it became apparent that we are all in this together, and our shared humanity is what makes the world go round.

During my trip, I dealt with many recurring thoughts, including a couple of big questions: How will this end? Why must I suffer? Will I survive?

I kept envisioning the documentary playing on someone's TV and ending abruptly with an obituary: "Robert DeLaurentis, 1966-2020. He died trying to bring peace to the planet, advance science, and inspire others to pursue their impossibly big dream."

Strangely and ironically, I knew that if I died attempting to complete this trip, my message would become even more impactful.

I prayed that the Universe's script might be different, that perhaps I was intended to go on into the world and share my story in person.

In any event, I set aside funds and left Susan instructions to complete the book and documentary if anything happened to me.

The Global Victory Lap, or, Breaking Me Open

After successfully crossing the South Pole, I felt I had completed the hardest part of the polar circumnavigation and jokingly referred to the rest of the trip as a "Global Victory Lap." I could not have been more wrong. The Universe continued to test and, I felt, torture me in ways I could not have dreamt or imagined.

What I later realized was that the South Pole crossing merely served to break me open and ready me for what was to come by giving me the opportunity to heal the inner and outer divide that existed within me. As weeks of coronavirus quarantine in Spain turned into months, it became clear that all those South Pole challenges were preparing me to respond to the pandemic, its impact on humanity, the earth, and our mission of global peace.

The virus seemed to split the world apart with great intensity. Many countries closed their borders. Isolation became the solution to global problems. Locking ourselves away, hunkering down, and fighting the natural order of things became the new normal for the world.

Robert holding the DeLaurentis Foundation mission flag high atop a sand dune in Mendoza, Argentina.

Our Flying Thru Life team, however, was and is dedicated to being a living example of what is possible when people from all countries work together. We are all stronger together. As "Citizens of the World for the World," we rededicate ourselves to our global community and our mission: "One planet. One people. One plane. Oneness for humanity."

Late Night Thoughts about the North Pole

With the North Pole looming a few days away, I couldn't sleep. My inner child was terrified because he knew I'd be taking him along, like it or not—again. I kept tearing up when I thought about all I'd been through so far. I'd been away from San Diego for seven months, and it was looking like it would be another two months before I got to go home. I had originally planned for a total journey of five months. I was exhausted, and people were still calling me crazy.

This North Pole crossing has been perfectly planned, but that didn't keep me from thinking about all the possible issues the Universe could throw my way. The *Citizen* was working well after the removal of one ferry tank and the repair of another. Who wouldn't have wondered what would happen next?

Pluses and Minuses

Summer, when temperatures are warmest, is the ideal time for an Arctic Ocean flight. All the great pilots from the past, including Charles Lindbergh, have picked this as the ideal time to cross. The warmer temperatures will help avoid potential fuel gelling and engine operating issues. But like everything in aviation, there is also a downside—in this case, a lot of low-lying fog. Low fog makes it difficult for an emergency landing, but, fortunately, my radar altimeter works pretty well for helping to determine my altitude above the ground or water in case I have to make a blind landing into ground fog.

I'm well prepared with respect to survival gear, training, and support. In fact, I couldn't be more prepared.

Unlike the South Pole, the North Pole is often crossed by commercial jets, and it gives me some comfort to know there might be more experienced commercial pilots in the air who could offer me assistance if needed.

I had charted my route to cross all three north poles—True, Magnetic, and the North Pole of Inaccessibility—along with the points where I would shift from magnetic to true navigation. And, in case my destination was unexpectedly fogged in, I had also laid out alternate landing sites, all of which were approximately five-hour flights from the North Poles.

Unfortunately, my permit to make a 24-hour refueling stop at Longyearbyen Airport in Svalbard, Norway, was denied after repeated attempts to convince the government to allow it. This pushed the distance of the North Pole leg to 3,000 nm and 11 hours of flight time, which would require me to use my more questionable ferry tanks.

Peace Moment

Many times on the expedition, I felt as if I were being prepared for something much bigger than myself. I just didn't know what it might be. I knew my trip was divinely inspired from beginning to end.

Chapter 27

Crossing the North Pole— Three Times

I took a minute for a few deep "Zen" breaths in the midst of the shit storm unfolding around me. I took a personal inventory and realized I was still in the air, flying straight and level, and wasn't out of options yet. This was fast becoming a test of my faith.

—Robert DeLaurentis, Peace Pilot

As I made final preparations for my first North Pole crossing, things were going smoothly. Almost too smoothly. I'm used to last-minute surprises. But I'd had more than two years to prepare for this leg of the journey. Maybe the Universe was finally going to throw me a bone.

The taxi showed up on time. The airport manager let him on the tarmac, which never happens. The new coordinates for my flight worked in the Flight Management Systems. There was no leaking fuel, the tires held air, the emergency oxygen was almost full, and the nitrogen charge was still within limits. The *Citizen of the World* was in all her fierce glory.

My good fortune continued when the airport allowed me to take off early without an extra charge. The tower operator showed up early and got me into the air traffic control system, and the engines fired

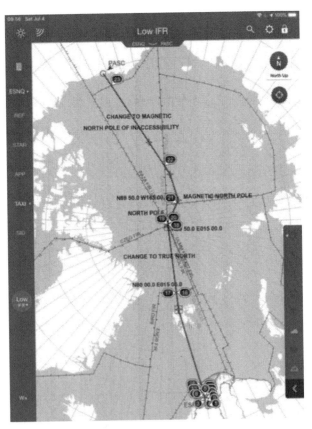

The flight route across the three North Poles

right up. All avionics systems came online immediately. Isn't life wonderful! I thought.

I started down the runway like a bat out of hell with enough fuel to get me to Alaska. At that point, six weeks still remained before I returned to my San Diego home, but I was getting closer.

As I climbed above the solid cloud layer things were going well. I had a great climb rate, even with the extra fuel. As I flew over Svalbard, Norway, it seemed to me that skipping this refueling stop had actually reduced my risk, because it was always safer to stay at a stable cruise altitude than it was to add in an additional landing and takeoff.

About two hours out of Kiruna, I was beyond VHF radio communication range when my luck seemed to change. My HF radio was not picking up anything, and I was at a wrong-way altitude for the direction of my flight. My satellite phone calls to Bodo Oceanic Control while I was over the most remote part of the planet, didn't work either. Considering I had eight hours of open-ocean-flying ahead, this loomed as a major problem.

One hundred fifty miles from the True North Pole, my two Flight Management Systems/GPS units started to fall offline because they weren't getting a satellite signal. How odd. That didn't happen until I was about seventy-five miles from the South Pole, and I figured there would be more satellite coverage over the North Pole, since it was a more traveled route. My autopilot would still hold in heading mode, so I made the adjustment and continued on my way using my iPad. No problem. This felt like old times over the South Pole.

When I was within twenty-five miles of the True North Pole, however, things started to unwind and get really scary. One of my Attitude Heading & Reference Systems (ADHRS) went offline. This was an in-flight emergency I had never experienced before. I was thankful to have two such systems, and I flipped the toggle switch to the back-up unit. Nothing. I lost the autopilot, and the plane immediately banked hard to the right side. "Oh, my God," I said to myself, "I'm losing control of the aircraft!"

I instinctively pressed the bright red yoke cut-off switch to disconnect the autopilot, which seemed to have become possessed. It chirped but didn't disconnect or stop the turn. Frantically fighting the autopilot so the plane wouldn't flip over, I reached my finger out, like shooting an arrow at a moving bullseye—and hit my mark. I pushed the "off" button on the autopilot unit, but it still didn't work. Now I felt like the Universe was conspiring against me. This was how the 737 Max planes went down. Would this be how my life ended?

Highlighted section of the track showing where Robert lost navigation over the North Poles and the remaining five hours of the leg

"F—k, no you don't!"

As the situation grew overwhelming, I was just about out of strength and ideas. I knew I wasn't strong enough to overpower the autopilot all the way to Alaska. On the Boeing 737 Max planes that went down, the cockpit voice records documented the fact that the pilots had used their feet and all their strength to try and overpower their autopilots. But they could not, resulting in hundreds of deaths.

In a last-ditch effort, while trying to hold the plane level and not caring much about the altitude or direction, I reached to the left and pulled the autopilot circuit breaker I had marked with a yellow cap so that it would be easy to find in an emergency. It was the one circuit breaker I could find with my eyes closed, in case there was smoke in the cabin. It was my last hope, short of shutting off the autopilot power completely over the North Pole, which was a terrifying thought. The autopilot is like an old friend who saves you time and energy, but also knows all your worst fears and vulnerabilities and, if possessed by a demon, will use them against you.

This emergency made no sense to me.

Just as I pulled the yellow breaker, the resistance faded as quickly as it had appeared, and I breathed a deep sigh of relief.

To put things into perspective, I was lost five hours from land and 30,000 feet over a cloud layer at a wrong-way altitude doing almost 400 mph over the North Pole with no communications, attitude, heading, or reference system. I was hand-flying in RVSM (Reduced Vertical Separation Minimum) airspace, which legally requires an autopilot to maintain precise flight level—except my autopilot was acting up. And I had no copilot to help me fly manually. My non-Zen words were, "I'm super f—ked!"

Rather than continuing to focus on what was not working, I took inventory of what still worked. I had a visual horizon for the time being, two rock-solid engines, two kick-ass MT 5-bladed nickel-tipped scimitar props, and about seven hours of remaining fuel. That could potentially extend my misery as I flew in circles around the North Pole while my followers wondered why my track on the InReach Explorer was so erratic. A directional gyro held my course for the time being, but I knew that as I turned from the True North Pole to the Magnetic North Pole and finally to the North

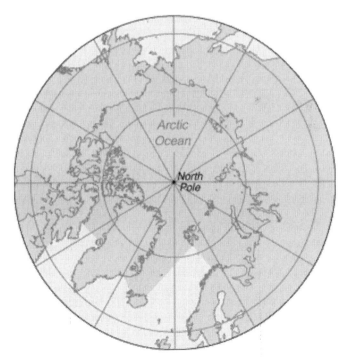

A map of the geographic North Pole

Pole of Inaccessibility, it wouldn't continue to work forever. As if to tease or taunt me, the Flight Management Systems would periodically come online but then fall offline a short time later. They were on for such a short time that I dared not rely on either one.

All of this felt like cosmic torture, complicated by the conflicting heading information I was getting from multiple sources on my panel. My magnetic compass said one thing, my two GPS units had different headings, and my L3 backup system said something else. My directional gyro offered another reading. Which one to believe? Meanwhile, I wondered if I would run out of fuel because I was flying in circles over the North Pole.

As I tried to hold my altitude constant in airspace separated by 500 feet from opposing traffic traveling at over 450 knots, I started shutting down and restarting the failed systems. Normally, this procedure takes 1 to 2 minutes per component, but in this altered version of reality, it seemed to take forever. The Altitude and Heading Reference System (ADHRS) tried to restart itself in motion but couldn't complete its two-minute start-up because the plane was bumping around in turbulence. I noticed that one of the GPS units would show the aircraft flying backward along the track for a time, then would right itself, and then go backward again. I was totally confused and trying to make sense of all the conflicting information. I remember feeling sweat dripping down my back and thinking that the laws of physics no longer seem to apply.

I was breaking open physically, emotionally, and spiritually. When something breaks us open, it allows in the light that heals and nurtures us. At our breaking point, we are vulnerable, scared, and unsure. It's an opportunity to work on our issues and heal. I was praying that I had the strength to do that. Recalling my time over the Drake Passage, I remembered that the Universe only gives us what we can handle. School was clearly in session, and I had to deal with this in the present moment. Apparently, I had not broken open completely before, and the Universe was doubling down on me. Now, almost three years since I began planning for this moment, I was again struggling for my precious life, alone and barely in control.

In the purest sense, I was suffering. The Universe continued to hit me with one issue after another. I was being beaten down day after day, wondering how much I needed to suffer. And then it hit me: Everyone suffers. Every creature on the planet knows suffering in some form. And suffering is something we share not just with humans but with every living thing on the planet. We are really all connected in this way. During the trip, I saw that people were connected in their love of family, their desire for health, happiness, and financial security, but I had not considered or understood that suffering is a critical element of life. I now realize that we would not experience suffering if we were in control of our lives.

Control is only an illusion.

As I moved from the True North Pole to the Magnetic North Pole to the North Pole of Inaccessibility, I continued to hand-fly. My autopilot could maintain altitude, and it seemed to fly on a heading once I set it, but I had to restart it every time I changed my heading. Oddly, my iPad—of all things—seemed to track a steady course to Dead Horse (Prudhoe Bay), on Alaska's northern coast. Flying like this was totally illegal, but I had no choice. I was doing what my instructors had told me to do, which was "just fly the plane." I was lucky to have a visual horizon above the clouds as far as the eye could see.

As things began to settle down to my new normal, the Universe surprised me with an ever-so-brief reward—a minor break in the clouds as I passed over the Magnetic North Pole. But when I saw what lay below the clouds, I immediately questioned whether it was a reward or a warning. There was no solid ice. The surface was a combination of ice and water. Ditching would now include the risk of sinking in frigid water.

I expected the failed systems to come back online in about thirty minutes as they had over the South Pole, but to my surprise, everything stayed offline until I reached the Alaskan coast almost five hours later. This was the longest five hours of my life. Navigating the "Zone of Confusion" where GPS doesn't work and we question our abilities, knowledge, and courage at one of the most isolated points on the planet. This was extremely stressful and tiring while I was also trying to get the failed systems to work and searching for the lesson in all of this. When the systems finally returned, they acted like a bad school kid who misbehaves when the teacher is out of the room and then almost

An aerial picture of the True North Pole showing only water and ice below and nowhere to land

magically reverts to being the perfect angel when the teacher returns. (Later, I learned that at the poles, the angle of the satellites relative to the Earth is much greater, which causes the units to lose contact.)

As I neared Prudhoe Bay/Dead Horse, I realized that the weather was not the broken clouds that had been forecast. Instead, the airport cloud ceiling was just 300 feet above the ground, which was about as low as it could be for me to land. Since I had been flying for so long with a healthy tailwind, I still had three and a half hours of fuel left. I decided to extend my flight for another hour and a half and land in Fairbanks when the weather was clear. I texted the film crew, who had left me months before in Bulgaria, to give them my new arrival point in the United States.

As a side note, on my first call to Customs and Border Protection the night before I departed on my North Pole leg, the Director told me he would arrest me, impound my plane, and fine me if I landed at my intended destination, Prudhoe Bay, where they didn't have an agent. When I told him my first priority was my safety, and that weather over vast distances was unpredictable, he told me that if I had planned better, I would not be having such a problem. I hung up, defeated. About two hours later, he called me back and said I could land in Prudhoe Bay for an overnight stay, but I would have to call Customs when I landed and then head on to Fairbanks the next day.

It's hard to put into words how I felt when I spotted the runway at Fairbanks. From ten nautical miles away, the weather was clear. It was like the things that happened 6 ½ hours before were part of a bad dream. The words elated, relieved, disbelieving, proud, in shock all come to mind. I also dropped a few select F-bombs.

So much had just happened so quickly. One moment I was confused about why all this was happening and wondering if I would survive the flight. Then the next moment the plane touched down, and it was done. As much as I wanted to jump up and down and kiss the ground, I also wanted to curl up in a ball and weep like a child for all that I had been through. I pulled into a spot designated for international traffic.

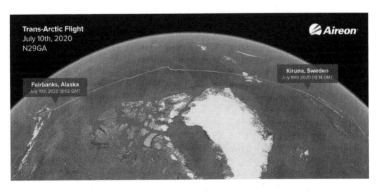

The Aireon ADS-B Out track from Kiruna, Sweden, to Fairbanks, Alaska

Customs and Border Patrol walked toward me as I ran through the shutdown checklist for the tired *Citizen of the World*. Heat radiated off the big Predator B Drone engines as they spooled down, and the oversized props eventually came to a stop to reveal their beauty.

Tired and smelling of sweat, fear, and jet fuel, I emerged from the plane in my bright red survival suit. The two agents standing there with a radiation detector in case I happened to be transporting illegal nuclear material stared for a second. They must have been wondering what I had just been through. One asked, "Are you Okay?" I said I was fine; I had been through a very difficult flight. In a friendly voice, the other agent asked me, "Where are you coming in from?"

I flashed a tired smile. "Kiruna, Sweden, via the three North Poles."

The agent looked at me incredulously. "In this?"

"Yes, in this."

After a brief inspection of the plane, they said I was free to taxi to transient parking.

As they left, I heard the sound of familiar voices calling my name. It was Jeremy Lá Zelle and Kristin Gates, the film crew. They had driven at over 100 mph to make it to my alternate landing site. True to form, they'd done what it took to get the video. I walked to the fence, overcome with emotion. They offered congratulations, and we had a brief conversation.

"Good flight?" Jeremy asked.

"Ya, good flight."

I was finally safe and sound on *terra firma* with friends and back in the United States.

At transient parking, a mechanic and Wendy, the owner of the East Ramp Pizza Parlor at the airport, came over and snapped a few pictures. Wendy invited the film crew and me for a delicious pizza. As we ate, I stared at the *Citizen of the World* and the tears started to well up. She was fierce, shiny, colorful, and perfect to my watery eyes. After what we'd just been through together, I never felt closer to her.

I was exhausted and in disbelief. I wanted to sleep for at least an entire day, and I couldn't yet really appreciate what I had just pulled off or the impact it would have on our peace mission and, I hoped, the world.

For the next two days, I continued receiving calls and messages congratulating my team and me. Although it was difficult if not impossible for them to understand what I'd been through, I was touched by those who reached out in the kindest way. One example was the messages I received from Eddie Gould, one of my handlers and biggest supporters at GASE (General Aviation Support Egypt).

"Adventures like yours do inspire and create so much more than what you have personally achieved. Having this adventure during one of the world's most horrific periods must rank high above many of the worthy exploits undertaken by pilots."

"I guess we, on the ground, have felt invested in your quest in a way that others would not. Your successes in the air are also ours. I have a massive smile, and I know Ahmed does too, when we get something approved, or a plan works out or even when you say 'this hotel is fantastic' and they say 'the work we do in the background can be enjoyable, satisfying and at times frustrating…like when you lose comms or someone doesn't answer a phone in an office 7,000 miles away. But your adventures create the memories for us too, and this adventure is yours and our crowning glory, you took on everything the planet could throw at you, faced dangers in every corner of the globe and even had to change everything you knew about to become a Spanish recluse and then a Viking hermit!'

"I hope you make the book at least half as exciting as the reality was and by the way the aircraft was amazing and beautiful :-)."

Tears flowed. I truly loved and respected Eddie and Ahmed as a friends and brothers, and I was so happy to have them supporting me every step of the way, dealing with every challenge, working to find solutions, helping to keep me motivated, and being my sounding board.

A Whole New Perspective

On the North Pole leg of my journey, I achieved several world firsts:

- Testing for microfibers in the atmosphere over the North Pole
- Flying a NASA Wafer Scale Spacecraft over the North Pole
- Flying the AOPA "Colors" over the North Pole
- Being tracked using ADS-B Out over the North Pole
- Using biofuels for the first time over both the North and South Poles

Upon crossing the three North Poles, I saw the world from all four corners. I knew it would never look the same to me again. I was now in the world in a different way. I had gotten my arms—and aircraft—first around the equator and now the poles. It was as if I had been looking for something, and when I got to the place where it was supposed to be, I realized, "Oh shit. It's not here."

What I was searching for could only be inside me, because I had looked everywhere else for it. What a cliché. Wasn't this the same inner journey I had started years before with my spiritual psychology studies? Had I just returned to where I started? Wasn't this the hero's journey Joseph Campbell wrote about in Hero of a Thousand Faces and other works? What I was experiencing was just too much to process in my exhausted state, and I knew that the answers I sought and the events that would define me happened only on God's time schedule, not mine. I felt that the answers to my questions would come in the quiet of my thoughts. Forcing answers would not work.

Peace Moment

The Universe was saying, "This will not be easy for you no matter how much planning and preparing you have done. It is important that you struggle and suffer to achieve this." My lesson in this place of awe and wonder was that I was not in control. No man or woman could possibly be in control of such a place.

Chapter 28

Alaska

Pushing to expand our knowledge is what's going to solve a lot of our problems. Not only does it build peace, but it also builds the economy, it builds the world, and it puts us in a position to think about the new things we need to do.

—Mead Treadwell, Former Lieutenant
Governor of Alaska

After the team and I filmed in Fairbanks, it was on to Anchorage, the birthplace of Alaskan aviation. Within the Anchorage municipality, known as the Cross-roads of Aviation, there are five airports with control towers, more than twenty without, the largest active seaplane base in the world, and a strategic U.S. Air Force base. All of these cater to Alaska's 8,000-plus active pilots (amounting to 7.9 pilots per 1,000 residents, by far the highest ratio in the United States, as well as 3,000 airframe and power-plant mechanics.

An aerial shot of the Citizen of the World *over Alaska taken by the wingtip camera*

Astoundingly, Anchorage records close to a million take-offs and landings per year.

Why does Alaska have so many pilots? Because flying is integral to life in the state's remote cities, islands, and vast landmass. Places like Barrow, north of the Arctic Circle, have ice highways that are available in the winter. I have heard stories about people learning to fly before they learn how to drive. Aviation has connected but not tamed the vast wilderness.

Ron Sheardown and Mead Treadwell— Anchorage, Alaska

The pleasure of coming home to the United States was made even more enjoyable by the warm reception of my Alaskan friends, Ron Sheardown and Mead

*Interviewing former Governor of Alaska Mead Treadwell (Left) and
North Pole aviation legend and mentor Ron Sheardown (Right)*

Treadwell. Ron and Mead are both members of the Explorers Club and have been helping me since 2018.

Mead, a former Lieutenant Governor of Alaska, and his wife threw a welcome back dinner party for the film crew and me. There were several influential people in attendance that evening when he led a discussion about our "One planet. One people. One plane. Oneness for humanity" Global Peace mission.

Because we didn't walk away from our mission during the pandemic, we showed our strength of heart, courage, and drive to be a positive force in the world. We proved that we would not shy away from this challenge or any others, no matter how hard things got or what the Universe threw our way. No single person, company, or country could resolve all the problems facing our planet, but collectively, we humans could overcome anything, be it plastics in the atmosphere, the COVID virus, or the issues that divide us.

By making innumerable introductions, Mead provided me the opportunity to attract publicity, generate sponsorship, and develop a deeper relationship with the Explorers Club. He also became a sponsor and helped to ensure that the *Citizen of the World* made it back home safely.

Ron Sheardown, one of Alaska's greatest aviation legends and one of my heroes, has amassed 19,000 hours of flight time in dozens of nations and is one of the few living pilots skilled enough to have navigated the polar regions of the far north nine times, including trips made to rescue less experienced pilots. Ron advised me on GPS and HF radio operations while I flew over the North Pole. He told me the proper frequencies to use and the best airports for re-entry into the United States. When I had an issue, he drove to the local Customs and Border Protection location to help.

Ron also made countless introductions while I was in Alaska, which resulted in sponsors picking up the cost of fuel throughout the entire state. Every day I was there, Ron checked in with me to make sure everything was going well. He helped get the *Citizen of the World* displayed at the Alaska Aviation Museum during my visit and offered my film crew a ride in a DHC-2 Beaver for filming, something I will never forget.

Both Mead and Ron agreed to be interviewed for the documentary, *Peace Pilot: To the Ends of the Earth and Beyond*, and shared their considerable wisdom related to aviation and life. I respect and admire these guys more than words can express for what they are doing in the world, for peace, and for aviation.

They are great men and examples of mankind for all of us.

Peace Moment

To me, being a citizen of the world doesn't mean global government, it means that each region of the world does its best to compete with other regions of the world in a friendly manner to sell and succeed. Being a citizen of the world is about building bridges.

People like to make decisions for themselves, and diversity helps us all to be stronger, but diversity works only when you have interaction. So that's the difference: you should always be building bridges because we need to work and trade together.

Chapter 29

The Future of Aviation

"When you navigate risk, fueled with a big vision, charted by an inner guidance system, your destiny unfolds."

—Susan Gilbert

I departed from Juneau, Alaska to Renton (Seattle), Washington, after flying three days over the snow-caped Canadian Mountains and set foot back in the continental USA, almost nine months since the expedition began.

While in Seattle, I met with Erik Lindbergh, grandson of famous Charles Lindbergh and owner of Verdego Aero to discuss global peace and the future of battery powered flight. After being gone for about eight and a half months, I'm curious how things have changed here in the lower 48 states. Curious also about how I changed. It's kind of like a piece of the puzzle that doesn't quite fit back into the same place; but, I'm confident that I will find my place again.

Wherever that may be. I left in mid November of 2020 on the Citizen expedition with the intention of doing something no one else has ever done in an aircraft like the Turbo Commander 900. But most importantly, my mission is to promote peace, to learn how others are looking to achieve global peace and to share this knowledge with the world. I believe aviation has changed and is changing the world for the better. Throughout history, the aviation industry has transformed the nature of our existence in such a profound way.

Arriving at the Museum of Flight, Erik and I sat down for our meeting with the backdrop of an extensive collection of airplanes.

"Erik, you have aviation in your blood—you're our go-to guy for electric power. I'm curious, where do you think the industry is going? How far away are we from having something that works?"

Excited to share his dream with me, he answered, "What we're looking at is rapid expansion of that small aircraft level in vertical takeoff and landing vehicles, because people want to realize that inexpensive, clean, quiet urban air mobility or rural vertical mobility really is promising that Jetsons future that we were all thinking about in the '50s and 60s we may be starting to realize in the next five years. That's our business with Verdego Aero is really freeing the science of this new technology to commercial flight. What we're looking at is rapid expansion at that small aircraft level in vertical takeoff and landing vehicles.

I replied to Erik, "When I was traveling through Europe just a couple months ago, what I found in Sweden was that they emphasized cooperation. I think in the United States, we focus on competition. When people are cooperating, I think that we can achieve more, because I don't think it's going to be one person, one company or even one country. Do you think aviation cooperates with other countries as well? Or what's our path forward?"

Erik paused before replying, "The greatest things we've done in history were cooperative, not competitive. Competition can help you when we compete with ourselves, but it defeats the purpose to compete with others. We can make it better but we gotta coordinate. It's like going out on a vision quest, adventure, a mystical journey. You do face dragons and sirens sweetly singing on the rocks and all of those challenges sort of forges you and leads you to become a different person. And that's something like my grandparents saw early in their flying career. So as they flew north to the Orient in the 30s through the Arctic, and up through Greenland and Europe, down across through South America, they saw the hurt. Then they saw the changes that they could see from above, as they traveled the globe for the rest of their lives and realized that this advanced technology gave us flying because it also improved our quality of life. And so how do we find that balance between technology and nature. We do know that's a threat that's happening right now—99.9% of scientists agree. We have global warming and we have carbon emissions problems we need to solve and it's happening."

I forged ahead asking, "What part do you think science will play in this role? Because you started with the Spirit of St. Louis. And now we have propulsion systems, right hybrid drives, vertical takeoff, air taxis."

"Our business is really providing the propulsion systems that will enable us to achieve electric flight not only me it's all but fixed wing. We have some people coming to us with amazing new design, even airships. asking us about hybrid electric propulsion for now and in some cases, all gathered. So we're talking about a lot of things and the challenges in life," said Erik.

"Can I challenge you with one final question? The name of my plane is the *Citizen of the World* and its role is to connect the south pole, north pole and everybody in between on this mission of global peace. So what does it mean to you to be a citizen of the world?"

"To be a citizen, you have your eyes wide, open your arms, cast a wide net and listen, even when you're afraid of something. Try to look at the fear—why am I afraid of this?—and go especially when you're dealing with other people. You need to look for the good in people—look for the rationale behind their statement not what might be hurting your feelings because then you find that commonality. You find that connection so you can empathize and start to understand that 'ah, it wasn't as bad as I thought'—when you get away from all the chatter."

When Erik's grandfather, Charles Lindbergh, who flew the world's first solo nonstop transatlantic flight, was met with extreme adulation across the world, that single event inspired generations of dreamers inventors, and pilots like Erik, like myself. All that enthusiasm for pushing the boundaries of aviation has really transpired into a world of aviation wonder, connecting us globally in such a profound way—achieving something everyone thinks is impossible, ultimately becomes a way forward for all of us.

Peace Moment

Cooperation not competition is the world's only way forward for peace.

Chapter 30

Coming Home

During hard times we must return to funda-mentals. When it is impossible to distinguish the truth within the conflicting interests of the media, politics, and the medical industry, the burden is on us to go into the world and see for ourselves what is true.

—Robert DeLaurentis, Peace Pilot

The world has changed since I started on this Pole-to-Pole expedition. Since the official departure, a global pandemic has raged, human rights protests engulfed cities across the US, and a global economic depression looms. As a citizen for world peace, I've learned so much more is needed.

A Return to Home
Time to embark on one last leg home to San Diego, California. Upon approach into San Diego's Gillespie Field I'm surprisingly accompanied by five vintage

The Tiger Squadron escorting the Citizen of the World
back home

aircraft from the world famous Tiger Squadron. Together we meet in the air along the Pacific Coast
near Long Beach and fly in tight formation.

One of my sponsors was Lift Aviation. Their president, my close friend, Guido Rietdyk, was a member
of the Squadron. The Tigers agreed to do an aerial
photo shoot with the *Citizen* and five of their Nan-
chang formation aircraft. Our cinematographers took
epic aerial footage from their positions in two different aircraft in the formation.

Chills ran down my spine while I was in formation
with the squadron as they turned on their smoke just
a short distance away. We did multiple passes, including the *Citizen's* overtaking and flying in formation with them. The best shot of the flight came as

the cinematographers flew across and above the formation at a 45-degree angle. The Tiger Squadron aircraft was trailing smoke, and it was a visually perfect piece of footage.

Coming home to San Diego was one of my favorite parts of the entire polar expedition, but it was filled with many conflicting emotions. I was overjoyed to be alive and back in my hometown, but at the same time, I was afraid. As in most places in the United States, San Diego's economy had been decimated as warring political parties, exacerbated by the media and their own election strategies, maneuvered to take control. It was clear to me that our political parties were no longer serving us as they had been intended to do. Nobody trusted the media or the medical community.

I felt that I had a unique perspective, because I had seen the pandemic roll out worldwide with my own eyes. I didn't need to determine if media reports were right or wrong—I'd seen it for myself across twenty-two countries, six continents, and the far reaches of the planet.

What I learned on my journey was that, during hard times we must return to what is fundamental. In a plane, the fundamentals are to aviate, navigate, and communicate. On the ground, it is to see our similarities, not our differences.

People interviewed by Robert in Mendoza, Argentina, South Africa, Brazil, Kenya, KwaZulu-Natal, South Africa, and Sofia, Bulgaria.

While away I learned to live simply. My life was contained in two suitcases filled with clothes that now smelled of jet fuel. I had become accustomed to constant change, moving between countries, hearing different languages, interacting with different people, experiencing different rules and political structures, and seeing vastly different scenery and cultures. Like my aircraft, I had become a "Citizen of the World."

I had been living in survival mode for eight months and twenty-three days having departed on November 16th, 2019 and returned on August 10th, 2020. I had become accustomed to the constant stress of the trip. I was writing blogs, writing this book, working on a documentary, preparing four flight simulations for Redbird, doing podcasts and TV, newspaper, internet, and magazine interviews, interacting with sponsors, posting to social media, and struggling to find my inner peace amidst the global chaos.

The final leg of the flight, into San Diego's Gillespie Field, was a short and enjoyable hop with Bill Allen, one of the Owner/Founders of Allen Airways Aviation Museum. Bill was excited beyond words to be involved and helped me and my team deal with the COVID restrictions at the airport. We scheduled interviews with each of the local TV stations and other media and had a touching meeting with some of my biggest supporters. I was overcome with emotion to see the people there to support me. Some came from out of state and others from various cities across California.

With respect to aviation, I had not missed much during my absence. COVID had eliminated all the events I would have normally attended or displayed the aircraft. Some venues had attempted online events to keep things alive, but with little success. Aviation has always been experiential.

Returning to the city of San Diego was also stressful in that I still deeply desired the quieter life I had experienced during the trip. It was as if I could hear and feel all the voices of the thousands of people around me. The monk's life, free from personal attachments with time for reflection, called to me. The tug grew stronger and stronger.

Was this something I was always intended to do? Ever since my earlier circumnavigation along the equator in 2015, my life has trended in the direction of simplicity, being solitary, and having few commitments. In actuality, this way of being had set me up perfectly for my endeavor. We all have different paths we choose to follow in our lives. This was mine.

Citizen of the World Day

San Diego Mayor, Kevin Faulconer, issued a proclamation declaring September 21, 2020, "Citizen of the World Day." which was also the United Nations "World Peace Day." World Peace TV requested a three-minute video segment of my trip to play on the U.N. website. We provided eleven minutes of our most impactful video, including nine interviews with people all over the world stating what it means to be a Citizen of the World. We expected that the good people at World Peace TV would edit the video down, but to our delight, and to the credit of our gifted cinematographers, they ran the entire segment. (You can view the video at https://youtu.be/sUGpHqD0Mw0).

With the 2020 election approaching, the timing was perfect. More than ever, the world needed the message of peace to bring us together in a world divided.

Peace Moment

People need to see others overcoming the most extreme circumstances possible while going deep inside themselves to find strength they never knew they had. It's the triumph of faith over fear that gives us the hope that we can find peace within ourselves and also in the world.

Chapter 31

Shocking Discoveries

You don't concentrate on risks you concentrate on results

—Chuck Yeager

A few chilling details came to light about three weeks after I returned home. During the Citizen's 150-hour inspection, the mechanics from Skywest Aviation in Midland, Texas, who had helped prepare her for the polar expedition, found that two bleed air lines in the high-tech environmental system had ruptured and were leaking. Two of the cooling fans were heat damaged. The temperature of the leaking air was 600 degrees Fahrenheit. The environmental system is located behind the baggage compartment, just below the tail where the #6 ferry tank was located. That much heat could have started a fire at any moment and damaged the control cables to the rudder and elevator, making the plane uncontrollable. That danger was made even worse by the 10.5 gallons of fuel from the multiple fuel leaks I sustained during the trip that the mechanics found below the floorboards.

The 10.5 gallons of Jet A1 fuel that remained under the floorboards of the Citizen of the World *at the completion of the trip*

As I digested this news, I tasted bile. Any of those failures could easily have brought the plane down over the most remote parts of the planet while I was totally alone. It was a recipe for disaster.

About six months later, the *Citizen* went in for new paint and a new interior at Art Craft Paints at the Santa Maria airport to prepare her for a year of visiting various aviation events and museums. She'd earned the major makeover after enduring the rough treatment Mother Nature had given her during the Polar Expedition. We made the *Citizen* two shades brighter, added pearl sparkle to her yellow and baby blue stripes, and placed two bright red stripes on the top of the fuselage to aid in search and rescue efforts. We were surprised to discover her entire interior was originally done using highly flammable materials intended for cars. These materials are generally forbidden in aviation because they turn the plane into a flying Roman candle, complete with large amounts of deadly black smoke.

Upholstery of the Citizen of the World *failing flammability test*

There was one other final chilling detail: Two of my three remaining metal ferry tanks were used for a ferry flight of a Pilatus PC12 from the mainland to Hawaii shortly after I returned. That aircraft suffered an engine failure and ditched in the Pacific Ocean as a result of low fuel pressure. No one died, thankfully, and the tanks were not the cause of the fuel starvation. But based on my challenges with the tanks, I was also pleased to hear they were no longer in use.

Each time I discovered another risk, I thought about Fred Sorenson's comment that he always vomited the night before and the morning of an open ocean flight, and then he was fine. In the end, I felt that I had rolled the dice in the game of life and death and somehow survived against all odds.

In this book, I have shared the countless obstacles my Flying Thru Life team overcame to prove that, in the face of impossible odds, you can prevail! Our mission was beyond borders, and on our journey we did our best to find peace within ourselves and bring it into the world. At times we failed, but we recognized our humanity, got up the next day, and put one foot in front of the other to keep going.

We hope that, God willing, through what has seemed like an endless series of trials and tribulations, we have inspired some of you along the way to take on whatever impossibly big dream seems beyond your reach. Perhaps others have told you it is impossible. Don't let anyone stop you. It is our wish that you simply go for it, shine as brightly as you can, and allow your dreams to become your reality.

I wish you all courage in the face of adversity and the opportunity for growth that comes with it. May your world be opened forever to what is available to you so that you may have the greatest positive impact on the world.

Peace Moment

The only way this mission was even possible was with the help of my angels. They supported and looked out for me throughout the Polar Circumnavigation. My continued luck had certainly been beyond probability.

PART FIVE

Reflections and Lessons Learned

Chapter 32

Lessons Learned as a Citizen of the World

The way I see it, somehow, somewhere along the line, people think the planet is there for them. They don't look at it as if they are part of the whole thing. They are part of the animal kingdom ... This is 2020, technologically it's amazing and there is some really cool stuff, but we ... dump everything in the water. For what is supposed to be an evolved society, it's uncanny. It's ridiculous.

— Drake Olson, Pilot, Haines, Alaska

Despite my fanatical concern for keeping the plane as light as humanly possible, I carried on the mission one full-size (3 inches in diameter) serialized Courage Coin and 200 lightweight smaller ones produced by the DeLaurentis Foundation. These lightweight coins were intended to be given to aspiring pilots to help them overcome the many challenges they face as they begin their lifetime journey of aviation learning. Once they become pilots, the intention is that they fly the coins forward to be passed along to other aspiring pilots they bring into the brother- and sisterhood. These coins will be auctioned at events to raise money for aviation scholarships once the documentary is released. The full-size coin was for Susan, for being my greatest supporter and never once giving up on me during this flight or in life.

After nine months spent meeting and talking with thousands of people across the planet and interviewing more than fifty of them about what it means to be a "Citizen of the World," I'd like to share what I learned along the way.

Once I left home, I was subjected to many new influences. The things that had defined and influenced me were gradually changing. When I was in Sitges, Spain, I realized I was becoming a product of my new environment. I would walk down the winding mountain road to the market, through the ancient city and along the beach. Most often, I was the only person on the street. At the market, I loaded up with bags of groceries and then walked home. Over time, I could carry more and more, while enjoying the view of the old town, harbor, ocean, and mountain. During these walks, I sometimes fell into a deeply meditative state and felt uniquely connected to everyone and everything in my new world. It was a beautiful experience and one of the many steps that redefined me as a "Citizen of the World."

I saw people cooperating rather than competing. In fact, in some places, like Sweden, both athletic and scholastic competitions were frowned upon until the age of twelve. Growing up, I was always encouraged to stand out and be better than others. On this expedition, I realized my old perspective, shaped by my upbringing, was a divisive way to see other people. All the people along the way who helped me, even when it wasn't necessarily to their benefit, got me to see that when we work together, we can accomplish much more. I came to understand that working together as Citizens of the World would be the only way ahead for the planet as we tackled unexpected events and circumstances like the coronavirus pandemic.

This transformation continued in each country I visited. My definition of myself and of home changed and expanded. Hearing what different people had to say about what it meant to them to be a Citizen of the World gave me greater clarity. In my time of personal evolution, I did not always feel comfortable about what was happening in the world. At times, I felt lost and confused, but I kept choosing faith over fear as the way forward even when that choicé flew in the face of what I had been taught. I came to realize the following things about what it means to be a Citizen of the World:

Adopting a World View

Citizens of the World formulate their worldviews based on their own global experiences, by traveling, meeting other people, shaking hands, looking them straight in the eye, and seeing that these "others" are struggling just as they are.

This face-to-face interaction helps us see we are more similar than different and helps us to develop new and lasting bonds. When we recognize our shared humanity, we are better able to work together to overcome hardships, participate in one another's successes, and shape a better future for everyone and the planet.

Being Willing to Listen

We all long to be truly heard, but not many of us are taught how to listen. Most try to anticipate what someone is going to say and formulate an answer before the other person has even finished speaking. We must try to be present, remain silent while others are speaking, and completely hear what they are telling us. This is a powerful bonding experience that allows our deepest thoughts, truths, and dreams to be revealed to one another, in the course of which we learn more about ourselves and about how powerful and empowering our connection with others can be.

Removing Borders

Citizens of the World keep borders open. When I'm flying between countries in the *Citizen of the World*, for example, there are no walls or boundaries. Flying is the ultimate metaphor for those things that do not divide, restrict, or limit. It allows us to spread our emotional wings and experience how it feels to connect to the rest of the world without labels, definitions, walls, and borders that separate us. Flying can bring us together as One.

Maintaining Perspective

Imagine standing next to a river as opposed to seeing it from 35,000 feet. From high above, we can connect the dots more easily, and things on the ground begin to make more sense. We start to think on a global scale, and see how all the players are impacted both upstream and downstream, which inspires us to act in a way that creates more unity and less separation.

Sharing Passions

Shared passions, even those so big that they scare us, inspire others to achieve their own greatness. Passion ignites a fire in others that encourages them to keep reaching for their impossibly big dreams. Passion can direct humanity to the next step in its collective evolution. Seeing people express their passion and watching them struggle to achieve their goals provide us with powerful lessons. Passion transforms fear into courage and inspires us to action.

Being In the World

On our journey of exploration and growth, we learn that we won't change the world for the better by sitting in front of a computer, posting on social media, or by texting on a mobile phone. To create positive change, we need to go out into the world, make contact with others, and show kindness and concern for everyone. It's a matter of seeing and taking the time to really understand the challenges we share, the emotions we feel, and our common language of pain and suffering, love, and joy. It's easy to miss our common bonds when we're lost in comparison, competition, separation, and isolation. The world puts barriers in front of us to test our clarity, inner strength, determination, and desire for growth. Overcoming these challenges through respect, listening, embracing diversity, perspective, life-long learning, and passion makes us all stronger and connects us globally as One.

One planet. One people. One plane. Oneness for humanity.

Peace Moment

The time for this global connection is now! No single person, company, or country can do it alone. The world needs this positive change now more than ever. It will take every one of us as "Citizens of the World for the World working together to manifest a better, more connected, loving, and peaceful world.

Chapter 33

Personal Lessons Learned on the Pole-to-Pole Flight

Taking ourselves to the limits of our existence on the planet forces us to consider our mortality, the depth of our emotions, our mental toughness, the strength of our faith, our ability to adapt, and our role on the planet as souls having a human experience. In this process, we must decide whether we will choose faith or fear for ourselves.

—Robert DeLaurentis, Peace Pilot

The expedition turned out to be so difficult at times that I thought death would be an easier way out for me. I was mentally and physically fatigued for much of the eighteen months of preparation and the nine months of the trip. A quick end would relieve me of the stress I was experiencing minute to minute, hour to hour, and day to day. It would have been a noble way to go.

I accepted whatever might happen to me, even my death, and as these pivotal moments came and went, I realized that I was being held here on earth for a reason. In fact, it seemed clear that nobody could cheat death so many times. What were the odds? There had to be divine involvement. Knowingly flying from country to country with Jet A sloshing around under the floorboards just inches from electrical components and not catching on fire seemed like further proof that there was a divine plan for me.

My spiritual beliefs helped me find peace with what was happening on a day-to-day basis as I struggled to find meaning in it all. What I came to understand is that we are all souls having a human experience and growing in what many call the "Earth School." Our lessons come in many forms; one day it could be something small, and the next, a life-altering event.

Take time to prepare

Don't rush your preparations. This is a vitally critical time to get into the zone and begin transitioning from a two-dimensional ground-based being to a three-dimensional airborne being. Methodically pre-flighting and thinking things through can prevent dangerous mistakes. If you are hurried, tell whoever is waiting for you that it's going to be a while longer. Take time out of the equation. If you feel like spending thirty minutes with the instruction manual for that new piece of equipment, pushing buttons on your panel, studying the approaches, walking yourself through the emergency checklists, or if you just want to sit quietly for a minute, then do it. The time is well worth it and will make your flying experience more enjoyable.

When I was in Sweden, I was instructed to park in a particular location that ended up partially blocking the taxiway. Because of my concern that the *Citizen* was in a taxiway, I rushed to move the plane the following day. As a result, I didn't properly prepare for the startup, and I forgot to remove one of the exhaust covers from the pilot-side engine. After shutdown, I found the burnt-up exhaust cover twenty-five feet away. I ran to the front of *Citizen of the World* to see if I had removed the intake cover. If it were sucked into the engine, the engine would need to be removed, shipped to a repair facility, and inspected at great cost and delay. Thankfully, I remembered to remove the intake cover.

Visualize handling different emergencies

When my environmental system failed at 34,500 feet, I handled the problem quickly and properly because I had previously done a "Zen Power" visualization during which I saw myself grabbing my oxygen mask over my left shoulder, placing it on my face, and then turning on the backup pressurization system. Thinking through these situations in advance was a great advantage when things started going south, no pun intended!

Pre-plan ways to get an answer while in flight or on the ground

I was 600 miles off the coast of California on the last leg of my equatorial circumnavigation in 2015 when my engine temperature jumped twenty degrees in less than an hour. I texted a mechanic from High Performance Aircraft, and he quickly helped to resolve my emergency situation.

What greater comfort could there be for a solo pilot than being able to ask for help from a mechanic or flight instructor when an emergency arises? Hand-held satellite texting devices and satellite phones by satphonestore.com offer an almost instant way to reach out in your time of need.

Don't wait to ask for help. Plan for it before you need it.

Override your reptilian brain

When you lose your cool in the cockpit, you pretty much become the family lizard and activate your reptilian brain. This is great if you need to kick the window out of your airplane or rip the hatch off the hinges like the Hulk. But the Hulk never flew an airplane.

It is natural to go through a brief period of confusion when you're angry or scared. When you practice your "Zen Power," you will calm your lizard brain and switch on your CEO brain to make critical decisions. Take a few deep breaths; remind yourself that you have a lot of great training, technology, and hours of flying, and then get down to business. You have all the external tools you need within arm's reach, and all the internal tools you need inside your head.

Listen to your inner voice!

If you keep thinking about a nagging problem or a concept you don't quite understand, delve deeper into the issue and find out why the Universe keeps tipping you off. During my polar flight, I kept thinking about the environmental system, which I was running hard. I flew the airplane using the environmental system to heat the ferry fuel stored in the cabin. When I got back to the United States, we found two cooked and burst stainless-steel bleed air lines. When the Universe talks, listen!

Silence your mind

My mind often gets busy before a flight. The voices of self-doubt remind me of all the reasons I'm a bad pilot: "You shouldn't have messed that approach up," "You should have tried harder," "You should have paid more attention during training." and "You should be smarter." The way out of this negative thinking is simply to say the words, "Cancel, cancel," and use your "Zen Power" voice to remind yourself of your successes: "You aced that check ride!" "You read the weather properly." "Remember that landing you greased!" If you are going to tell yourself a story, you might as well make it a good one!

Overcome your fears by going deeper into them

Rather than running from the things that scare you, as most people do, I'm going to suggest something that may seem even more frightening: Go deeper into the things that scare you. Take them head-on. Visualize what you fear most—think about it, feel it, and really get into it for a few seconds. You need to feel the fear completely before it will go away.

For me, one fear was how I would navigate the poles when I lost my GPS and magnetic compass. I visualized getting close to the South Pole, and seeing my magnetic compass start to spin and my GPS fail. I closed my eyes and felt the panic, confusion, and stress, but I kept going deeper into it. For a time, it felt even scarier, but I held the energy. I had a bit of an emotional response and continued to hold and feel it. Then something amazing happened—the fear started to fade. In a few minutes, it totally disappeared. I could breathe again. I received the message from my unconscious: dead reckon, keep the sun in the same position, switch the GPS from magnetic to true north, and put a viable waypoint before and after the pole.

Whose fear is it?

Before I departed on my first circumnavigation, three people voiced their concerns. My girlfriend said, "I had a dream that you died a terrible death ALONE in the Pacific." My dad said, "You are taking unnecessary risks. You're just going to get yourself killed!" My best buddy suggested, "Wait until you can afford a turbine aircraft, which is 100 times more reliable." My impending flight brought up the fears of my top three supporters, but those were their fears, not mine. I listened and gave them empathy: "I hear your concern; thank you for caring." You can't control another person's reactions, but you can control your own. They had to deal with their fears; I needed to handle my own.

Hyperfocus

A polar circumnavigation can be extremely complicated when it also involves finding and maintaining
sponsorships, managing speaking engagements and
social media, planning flight routes, getting permits,
and overseeing maintenance and repairs to the
plane. When it's time to fly, though, you need to focus on nothing but flying. Erik Lindbergh said it best
before I left the U.S.: "You have only one mission,
and that is to stay alive!"

What happened to you last week at work or this
morning at the breakfast table is not in the past.
Leave it there. Don't let anything other than what's
happening in the present moment distract you. None
of the other things going on in your life will help your
decision-making skills in the cockpit. Your ability to
stay 100 percent in the moment will allow you to fly
at your best. If you feel distracted, visualize removing
the issue from your mind, stuffing it into a little
wooden box, and closing the lid. Open the box when
you are back on the ground and have the where-
withal to deal with it.

Never give up on your passion

There were times when things went terribly wrong on
my Polar Circumnavigation, and I could have quit.
When my #1 ferry tank burst inside the airplane in

Dakar, Senegal, spraying fuel in my eyes, on my legs, stomach, arms, chest, and groin, was one of those moments. I could have stepped back and watched the plane be destroyed, packed it in, and called it quits. Instead, I splashed water in my eyes, jumped back into the plane, deflected the fuel out of the cabin, and did what I could to save the aircraft while others looked on in disbelief. I skipped the judgments and got on with the mission. No excuses.

Have faith in your ability to accomplish the impossible

For eighteen months, the industry leader in flight planning told me they would be able to get me permits to fly to the South Pole. Then, two days before my scheduled departure from the United States, they told me they had been unsuccessful, and I would need to get permission from the Chilean scientific community, a process that would take six more months.

I felt defeated and betrayed. After making promises to 95 sponsors, spending hundreds of thousands of dollars, and working harder than ever in my life, things looked grim. I turned to the U.S. State Department and they refused to help me despite the fact that the Antarctic Treaty permitted all member nations free movement in the airspace over the continent.

Within 24 hours, my team and I shook off the setback and shifted into high gear. Our senior scientist, Dr. Dimitri Deheyn, reached out to the senior scientist for Chile, asking for an exception. General Aviation Support Egypt reached out to a British military base in the Falkland Islands asking for permission to depart from there. Circumnavigator Michel Gordillo also reached out to his contacts in Ushuaia, Argentina. In the end, we got approval from all three countries and pulled off what the industry leader could not. It was an epic win for our team and a testament to what is possible when you choose faith over fear and don't give up!

Stretch your comfort zone on every flight

If you aren't growing, you are stagnating. It's an easy space to slip into, and before you know it, you are afraid to leave it. I'm not advocating taking major chances, but I am suggesting that you try new functions on your panel, simulate various emergency procedures, and memorize the location of critical circuit breakers. With time, you'll become a more confident and skilled pilot. You may feel uncomfortable at times, but my guess is that from time to time you have felt a little awkward during your training and worked through those issues—for which you were rewarded with a heightened sense of accomplishment and confidence.

Mitigate the risk of flight

Every flight is an opportunity to identify and mitigate the risks involved. Before each flight, sit for a moment and review the potential risks you could encounter on this flight. What can you do to improve your chances of success?

Most flights offer one or more of a variety of challenges including weather, distance, terrain, day/night conditions, complicated airspaces, corruption, and runway length/surface challenges. One of my most challenging risks was dealing with extreme cold. To mitigate the risk, I flew during the warmest time of the year, installed an additional outside-air-temperature sensor and a new environmental system with higher heat capacity, heated my fuel inside the cabin, wore a survival suit, and used a Prist fuel additive icing inhibitor and biofuels, which have a lower gel point than Jet A-1. I spoke with people who had flown my type of aircraft in the extreme cold, and even considered burning Avgas, (which is the aviation fuel most commonly used in piston engine aircraft) in my turboprop engines which is permitted on occasions, in hopes that the fuel would help to make flying in extreme cold safer. How far are you willing to go to make your flight safe?

Fear Polarizes, Love Unifies

What we have hoped to show you with the actions, risks, and adventures we have shared is that ultimately fear polarizes and love unifies. This love is for our planet, our families and friends, and perhaps most importantly, ourselves. For it is only when we love ourselves that we can go out into the world and love others.

In this book, I have shared the countless obstacles that my Flying Thru Life team overcame to prove that in the face of impossible odds, you can prevail! Our mission was beyond borders, and on our journey we did our best to find peace within ourselves and bring it into the world. At times we failed, recognized our humanity, got up the next day, and put one foot in front of the other to keep going.

God willing, through what has seemed like an endless series of trials and tribulations, we hope we have inspired some of you along the way to take on whatever impossibly big dream that seems beyond your reach. Perhaps others have told you it is impossible. Don't let anyone stop you. It is our wish that you simply go for it, shine as brightly as you can and allow your dreams to become your reality.

I wish you all courage in the face of adversity and the opportunity for growth that comes with it. May your world be opened forever to what is available to you so that you may have the greatest positive impact on the world.

Peace Moment

With every challenge comes an equal opportunity to learn, grow, and connect with others. Navigating uncertain times ultimately brings us together. We will emerge from this pandemic Choose to see the similarities, not differences in people, and you will contribute to world peace. We are all Citizens of the World.

Chapter 34

Aircraft Lessons Learned on a Polar Circumnavigation

A Citizen of the World is someone who doesn't wait around for others to change the world for them. Instead, Citizens of the World have the courage to go out into the world using whatever resources they can draw upon to become the change they want to see in the world.
　　　　　　—Robert DeLaurentis, Peace Pilot

Flying a plane to the South and North Poles creates stresses on an aircraft that it was never designed to endure. Furthermore, modifying a stock aircraft in more than 50 ways and hoping all those systems will work in perfect harmony for eight months over 26,000 nm is total insanity. But, somehow, I did it— on the first attempt—with the help and support of some of the most talented, brilliant and skilled mechanics, engineers, and aviation enthusiasts on the planet. And along the way, we learned a lot about what a 1983 Turbo Commander is really capable of. I'd like to share some of those important lessons in the hope that they will help others operate their aircraft in the safest and most reliable way possible.

Be protective of your plane

Before anyone puts a wrench to my airplane, I make sure that they have lots of experience and are able to focus 100 percent on the job. If they are dealing with a major life event or anything that will distract them, they need to resolve their issues first. Pilots must be in a positive mental state of mind to fly, so why shouldn't the person you are trusting to keep your machine running over oceans, mountains, and deserts in the dark and in bad weather also be required to have that same mindset? The aviation industry says the most likely cause of flying accidents or incidents is pilot error, but I would disagree. New mechanics today are taught component replacement but many do not necessarily have the critical thinking skills required to diagnose and resolve problems.

Critical aircraft components fail regularly

If you think you will never experience a major component failure in flight, then you are in for a few big surprises. Planes are machines, and all machines eventually fail. In fact, the more we ask from these systems, the shorter their lifespan. With just 2,000 hours of flying time, I've had engines, avionics, hydraulics, props, environmental systems, tires, fuel tanks, batteries, and even windows fail at critical moments. Using the most skilled mechanics and equipment money can buy can't stop failures from happening.

The thing that surprised me was that even new parts can fail. I experienced this while test-flying my new, high-tech environmental system at 34,500 feet and lost pressurization when the turbocharger blew out. The problem was eventually traced to a poorly designed turbocharger and weak bleed air lines.

Install multiple redundant systems

As I watched the failures of my flight-management systems, attitude-heading and reference systems, and autopilot while flying over the Poles, the importance of having backups never felt more vital. Redundancy, and not becoming attached to any one piece of gear for any critical phase of flight, can save your life. Luckily, a variety of backup avionics systems are plentiful and relatively inexpensive today. With just an L3Harris ESI 500 standby instrument with battery backup, an iPad, and an Icom handheld radio, you can pretty much fly your aircraft even if you lose the rest of your panel. Having these independent backup systems allows you to troubleshoot when things go awry.

Go high tech and low tech

Technology has many advantages, but let's not forget about our heavier, older, often rock-solid steam gauges. I have both in the aircraft I fly, and while it makes for a busier panel that may not look as cool as all-glass, you are covered in most emergencies. Additionally, just about any avionics shop in the world can replace old school steam gauges.

In preparation for the Polar Circumnavigation, we reinstalled a directional gyro that was crucial to navigating the *Citizen* over both poles, as well as an automatic direction finder (ADF) that's required for flight in Europe. Both these systems probably came with the plane when it was built, but they'd been removed for newer glass panel equipment with digital displays.

Planning your flight may be the most critical part of your flight

Every minute you spend on the ground planning your flight, and what your responses will be to critical issues during the flight, can save your life. When you are on the ground, thinking calmly and not under stress, you will do your best planning. Spend extra time reviewing your approach plates, charts used for approach procedures, and the frequencies you will use, studying the weather, selecting alternate airports, and thinking about the "What if's?"

When I was in Madagascar, two days before departure for Kenya, I spent time reviewing the local weather patterns. I saw the winds starting to swirl between the mainland and the island. It was the beginning of a tropical cyclone, and knowing that, I left a day early, which saved my plane, the mission, and possibly my life.

During moments of crisis, focus on what is working

When I was flying over the North Pole without communications, autopilot, magnetic compass, attitude heading and reference systems, or flight management systems, it would have been easy to fixate on the avionics that had gone offline and try to fix them. Instead, in a moment of clarity, I decided to search for what *worked* and use it. My Apple iPad was working perfectly, I was above the cloud deck with a clear view of the horizon, and the Honeywell TPE 331-10t engines and their five-bladed props were perfection in motion.

Check the work of your mechanics

I usually allow a half-day after completing any kind of major maintenance to look over the airplane with the mechanics. Take a wrench to the fittings that have been worked on. Run the systems, and stress the aircraft. You are the pilot in command, the one whose life is on the line. With the exception of High Performance Aircraft, Inc. in San Diego, I don't know any repair facility that takes the plane up in the air after completing major work to test it. This alone is reason enough to pay a premium for the work done on your plane.

In my ten years of flying, I've never experienced a truly perfect flight. If you think you have, I can almost guarantee that you missed something. Aviation is a great way to hone your skills, refine your equipment, and learn valuable lessons about life. See your plane as a training ground to grow your mind, body, and soul. Knowing that you are prepared for whatever may come your way will make your flights safer and more enjoyable and will allow you to better experience all the wonders available to you.

Peace Moment

Making preparations for the challenging times in life is part of your journey. This includes the mental, physical and spiritual parts of the experience. These preparations help us experience ease and grace during the most difficult times.

Chapter 35

Upset Training

Don't let the behavior of others destroy your inner peace.

—Dalai Lama

In Chapter 21 I talked about how the upset training I'd taken while preparing for my polar circumnavigation had helped me to escape potentially explosive human encounters during the lockdown in Spain, when the whole world seemed to be out of control. Having found those lessons so helpful, I'd now like to share four quick suggestions to help you return to a more peaceful and compassionate space if and when you are confronted with your next challenging encounter.

1. See the world through their eyes

In the space of one week during COVID, I twice encountered another person's pain related to the pandemic. In the first instance, it happened to be a person who had checked all the vulnerability boxes and was at high risk of dying from the coronavirus. In the second case, the person was dealing with stage-four cancer, so her immune system was already challenged before the coronavirus came into the picture. The bottom line? You never know what another person is dealing with in their life, so be gentle.

2. Practice compassion

When someone has been triggered and is out of control may be the absolute hardest time to practice compassion, but it is also the most important. You have squared off with another human who is dealing with life's challenges, just as you are.

Take a few deep breaths and don't respond.

In most stressful situations, I sometimes literally hold my breath, which doesn't help. My heart beats a million miles an hour, and my rational mind can't respond with the answers I prefer. If time is an option, wait until cooler minds prevail, and remember that you can't take your words back or un-ring the bell.

3. Don't add fuel to the fire. Say something positive or neutral.

Say something that lets the other person know you value his opinion. If you can't come up with anything positive at the moment, simply make a neutral comment and let the person know you heard what he said by repeating his key points. Sometimes I find it helpful to imagine myself as someone I respect and think about how that person would respond in this situation.

4. Walk or run away!

Avoiding confrontation may be the best thing to do in some situations where the result is not critical to the outcome of your mission. Instead of standing your ground on principle and fighting it out in every instance, you can simply leave and fight another day. You don't even need to say a word. This can prevent you from getting hurt and your mission from being derailed. When danger or discomfort arises, get the hell out of Dodge as fast as you can. Become an Olympic sprinter the likes of which the world has never seen, and live to fight another day. I sometimes refer to this as my Forrest Gump strategy because I hear the words in my mind: "Run, Forrest, run!"

When we see these difficult situations as opportunities for us to evolve and learn in the Earth School, they lose some of their emotional energy, and maybe, just maybe, we can smile in the face of adversity and continue on our way, giving the other person the dignity of his or her process.

Peace Moment

How you handle the issue is the issue.

Chapter 36

Seeking Safe Harbor

*Be assured that there is a safe harbor. You can
find peace amidst the storms that threaten you.*
— Robert DeLaurentis, Peace Pilot

As pilots, we are naturally curious and restless souls
who want to explore the world and seek new adventures. As Citizens of the World, we travel to connect
with those around us, gain perspective, and see our
place within the universe. But, at some point in our
journey, we all need time to return to our roots or a
place of safe harbor. We can go beyond our comfort
zone for just so long, but not indefinitely.

This safe harbor I am describing is one protected
from the storm, but also welcoming. Without a safe
harbor, we don't feel grounded, and our souls are unable to reconnect with the earth. I felt this more than
ever as I ventured to more and more distant places
and my polar circumnavigation was extended from

five months to nine months because of the COVID virus.

So, what does a safe harbor look like? How can we find one? Here are a few of what I consider to be its defining elements.

Kind and welcoming people

The power of a smile helps us to feel a human connection after a long journey. When a handshake wasn't appropriate during the height of the pandemic, an elbow tap, wave, or toe tap worked just fine. And still does. It satisfies, in part, our desire to be in a place where we can connect emotionally with others. Sharing stories from our journey is a way to process what we have experienced and fulfills a critical element of what it means to be human.

People who look out for one another

Aviation legend and philosopher Fred Sorenson said it best: "A safe harbor is one that is protected from the storm, but also welcoming, with support from others and a mutual understanding that if you don't protect and secure your own vessel, it could cause damage to the other vessels nearby. You take your responsibility seriously, and the others do the same. You all meet at the harbor pub knowing everyone has done their part, and others have even helped you do your part. It's not policed. It's mutual help, mutual responsibility, and mutual trust."

A place to recover from life's adversity

We can't be out in the world and moving about indefinitely. We need to return to a place where we can regroup, rest, and reflect on what has happened. We need to figure out what lies ahead, and this quiet place allows us to catch our breath, clear our minds, and regain our strength in peace, away from the congestion, pollution, and noise of society.

Safety

Above all else, safety is critical for all humans, regardless of their country of origin, political affiliation, religion, or the color of their skin. If we don't feel safe, we can never put our heads down and relax or drop our guard to find our center. Safety from the elements, crime, and other outside influences is critical if we hope to continue on our journey.

A good meal and restful sleep

At the end of a long journey, having a good meal and getting a good night's sleep allows us to recharge our batteries, fill up the tank, and replenish our reserves of energy. Call it what you want, but for me, a good meal after a long day is a reward for a job well done as well as a chance to come together with others. We associate happy times with good meals. And there is no better way to prepare oneself to take on the world than enjoying a restful night's sleep. Being physically satisfied is important for our mental well-being.

Peace of mind

Mental relief is one of the most cherished aspects of a safe harbor. Putting your worries in park and being able to clear your mind for a time is priceless. This is when I can focus again on the moment and return to a place of gratitude. When I'm at peace I can connect with the collective conscience, the storehouse of all human knowledge.

Finding a safe harbor allows my soul to reconnect with the earth and with others, recharge, and find my true north, so that I am ready to continue my journey and our mission: One planet. One people. One plane. Oneness for humanity.

Peace Moment

Lifting off from the earth allows us to explore, experience, and exist in a place and time that are different from those to which we are accustomed. That way of being is much closer to who we truly are.

Chapter 37

A Primer for Overcoming Stress

As we sit in silence, free of the many distractions of life, we are forced to figure out how to be with ourselves.
—Robert DeLaurentis, Peace Pilot

Here are some of the ways I dealt with the enormous stress I was feeling during my journey, including my COVID isolation.

Remember that this too shall pass

Contrary to what you may think in the moment, the Universe gives you no more than what you can handle. It may feel like more than you have dealt with before, but what is happening is helping you learn and for your continued evolution. You will experience moments when things seem to be totally out of control. That is normal and will pass in time—sooner rather than later. Press pause and ground yourself by slowing down your breathing and your pace. Count to ten or say your favorite prayer or mantra. Recognize and acknowledge that you are in this space, and it is temporary. Mentally revisit your greater purpose and what matters to you, then ask yourself what step to take next. Action, positive or negative, follows intention. Aim for positive.

Identify the real issues

If you could magically look down on your situation from 35,000 feet above while letting go of fear and panic, what advice would you give yourself (or a good friend, if that is easier to imagine)? How could you look at the situation more realistically?

When I was just about two months out from departure, I had an opportunity to rent my home out early and raise some additional money for the expedition. This left me without a place to stay for those two last critical months and left me feeling a bit homeless and out of sorts. My perceived deprivation was not real but imagined. I ended up moving into a rental property that was undergoing extensive renovation. Amidst the dust and debris, I was able to carve out the room in a small bedroom for a bed and desk. This space was void of my creature comforts but helped change my mindset to the mission at hand and started my transition to the more challenging lifestyle I would experience on the Circumnavigation.

What are the immediate and real issues that you have to deal with?

What if you did absolutely nothing?

Drawing upon resources

Did you know that the number-one factor that keeps people alive in challenging situations is the will to survive? People with loved ones, causes they believe in, or a strong desire to live, survive much longer than those who check out mentally. Don't underestimate the force of your will. You are capable and strong. Never in the history of the planet has there been a living being with a better combined skillset and capacity to survive than a human being. Take an inventory of all the people you love, those who love you, and those who need you in the world. You are awesome—own it.

Questioning how much I really needed

Chances are that you need much less than you have become accustomed to having. Think about it. In the short term, we need air, water, shelter, warmth, food, a sense of belonging to something greater than ourselves—and not a lot more. The happiest people I saw on this polar circumnavigation were people in the Tigray region of Ethiopia. They didn't have cars, beds, medical care, cell phones, TVs, or social media. They have each other and nature.

Parking my ego at the door

Whatever you're going through, chances are you will be eating some humble pie, so accept it and let the resistance fall away. Maybe it's time to call in a favor from a friend or family member, ask for help from others, or wear the same socks for a few days at a time. Try to see what is happening as an opportunity to show how strong and courageous you are and that you can take things in stride. Offer to help others, too. Altruism relieves stress and increases well-being.

Never giving up.

When my fuel tank burst and spayed 75 gallons of Jet A inside my plane and all over me, I splashed water in my eyes, pulled off my clothes, put on dry ones, and kept fighting to save the *Citizen* and my mission. Don't give up, no matter how bad things look. You are much stronger than you will ever know. Trust yourself. Choose to believe this is all happening for a reason, and let your intuition and the Universe guide you.

Finding a way to recharge and regroup

You may be operating at a pace you cannot maintain for the duration of the issue you are facing. Take time for yourself and replenish your spirit. I re-energize myself and regain my inner peace by walking in nature, being in a quiet place, or sleeping restfully. In the silence, I'm open to whatever guidance the Universe has for me. By shutting out the distractions of life I can receive the messages meant for me and learn whatever lessons are intended to move me past the challenges I'm facing.

During the pandemic, I came to understand that what was happening in the world was not any type of cosmic punishment. Viruses and "dis-ease" have occurred for thousands of years as part of the natural order in "Earth School." Much as we might wish otherwise, our bodies are not immortal, even though we may believe our souls are eternal. So, we need to get used to the fact that even with all the current scientific advances, our time on the planet is still limited. Let's slow down, take deeper breaths, and look for the good in whatever this brings.

Peace Moment

Take a deep breath. Inhale peace. Exhale happiness.

Appendices

List of Sponsors

ABCI (Aviation Business Consultants International, LLC)
Access Flight Training Services
ACR Electronics, Inc. (ARTEX)
Aero Air
Aero Club of SOUTHERN CALIFORNIA
AeroMech Incorporated
Aero Marine Tax Pros
Aerox—Aviation Oxygen Systems
Aircraft Spruce
Airport Coloring Book
Allen Airways Flying Museum
Allison-McCloskey Escrow Company
AmSafe
Artcraft Paint
Artex
Astronics – Max Viz
Atlantic Radio Telephone
AVI Aviation
Avidyne Avionics

AX Center for Experimental Cosmology (ACEC)

BH Gold Insurance Agency

Blacart Creative Group

BNC Bank

Breatheology

CAPS Aviation

Club Glove

Commercial Openings

Concorde Battery

David Nicklas Organ Donor Awareness Foundation

DeLaurentis Foundation

Desser Tire and Rubber

Don Harrison CPA

Fire Containment Concepts

Flight Contract Services

FlightHelmet.com

Frank Rogozienski Photography

FutureWAVE

GASE General Aviation Support Egypt

Gemini Air Group

GENESYS Aerosystems

Gibson & Barnes

Gleim Aviation

Global Parts Group

Golden State Flying Club

GTEC Inc., Gatz Technical Engineering Consultants

Gulfstream Aerospace

High Performance Aircraft

Honeywell

Icom

Iridium Satellite Communications

Jeppesen

KidderCorp Coins

L3 Aviation Products

Lift Aviation

Lightspeed

Mary Marcdante

Mead Treadwell

MT-Propeller USA

My Go Flight

Neal Aviation

NFlight Technology LLC

Online Promotion Success, Inc., Susan Gilbert

Passey-Bond Co., Inc.

Pilot Getaways

PRO Compression

RedBird Flight Simulations

Roseanna Banana All Natural Products

Ross Patent Law Office

Ryan Air

Safety and Survival Education, Inc.

SatPhoneStore

Scheyden Precision Eyewear

Shadin Avionics

Shell

Shiny Jets

Sirius XM

Start Pac

Steven Rodriquez

Survival Educators

TAE Aerospace

Tahoe Truckee Airport

The Muns Law Firm

Tricor

Twin Commander

University California Santa Barbara

USM

Winkler Designs

Whelen Engineering Company

Wolfe Air

Women in Aviation

World Citizen

X-Naut

Support Provided by:
AOPA

Contact us at www.FlyingThru Life.com to find out how you can become a sponsor.

Appendix 2

Pole-to-Pole
Expedition Route

Polar Circumnavigation route

Date	Leg and Sponsor
11/16/19	San Diego, California (KSEE)/Mojave, California (KMHV)
11/17/19	Mojave, California (KMHV)/Mojave, California (KMHV)
11/18/19	Mojave, California (KMHV)/North Las Vegas, Nevada (KVGT)
11/18/19	North Las Vegas, Nevada (KVGT)/ Mojave, California (KMHV)
11/19/19	Mojave, California (KMHV)/Phoenix, AZ (KDVT)
11/20/20	Phoenix, AZ (KDVT)/Midland, Texas (KMAF)
11/21/20	Midland, Texas (KMAF)/Brownsville, Texas (KBRO)
11/22/20	Brownsville, Texas (KBRO)/Panama City, Panama (MPTO)
11/29/20	Panama City, Panama (MPTO)/ Cartagena, Colombia (SKCG)
12/02/20	Cartagena, Colombia (SKCG)/ Guayaquil, Ecuador (SEGU)
12/04/20	Guayaquil, Ecuador (SEGU)/Mendoza, Argentina (SAME) Desser Tire & Rubber Co.
12/08/20	Mendoza, Argentina (SAME)/Santiago, Chile (SCEL) Aero Club of Southern California

12/12/20	Santiago, Chile (SCEL)/Ushuaia, Argentina (SAWH)
	CAPS AVIATION
12/17-18/20	Ushuaia, Argentina (SAWH)/South Pole/Ushuaia, Argentina (SAWH)
	Delaurentis Foundation
12/20/20	Ushuaia, Argentina (SAWH)/Falkland Islands (EGYP)
	General Aviation Support Egypt
12/26/20	Falkland Islands (EGYP)/Rio De Janeiro, Brazil (SBGL)
	MT Propeller
01/02/20	Rio De Janeiro, Brazil (SBGL)/Recife, Brazil (SBRF)
	Airplane Owners and Pilots Association (AOPA)
01/04/20	Recife, Brazil (SBRF)/Dakar, Senegal (GOBD)
	L3Harris
01/05/20	Dakar, Senegal (GOBD)/Accra, Ghana (DGAA)
	Flight Contract Services
01/06/20	Accra, Ghana (DGAA)/Maun, Botswana (FBMN)
	Nicholas Foundation
01/07/20	Maun, Botswana (FBMN)/La Mercy, South Africa (FALE)

Concorde Battery

01/16/20 La Mercy, South Africa (FALE)/ Plaine,
Mauritus (FIMP)

Susan Gilbert representing all Female
Pilots

01/19/20 Plaine, Mauritius (FIMP)/Mahajanga,
Madagascar (FMNM)

SatPhoneStore

01/21/20 Mahajanga, Madagascar (FMNM)/
Nairobi, Kenya (HKJK)

Online Promotion Success

01/27/20 Nairobi, Kenya (HKJK)/Addis Ababa,
Ethiopia (HAAB)

Scheyden Precision Eyewear

01/31/20 Addis Ababa, Ethiopia (HAAB)/Cairo,
Egypt (HESX)

Twin Commander

02/02/20 Cairo, Egypt (HESX)/Tbilisi, Georgia
(UGTB)

Rocket Route

02/06/20 Tbilisi, Georgia (UGTB)/Sofia, Bulgaria
(LBSF)

Mary Marcdante

02/10/20 Sofia, Bulgaria (LBSF)/Genoa, Italy
(LIMJ)

TAE Aerospace, Inc.

02/15/20	Genoa, Italy (LIMJ)/Madrid, Spain (LECU)
	High Performance Aircraft
02/28/20	Madrid, Spain (LECU)/Menorca, Spain (LESL)
	Lift Aviation
03/03/20	Menorca, Spain (LESL)/Madrid, Spain (LECU)
	Art Craft Paint
05/15/20	Madrid, Spain (LECU)/Malmo, Sweden (ESMS)
	Skywest Aviation
06/03/20	Malmo, Sweden (ESMS)/Farosund, Sweden (ESVB)
	Aerox
06/20/20	Farosund, Sweden (ESVB)/Pitea, Sweden (ESNP)
06/23/20	Pitea, Sweden (ESNP)/Borlange, Sweden (ESSD)
	GLEIM Aviation
07/06/20	Borlange, Sweden (ESSD)/Kiruna, Sweden (ESNQ)
	Start Pac
07/10/20	Kiruna, Sweden (ESNQ)/Fairbanks, Alaska (PAFA)
	Honeywell Aerospace

07/13/20	Fairbanks, Alaska (PAFA)/Anchorage, Alaska (PANC) Aero & Marine Tax Pros
07/23/20	Anchorage, Alaska (PANC)/Juneau, Alaska (PAJN) Global Parts Group
07/27/20	Juneau, Alaska (PAJN)/Renton, Washington (KRNT) Icom America, Inc.
07/31/20	Renton, Washington (KRNT)/San Diego, CA (KMYF) Genesys Aerosystems
08/05/20	San Diego, CA (KMYF)/North Las Vegas, Nevada (KVGT)
08/07/20	North Las Vegas, Nevada (KVGT)/San Diego, CA (KMYF) Astronics/Max-Viz
08/08/20	San Diego, CA (KMYF)/(KTOA) Torrence, CA
08/08/20	Torrence, CA (KTOA)/(KTOA) Torrence, CA Tiger Squadron
08/08/20	Torrence, CA (KTOA)/San Diego, CA (KMYF)
08/10/20	San Diego, CA (KMYF)/San Diego, CA (KSEE) Avidyne

Plane Modifications

In addition to the modifications described in Chapter 5, I went to my former sponsor, MT Propeller and told them I needed a propeller that was lighter, more efficient in climb and cruise, quieter and with less vibration that would also allow the engines to start faster with more prop clearance. MT had been working on a 5-bladed nickel-tipped Scimitar composite prop (wood with a composite covering) on Piper Cheyennes that had been tested at 41,000 feet. My Turbo Commander 900 was the first to get field approval from the FAA. Eventually, I gained the STC (Supplementary type certificate) through a distributor.

Some of the fifty plus modifications included:

- Upgraded Concorde batteries suited for extreme cold.
- AMSAFE seatbelt airbags for the pilot and copilot.
- Avidyne AMX240 audio panel, IFD 440 & 550

- L3 Harris NGT 900 ADS-B Out transponder
- Free Flight Systems ADS-B In
- Shadin F/ADC 2000 fuel data computer
- Astronics Max-Viz 1400 infrared camera
- X-Naut iPad cooler
- New environmental system
- High frequency (HF) radio
- Satellite weather, communications, and music
- L3 ESI 500 attitude indicator with synthetic vision and battery backup
- Apple iPad
- The best of the past – an ADF and a directional gyro

The Citizen of the World *getting her new MT Scimitar 5-bladed nickel-tipped composite props*

- Active traffic
- Terrain avoidance
- Lightspeed Zulu "Zen" noise-canceling headsets
- WAT LED light upgrades
- Desser Tires upgraded 16-ply tire on the nose wheel and 10-ply on the mains. Inner tubes added.

Avionics

Since I'm a self-proclaimed button pusher in the air and on the ground, I had a great excuse to load the plane up with the latest avionics of the day. This included a Bluetooth connection between the flight management system and an iPad, a ground circuit, L3 synthetic vision with battery backup attitude indicator, Avidyne glass panel flight management systems, Sirius satellite weather and music, active traffic, terrain avoidance, ADS-B In and Out, X-naut iPad cooler, Lightspeed noise canceling Zulu "Zen" ANR technology, and a Max-Vis Enhanced Vision System (EVS) infrared camera to turn night into day.

At the same time, it made sense to install old-school equipment as well. We put in an ADF (Automatic Direction Finder) and a directional gyro to navigate over the poles, where the magnetic compass was not expected to work and we were unsure about

Upgraded avionics panel by Neal Aviation.

GPS. The most reliable panel would include both the newest and oldest technology. While dramatically more-expensive integrated systems existed, they weren't in the budget and were difficult to get fixed internationally.

I had intended to strip the plane down to metal to save weight but I realized the weight savings was negligible and that Commanders were not nice looking without paint. Adding paint and a ceramic coating made the plane more slippery and helped increase the range.

We had originally intended to go for something quite outrageous with the paint scheme. At first, we

The Citizen carried the Airplane Owners and Pilots Association 80th Anniversary logo and colors signed by all the senior executives in support of their contribution to aviation.

selected a bird of prey with a map of the world spread across the fuselage and feathers on the wing tips, but the look was not in line with our Peace Mission. Since the plane was quite impressive on her own, we decided to go with a cleaner scheme, changing the color of the stripes on the sides of the fuselage and the tail to our yellow and blue Flying Thru Life logo colors. Additionally, we added our logo, sponsor decals, the national flags of countries I would visit, and her name, *Citizen of the World*. These changes took the plane to an entirely different level.

An additional motivation for the upgrades was to make the aircraft the star of one of the best video games on the planet, one that no kid or aspiring pilot could resist. This was a great opportunity to promote aviation to the world, and our avionics panel would be part of the global billboard.

World Records Set

- First use of biofuels over the poles
- First Polar Circumnavigation in a single or twin turboprop
- Fastest Polar Circumnavigation in a single or twin turboprop
- First Polar Circumnavigation with a NASA Wafer Scale Spaceship
- First to test the atmosphere over the poles and around the planet for microfibers
- Longest flight in a twin engine turboprop
- First Use of ADS-B In/Out over the North and South Poles

Appendix 5

Music Playlist during the Polar Circumnavigation in the Order Played

Superstition by Stevie Wonder
Thunder by Imagine Dragons
Steel Bars by Michael Bolton
Caught Up In You by 38 Special
Rocky Mountain High by John Denver
Rich Girl by Daryl Hall & John Oats
It's My Life by Bon Jovi
Angel by Shaggy
It Wasn't Me by Shaggy
Karma Chameleon by Culture Club
I Want It That Way by the Backstreet Boys
One Night in Bangkok by Murray Head
One Call Away by Charlie Puth
Heartache Tonight by the Eagles
Perfect by Ed Sheehan

Someone New by Hozier

Whatever It Takes by Imagine Dragons

This Embrace by Kirtana

Shallow by Lady Gaga & Bradly Cooper

Little Drummer Boy by Pentatonix

California by U2

Viva la Vida by Coldplay

21 Guns by Green Day

Rolling in the Deep by Adele

Pompeii by Bastille

Life in the Fast Lane by the Eagles

Lyin' Eyes by the Eagles

Take It Easy by the Eagles

Superman by Five for Fighting

Bailando by Enrique Iglesias

Ex's & Oh's by Elle King

H.O.L.Y by Florida Georgia Line

Take Me to Church by Hozier

21 Guns by Green Day

Bad, Bad, Leroy Brown by Jim Croce

Somewhere Over the Rainbow by Israel Ka-makawiwo'ole

Sunshine On My Shoulder by John Denver

Leaving on a Jet Plane by John Denver

Fly Away by John Denver

Fly Away by John Denver

Queen of Hearts by Juice Newton

Angel of the Morning by Juice Newton

Good Life by OneRepublic

Phantom Limb by the Shins

Play that Song by Train

Riptide by Vance Joy

Jive Talkin' by the Bee Gees

American Boy by Estelle

Hey Soul Sister by Train

Grenade by Bruno Mars

Moves Like Jagger by Maroon 5

If I Die Young by the Band Perry

The Things We Do For Love by 10cc

Stressed Out by twenty one pilots

Uptown Funk by Mark Ronson

Time for Me to Fly by REO Speedwagon

100 Years by Five for Fighting

Beat of the Music by Brett Eldredge

You Make My Dreams Come True by John Hall &
John Oates

Tusk by Fleetwood Mac

Script for the Redbird Antarctica Flight Simulation

"The *Citizen of the World*, a highly modified Turbo Commander 900, is holding short runway 025 at Ushuaia, Argentina. She is a wonder of modern aviation technology, with every speed, distance, power, and altitude modification that is available on the planet today. She has spent the last three years in and out of different repair shops being upgraded. She was built in 1983, and you are wondering if she can handle all you are asking of her. Some people tell you that you are crazy. Others say you are the bravest person they know. You are unsure who is right, but you decided a long time ago to go for it and ignore the naysayers. Nothing is stopping you in your quest to set world records, advance science, carry the AOPA logo across the South Pole in support of their 80th anniversary, and showcase the latest in aviation safety and technology. Your moment is finally here!

"Last night the wind reversed, so you are forced to take off in the opposite direction from the one you had planned. This will require you to do a 180-degree turn in the narrow Beagle Channel right after takeoff, when the plane is heavily laden with fuel. This makes you very nervous because you had planned to fly in the ground effect for up to 50 miles as you burned off fuel, and that is not now possible. The weather reports are favorable today; you may not get another day like this for weeks. You have never flown the *Citizen of the World* this heavy, even during the test flight in the Mojave Desert, because you would never want to fly the plane this heavy twice. The *Citizen of the World* is shining and looking good with her ceramic coating designed for speed and all the logos, including Redbird's.

"You are strapped into the pilot seat in a bright red neoprene survival suit intended to keep you alive in the frigid Antarctic waters of the Drake Passage, but it is awkward at best and hot. You don't have much room to move, and you start to wonder if you would be able to get out of the plane in a hurry in this "Gumby Suit." Will you have to use your extensive survival training? You also wonder if the last two years have been worth it, or if you are just going to get yourself killed in the most spectacular way. You can hear the roar of the two big Predator B drone engines in the background, each producing 1150 hp, and the wiz of the massive 5-bladed nickel-tipped Scimitar composite props built exclusively for this trip by MT.

"Sweat is dripping down your back despite the freezing temps, your legs are shaking, and the voices of self-doubt are rolling through your mind. You are wondering if the calculations by the Gulfstream engineer who designed the wing almost 30 years ago are correct. If he is wrong, you are dead. Palms sweating, you are wondering if you have enough runway and if the weakest point on the plane, the bulging tires, will hold.

"You added inner tubes to the heaviest ply tires approved for the plane, but you had to over-inflate them to hold the excess weight as you fueled, so who knows if they will even retract into the wheel wells.

"The next two hours will be the most dangerous of the trip as the *Citizen of the World* struggles to climb out from Ushuaia, Argentina. The *Citizen* is overloaded with Jet A1 fuel in six extra fuel tanks, five spread through the cabin and one in the unpressurized luggage compartment. There is barely enough room to breathe. In fact, the cabin smells of Jet A1 fuel from an earlier leak that spilled 75 gallons of fuel. The mechanics cleaned up most of it, but you can still smell and taste it in your throat when you swallow. Your eyes and sinuses burn a bit, making you uncomfortable and more stressed. You are used to stress at this point, but it is starting to feel crushing, just like the weight of the extra fuel.

"Your radio crackles to life, and it's the tower. 'Citizen two nine golf alpha, cleared for takeoff runway 25.' You were told by one expert that a rolling start from the taxiway is critical to build up enough speed for liftoff, but another told you that when the plane is heavily weighed down, the lateral force can collapse the gear before you get off the ground. The struts were topped off with nitrogen before you left the aviation maintenance facility in anticipation of the extra weight, but now you only have about an inch of clearance on each. Any bouncing and you will have metal-on-metal contact, which is dangerous.

"You push the prop condition levers forward to 100 percent and then lock them in place. Next, you push the throttles on those massive, gear-driven Honeywell TPE 331-10t engines forward to a screaming 100 percent power. The bulging tires start to roll, and the *Citizen* is slow to accelerate down the 9,300-foot runway. Mountains on three sides make the takeoff even more challenging. The takeoff roll takes an eternity, seemingly in slow motion. A quick look out the side window and you see the tower passing, with the big white snow-capped mountains in the distance. The plane continues to accelerate as you note that you are past the point where you can safely abort. You are either going into the water or barely making it into the air. The plane bounces a bit. You hope you don't bottom-out those struts! You are running out of runway as you accelerate past your normal rotation speed of 85 knots. On the speed tape of the L3 ESI 500 you see 90 knots, 95, 100, 105, 110, but the plane is not lifting off. You begin pulling back on the yoke at the risk of dragging the tail, but nothing is happening! Why won't the plane lift off? The end of the runway is fast approaching. Beyond that is the icy water of the Beagle Channel and a mountain.

"Your only solution seems to be to get into ground effect and accelerate. That's the only way you are going to make it. You are tapping the yoke back with your fingertips, asking God to let you climb just this one last time! You promise never to make such a request again. No answer! You jerk the yoke back, hoping not to stall the plane out. The drone of the engines becomes deafening, and the wingtips bend upward like you have not seen before. Slowly the nose wheel lifts off and hangs for a second. Then it settles down again. You pull back a little more, and the nose of the Citizen lifts again as you hear a sound from behind. The extra ferry tanks shift back a fraction of an inch, changing the center of gravity—for the worse. You hold on as the plane slowly lifts off.

The engines let out a deep groan, like you're asking more of them than was ever intended. "Hold on, you can do this." You look at the airspeed again and there's no change. You say, "COME ON! COME ON!" Still nothing, then you see the airspeed increase by one knot... then another... and another.

[A view from outside the plane shows the beautiful scenery in the middle of the channel. The plane looks small from a distance but gets bigger and bigger as it gets closer. The *Citizen* zooms by and you hear the thunderous sound of those two giant Predator B drone engines.]

"The plane starts to climb faster and faster. You have a fighting chance. You are out of the ground effect! A quick look at the vertical climb indicator shows the plane climbing at 100 feet per minute, then 150, then 200, then 250. Wow, this plane has a ton of power! In no time, you are clear of the mountaintops and start to bank the plane to the left on your way to flight level three five zero.

"You are on your way to the South Pole!"

The DeLaurentis Foundation

The goal of the DeLaurentis Foundation is to inspire people and organizations to live their impossibly big dreams through the wonder of aviation and courage. Led by philanthropist, entrepreneur, and Peace Pilot Robert DeLaurentis, the foundation is the charitable division of Robert's adventure publishing company, Flying Thru Life.

The mission of the DeLaurentis Foundation, a 501©(3), is to raise and distribute funds for aviation-related charitable causes that support innovation, safety, and education in the air, and that connect people worldwide in Oneness, Peace, and Love.

Find our books and videos (listed below), keychains, commemorative coins, stickers, patches, DVDs and more at www.delaurentisfoundation.org/shop/

Books:

Flying Thru Life

Zen Pilot

The Little Plane that Could

Let's Fly

Video:

Overcoming the Fear of Flying

Acknowledgments and Special Thanks

The Polar Circumnavigation was a mission undertaken by many inspired people and organizations.

While I am thankful beyond words for each and every one of them, I want to extend special thanks to Susan Gilbert. Susan is my number-one tactician, supporter, cheerleader, and voice of reason. Since 2014, when I started planning the circumnavigation from West to East and then in 2017, South to North, Susan has been with me every step of the way. She is my personal and moral compass. No major decision has been made without first consulting her. I have come to rely on her inspired perspective, rational thought process, and other-worldly intuition. Together we have weathered everything the Universe could throw at us. I know that without her guidance my life would not and could not be what it is today. I am truly blessed to have her as my True North.

In addition, I want to express my thanks for one of my non-human angels without which this book would not be what it has become. Aireon's satellite tracking images in these pages were made possible with the help of Iridium's newly launched 66 NEXT Satellites. Aireon's payload on the Iridium NEXT satellites picked up our ADS-B Out signals from the L3 Harris NGT-9000. The images are proof of how well ADS-B Out works, thanks to space-based ADS-B extending traditional ADS-B ground coverage across the oceans and beautiful planet.

And finally, I would like to thank the editors who helped make this story even more compelling, inspiring, and interesting. Each of them taught me on my journey and I'm sincerely thankful for their patience, experience and wisdom. Our editors included Judy Kern, Susan Gilbert, Mary Marcdante, and Joni M. Fisher.

About the Author

Robert DeLaurentis sitting in the Citizen of the World, *holding a copy of* Zen Pilot, Flight of Passion and the Journey Within, *and flipping his Scheyden Titanium "Zen" sunglasses*

Robert DeLaurentis loves to fly and is passionate about helping people face their fears and live their impossibly big dreams. He is a successful real estate entrepreneur and investor, pilot, speaker, author, and philanthropist. He has an undergraduate degree in accounting from the University of Southern California and an advanced graduate degree in Spiritual Psychology with an emphasis on Consciousness, Health, and Healing from the University of Santa Monica.

A Gulf War veteran, Robert served in the Navy for fourteen years. After receiving his pilot's license in 2009, he began flying solo in his single-engine Piper Malibu Mirage, *The Spirit of San Diego*. He completed his first solo circumnavigation in August 2015, visiting 23 countries in 98 days.

Robert's first book, *Flying Thru Life: How to Grow Your Business and Relationships with Applied Spirituality*, shows people how to find the resources to live their impossibly big dreams with grace and ease. His second book, *Zen Pilot: Flight of Passion and the Journey Within*, offers real-life adventures along with tips and advice, including "Zen Moments," gleaned from his many trips, and especially his first circumnavigation.

Robert is an aviation and spiritual thought-leader, a sought-after media guest, and is frequently called upon to speak to business groups and pilot organizations, at personal and professional business development conferences, non-profit fundraisers, schools, and youth groups.

For more information about speaking engagements or media appearances, please contact him at: www.FlyingThruLife.com/contact.

Important Media Links
Links to over 50 news articles and videos about the polar circumnavigation can be found at: https://flyingthrulife.com/media/

Connect with the author and his team here:
www.FlyingThruLife.com
www.DeLaurentisFoundation.org
www.PoletoPoleFlight.com

Join the discussion on social media.
What does it mean to you to be a Citizen of the World?

Twitter:	@flyingthrulife
Facebook:	www.facebook.com/flyingthrulife
YouTube:	www.youtube.com/flyingthrulife
Instagram:	www.instagram.com/flying_thru_life
Pinterest:	www.pinterest.com/flyingthrulife
Email:	robert@flyingthrulife.com